SQL Weekend Crash Course™

SQL Weekend Crash Course™

Allen Taylor

Hungry Minds™

Best-Selling Books • Digital Downloads • e-Books • Answer Networks • e-Newsletters • Branded Web Sites • e-Learning

Cleveland, OH • Indianapolis, IN • New York, NY

SQL Weekend Crash Course™
Published by
Hungry Minds, Inc.
909 Third Avenue
New York, NY 10022
www.hungryminds.com

Library of Congress Control Number: 2001098038
ISBN: 0-7645-4901-4
Printed in the United States of America
10 9 8 7 6 5 4 3 2 1
1B/SY/RS/QR/IN
Distributed in the United States by Hungry Minds, Inc.

Distributed by CDG Books Canada Inc. for Canada; by Transworld Publishers Limited in the United Kingdom; by IDG Norge Books for Norway; by IDG Sweden Books for Sweden; by IDG Books Australia Publishing Corporation Pty. Ltd. for Australia and New Zealand; by TransQuest Publishers Pte Ltd. for Singapore, Malaysia, Thailand, Indonesia, and Hong Kong; by Gotop Information Inc. for Taiwan; by ICG Muse, Inc. for Japan; by Intersoft for South Africa; by Eyrolles for France; by International Thomson Publishing for Germany, Austria, and Switzerland; by Distribuidora Cuspide for Argentina; by LR International for Brazil; by Galileo Libros for Chile; by Ediciones ZETA S.C.R. Ltda. for Peru; by WS Computer Publishing Corporation, Inc., for the Philippines; by Contemporanea de Ediciones for Venezuela; by Express Computer Distributors for the Caribbean and West Indies; by Micronesia Media Distributor, Inc. for Micronesia; by Chips Computadoras S.A. de C.V. for Mexico; by Editorial Norma de Panama S.A. for Panama; by American Bookshops for Finland.

For general information on Hungry Minds' products and services please contact our Customer Care department within the U.S. at 800-762-2974, outside the U.S. at 317-572-3993 or fax 317-572-4002.

For sales inquiries and reseller information, including discounts, premium and bulk quantity sales, and foreign-language translations, please contact our Customer Care department at 800-434-3422, fax 317-572-4002 or write to Hungry Minds, Inc., Attn: Customer Care Department, 10475 Crosspoint Boulevard, Indianapolis, IN 46256.

For information on licensing foreign or domestic rights, please contact our Sub-Rights Customer Care department at 212-884-5000.

For information on using Hungry Minds' products and services in the classroom or for ordering examination copies, please contact our Educational Sales department at 800-434-2086 or fax 317-572-4005.

For press review copies, author interviews, or other publicity information, please contact our Public Relations department at 317-572-3168 or fax 317-572-4168.

For authorization to photocopy items for corporate, personal, or educational use, please contact Copyright Clearance Center, 222 Rosewood Drive, Danvers, MA 01923, or fax 978-750-4470.

About the Author

Allen G. Taylor is the author of 19 computer books, including *Database Development For Dummies* and the best-selling *SQL For Dummies*. In addition to databases, Taylor has also written about operating systems and hard disk storage. Taylor has worked as a systems analyst, database developer, Web developer, electronic design engineer, high technology marketing executive, and college professor. He enjoys writing about and giving seminars on database design and broad technology issues.

Credits

Acquisitions Editor
Terri Varveris

Project Editor
Andrea C. Boucher

Technical Editor
Bill Morrissey

Editorial Managers
Kyle Looper
Ami Frank Sullivan

Senior Vice President, Technical Publishing
Richard Swadley

Vice President and Publisher
Mary Bednarek

Project Coordinator
Maridee Ennis

Graphics and Production Specialists
Kristin McMullan, Jill Piscitelli, Erin Zeltner

Quality Control Technician
Andy Hollandbeck, Angel Perez

Permissions Editor
Laura Moss

Media Development Specialist
Angela Denny

Media Development Coordinator
Marisa E. Pearman

Proofreading and Indexing
TECHBOOKS Production Services

Cover Design
Clark Creative Group

This book is dedicated to Brandon Ferguson,
who has a boundless future ahead of him.

Preface

Welcome to *SQL Weekend Crash Course*. You may wonder why I have written another SQL book when there are already a number of SQL books on the market, including some that I have written. Unlike many computer books, the *Weekend Crash Course* series is designed to give you quick access to the topics you want to learn. You won't need to be a weightlifter to pull this volume off the shelf, and you won't find pages and pages of dry reference material in it. Instead, you find the information you need to do the job at hand.

SQL is the language of databases, and the most important information possessed by corporations, governments, businesses of all types, and non-profit organizations is kept in databases. Knowledge of databases and of the language used to extract data from them is important for anyone who deals with data or anyone who manages people who deal with data.

Who Should Read This Book

This crash course is designed to provide you with a set of short lessons that you can grasp quickly — in one weekend. The book is for two audience categories:

1. Those who want to learn SQL fast. You may need to learn SQL for employment or you just want to create databases at home. Perhaps you are taking a course in database development and need a quick supplement. If you are entirely new to the world of database, relax. The 30 sessions assume no prior knowledge of SQL or of databases. As long as you have access to a computer, you are ready to learn SQL.

2. Those who have some knowledge of SQL, but who have not written SQL code in a while. This book serves as a handy reference to the new features of ANSI/ISO SQL:1999 as well as the traditional functions of SQL-92, whose details may have grown dim in your memory.

To get the most out of this book, you should have access to at least one database management system, such as Microsoft Access 2000, Microsoft SQL Server 2000, Oracle 9i, MySQL 4.0, or PostgreSQL 7.1. If you don't have any of these, you can use the copy of MySQL that is included on the CD-ROM that accompanies this book.

What Results Can You Expect?

Is it *possible* to learn SQL in a single weekend? Yes and no. It is certainly possible to learn all the things you need to know to create, maintain, and extract information from relational databases. That is the "yes" part. The "no" part stems from the fact that there is a richness to SQL that many people never tap because they never need to. This book does not cover many of SQL's more obscure features. You may never need to use any of those features. If you ever do, it will probably be after you have been working with SQL for quite a while.

Weekend Crash Course's Layout and Features

This book follows the standard Weekend Crash Course layout and includes the standard features of the series so that you can be assured of mastering HTML within a solid weekend. Readers should take breaks throughout. We've arranged things so that the 30 sessions last approximately one-half hour each. The sessions are grouped within parts that take two or three hours to complete. At the end of each session, you'll find "Quiz Yourself" questions, and at the end of each part, you'll find part review questions. These questions let you test your knowledge and practice exercising your newfound skills. (The answers to the part review questions are in Appendix A.) Between sessions, take a break, grab a snack, and refill that beverage glass or cup before plunging into the next session!

Layout

This Weekend Crash Course contains 30, one-half-hour sessions organized within six parts. The parts correspond with a time during the weekend, as outlined in the following sections.

Part I: Friday Evening

In this part, I set the stage for the rest of the book. You'll learn about how data is structured in databases, the various types of data that you may find in a database, and how to retrieve data from a database using SQL.

Part II: Saturday Morning

This part consists of six sessions that introduce you to the SQL tools for data retrieval that enable you to pull from the database exactly the information you want, while leaving behind all the rest that is not currently of interest to you.

Part III: Saturday Afternoon

In this afternoon session, you expand your information retrieval prowess by learning how to extract the information you want from multiple database tables simultaneously. You also learn how SQL works with other computer languages to give you tremendous flexibility in dealing with databases.

Part IV: Saturday Evening

During this evening session you learn how to design reliable databases and then create them using SQL. Also covered is connecting to remote databases that are connected to your computer by a network. Such client/server and Internet-resident databases are widespread and becoming ever more popular.

Part V: Sunday Morning

This session gives you the information you need to build high performance, reliable, and robust database systems. You will learn the most common problems of database design and how to avoid them. You will also learn how to protect your database from corruption caused by either mechanical or human error.

Part VI: Sunday Afternoon

In this concluding session, I discuss which standard SQL features are either present or missing on some of the most popular database management systems available today. I also describe how SQL deals with errors and what you can do to assure that when errors happen, they are handled gracefully. I also cover how to build SQL statements "on the fly" while your database application is running.

Features

First, as you're go through each session, look for the following time status icons that let you know how much progress you've made throughout the session:

30 Min.
To Go

20 Min.
To Go

10 Min.
To Go

Done!

The book also contains other icons that highlight special points of interest:

 This is a flag to clue you in to an important piece of information that you should file away in your head for later.

 This gives you helpful advice on the best ways to do things or a tricky technique that can make your HTML programming go smoother.

 Never fail to check these items out because they provide warnings that you should consider.

 This states where in the other sessions related material can be found.

Other Conventions

Apart from the icons you've just seen, only three other conventions appear:

1. To indicate a menu choice, I use the ⇨ symbol, as in:

   Choose File ⇨ Open to display a list of files.

2. To indicate programming code or an Internet address within the body text, I use a special font like this:

   The Web site appears at www.idg.com/ and displays the corporate Web presence.

3. To indicate a programming example that's not in the body text, I use this typeface:

   ```
   <p><font face=Arial>Italy ice cream.</font></p>
   <p><font face=Times New Roman>called
   gelato.</font></p>
   <p><font face=Arial>is the richest, creamiest
   ice cream in the world.</font></p>
   <p><font face=Times New Roman>Buon Apitito!</font></p>
   ```

Accompanying CD-ROM

This Weekend Crash Course includes a CD-ROM in the back. The CD-ROM contains a skills assessment test, source code for the longer examples in the book, MySQL, and more. For a complete description of each item on the CD-ROM, see Appendix B.

Reach Out

The publisher and I want your feedback. After you have had a chance to use this book, please take a moment to register this book on the http://my2cents.idgbooks.com Web site. (Details are listed on the my2cents page in the back of this book.) Please let us know of any mistakes in the book or if a topic is covered particularly well. Please write to:

Dittos@email.msn.com

You are ready to begin your weekend crash course. Stake out a weekend, stockpile some snacks, cool the beverage of your choice, and get ready to learn SQL the easy way. Turn the page and begin learning.

Acknowledgments

I am grateful to my acquisitions editor Terri Varveris, who has kept on top of this project all the way from beginning to end. I also appreciate the work of editor Andrea Boucher, whose suggestions and improvements on my writing have made the book much better than it otherwise would have been. I want to thank my technical editor Bill Morrissey, who made a large number of helpful suggestions as well as making sure that everything I said was technically correct. Thanks, too, to my agent Matt Wagner, who has given a real boost to my writing career.

I am most thankful for the support of my writing that I continue to receive from my lovely wife Joyce, from my children, my Mom, and my brothers.

Contents at a Glance

Contents

SQL Weekend Crash Course™

☑ **Friday**

☐ Saturday

☐ Sunday

Part I — Friday Evening

PART

I

Friday Evening

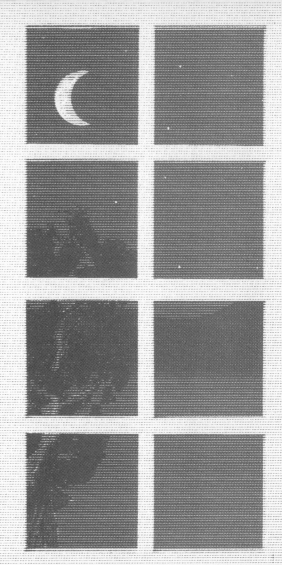

Introduction to Databases and SQL

Session Checklist

✔ The value of structured data

✔ Using relational databases to structure data

✔ What SQL does to relational databases

✔ What's next, after relational databases?

**30 Min.
To Go**

This evening's sessions describe why, after thousands of years of keeping written records of data people care about, they suddenly need databases to keep track of these things. The sessions also cover how computer databases are different from the record repositories of the past and how SQL works with databases to give you the information you want.

Data — Structured versus Unstructured

By the 1960s, computers could store a lot more information than had ever been feasible with paper files. Data started accumulating at an ever-increasing rate, and it soon became clear that retrieving useful information from the masses of data stored on computers was becoming more difficult. The solution to this problem was to impose a rigid structure on the data so that important information would not get "lost" like a needle in a haystack. Haystacks are totally unstructured, which is why it is so hard to find needles buried in them.

Unstructured data

Unstructured data is common in a number of business as well as personal contexts. For example, a small businessperson may investigate a variety of sources, looking for prospective customers. One source may have a business's name and phone number; another source may show a street address in addition to the business's name and phone number. A third source may only show the business's name and Web address. If you take notes on each of these, either on whatever pieces of paper happen to be handy or in a computer document file, you have a prime example of unstructured data.

Unstructured data has definite value but is not as useful as it can be. You don't have all the same facts about all the same prospects, making it difficult to take coordinated action. Furthermore, if you are not careful, you may misplace one or more of your notepapers. Nonetheless, if you don't have more than a few dozen prospects, you can get by with unstructured data. If you have hundreds or thousands of prospects, you cannot deal with them effectively with unstructured data.

Flat files

Computer companies in the 1950s developed a solution to the problem of unstructured data by imposing structure on the data stored on computers. These computers, running languages such as COBOL and Fortran, dealt with data in flat files. A *flat file* is composed of multiple fields, each containing a specific category of data. Each field is assigned a predefined number of characters. For example, the CompanyName field may be assigned 30 characters, the Street field 25 characters, the City field 20 characters, and so on. If a company name was less than the allotted space, the remainder of the field was filled out with blanks. Figure 1-1 shows a few records in a flat file.

Harold Percival	26262 S. Howards Mill Rd	Westminster	CA92683
Jerry Appel	32323 S. River Lane Rd	Santa Ana	CA92705
Adrian Hansen	232 Glenwood Court	Anaheim	CA92640
John Baker	2222 Lafayette St	Garden Grove	CA92643
Michael Pens	77730 S. New Era Rd	Irvine	CA92715
Bob Michimoto	25252 S. Kelmsley Dr	Stanton	CA92610
Linda Smith	444 S.E. Seventh St	Costa Mesa	CA92635
Robert Funnell	2424 Sheri Court	Anaheim	CA92640
Bill Checkal	9595 Curry Dr	Stanton	CA92610
Jed Style	3535 Randall St	Santa Ana	CA92705

Figure 1-1 *A flat file, with fixed length fields*

Flat files allowed computers to handle collections of data involving thousands of records, which was a big improvement over unstructured data. The downside of flat files is that an application program must be written that "knows" exactly where each field begins and ends. If you ever change the structure of the data, due to changing business needs or any other reason, all the application programs written for that data "break." The data the programs try to use is no longer located where they expect it to be. A single change to the structure of a data file probably means that all applications that use that data have to be changed also. The extra work of changing all the applications is one of the reasons corporate data processing departments in the 1950s, 1960s, and 1970s had such large backlogs of work, making it virtually impossible for users to get needed modifications in a timely fashion. Figure 1-2 shows a block diagram of a flat file data processing system.

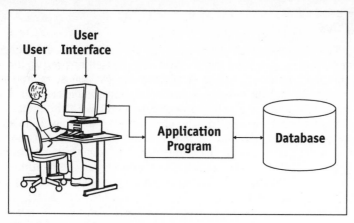

Figure 1-2 *A flat file data processing system*

Databases and metadata

Although flat files are structured in comparison to unstructured data, it is structure of a very rudimentary sort. A major weakness of flat files is the fact that the definition of the structure of a flat file is external to the file itself, which is why programs that deal with flat files break when the structure of the file changes. Each application must contain the knowledge of the file's structure. When that structure changes, the applications no longer reflect reality.

The central idea of a database is that not only is the data contained in the database, but the knowledge of the structure of that data (the *metadata*) is also contained in the database. Applications written to a database do not have to know how the data is stored. They only have to specify what data they want. The database management system (DBMS) figures out where to find the data and performs the desired operation on it. Figure 1-3 is a block diagram of the main elements of a database processing system.

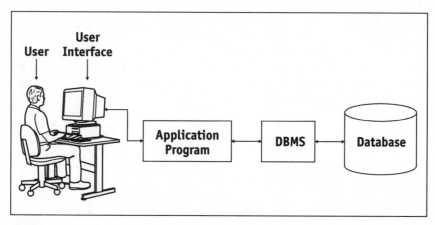

Figure 1-3 *A database processing system*

**20 Min.
To Go**

Relational Databases

The first commercial database systems, which appeared in the early 1960s, were designed according to either a hierarchical or a network model. They were fast and powerful, but rather inflexible. Changing the structure of a hierarchical database was almost as problematic as changing the structure of a flat file system. Network databases were easier to change but were much more complicated. There was clearly a need for a database architecture that was both flexible and conceptually simple. Dr. Ted Codd of IBM invented just such an architecture in 1970 known as the *relational database*. It took a decade from the publication of Codd's original academic paper on relational database until the first commercial relational database management system (RDBMS) hit the market. The superiority of the relational model caused it to dominate the database market, despite the 20-year head start that the hierarchical and network products enjoyed.

Tables

The relational model is based on two-dimensional tables made up of columns and rows, similar to the columns and rows in an electronic spreadsheet. Each table in a relational database represents an entity of interest. For example, say a business is interested in customers, products, employees, and prospects. Each of these entities can be represented by a table. The columns of each table hold the attributes of its associated entity. Thus, the EMPLOYEES table may have columns for EmployeeID, FirstName, LastName, and HireDate. Each individual employee is recorded in a row of the table. Figure 1-4 shows a sample table structure and Figure 1-5 shows a retrieval of rows from that table.

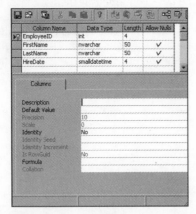

Figure 1-4   *Table structure, showing column names and data types*

Figure 1-5   *Rows retrieved from the* EMPLOYEE *table*

Relationships

If tables made up of columns and rows were all that is involved in relational databases, the databases wouldn't be very relational. The defining characteristics of a relational database are the relationships between tables. Using those relationships, users can combine data from multiple tables to obtain the information that they want. A corporate manager who wanted to know which customers were buying a particular class of product and who was selling it to them would want to pull data from the CUSTOMER table, the PRODUCT table, and the EMPLOYEE table. Pulling this data is possible because those three tables are all related to each other through the INVOICE table.

Saturday afternoon, in Sessions 11, 12, and 13, we cover several ways to use relationships to retrieve data from multiple tables.

SQL

SQL is the internationally recognized standard language for dealing with data in relational databases. Originally developed by IBM, SQL became an American National Standards Institute (ANSI) standard in 1986 (SQL-86). The standard was expanded in 1989 (SQL-89), again in 1992 (SQL-92), and yet again in 1999 (SQL:1999) to incorporate new capabilities.

SQL is not a general-purpose language such as Basic or C++. It is strictly designed to deal with data in relational databases. With SQL, you can do everything that you need to do with a database. You can:

- Create a database, including all tables and relationships
- Fill database tables with data
- Change the data in database tables
- Delete data from database tables
- Retrieve specific desired information from database tables
- Grant and restrict access to database tables
- Protect database tables from corruption due to access conflicts

Creating databases

You can create a database "from scratch" with SQL by specifying its tables, the columns that make up the tables, and the relationships between the tables. All of these things are accomplished with the CREATE TABLE statement.

Session 23 discusses the basics of table creation and Session 24 builds on that base by showing how to establish relationships between tables. The CREATE TABLE statement is a part of SQL's Data Definition Language (DDL).

All the SQL commands fall into one of three categories. The Data Definition Language includes all the commands that have to do with creating database structure. The Data Manipulation Language (DML) includes all the commands that add, change or delete database data. The Data Control Language (DCL) includes all commands that pertain to assuring the security and integrity of the data in a database.

Populating a database with data

After you have created database tables, the next step is to fill them with data. The DML INSERT statement is SQL's tool for this job.

Session 14 describes the use of the INSERT statement to populate database tables. In the same session, you learn how to change table data with the UPDATE statement and remove data that you no longer want with the DELETE statement.

**10 Min.
To Go**

Retrieving database data

Creating database tables, filling them with data, and deleting unwanted records are all relatively straightforward operations. The most challenging operations in SQL are retrieval operations. Specifying the precise information you want to retrieve so that you get all the data you want and none of the data you don't want can be a sophisticated operation requiring great insight into your data and skill in formulating retrieval queries. The SELECT statement is the tool of choice for this job. SELECT statements can be trivially simple, almost incomprehensively complex, or anywhere in between.

A major fraction of this book, including Sessions 2 through 13, deals with retrieving database data. Composing queries to retrieve database data is the biggest part of the job of any database programmer or database user.

Protecting database data

There are two main categories of threats to database data. One has to do with security and the other with integrity. Regarding the security threat, there may be information in your database that you do not want unauthorized persons to see or malicious persons to alter or destroy. SQL's DCL gives you tools to address these concerns. Data integrity can be compromised, even if everyone involved is authorized and means well. DCL also provides mechanisms to prevent data corruption during the normal course of operations.

Sessions 25 and 26 go into detail on how to use DCL statements to assure your database remains secure and uncorrupted.

Post-Relational Databases

Relational databases were a terrific solution to most people's needs for maintaining information as long as that information was of a few common types, for example, text, numeric, date, currency. For decades, these common types were the only ones that most people cared about, so relational databases achieved and maintained a dominant position in the market. In recent years, however, particularly with the rise of multimedia, other types of data such as graphical images, movies, music, and other sounds have gained in importance. These data types do not fit in well with the relational model. A new paradigm was developed, which considered database entities as objects rather than as two-dimensional tables.

Object-oriented database management systems (OODBMS)

Database management systems developed according to the object model that could handle the new data types, which was a big advantage. There was a corresponding disadvantage, however. Object-oriented systems were incompatible with the installed base of relational systems. Companies that had made large investments in their existing relational systems could not afford to convert to a completely new architecture. The solution to this dilemma was to take the best of both worlds, relational and object-oriented (see the following section).

Object-relational database management systems (ORDBMS)

The new object-oriented features of SQL:1999 enable object-relational database management systems to handle the newer, less structured data types such as graphical images and sounds. Furthermore, users can define their own data types. ORDBMS designers need not conceive of every possible data type in advance. ORDBMSs are significantly more flexible than traditional RDBMSs due to their object-orientation. However, they also have the advantage of being compatible with existing relational databases. This means that developers and administrators familiar with relational systems do not have to undergo massive retraining to use the new system. It also means that SQL-based applications that were originally written to operate on a pure relational database can run on a new object-relational database with little or no modification. The latest releases of Microsoft SQL Server and of Oracle, which were traditional relational database management systems, now have many object-relational features. As time goes on, all popular RDBMS products are migrating toward being ORDBMS products. Some products, such as the PostgreSQL database management system, had object-orientation built in from the start.

Done!

REVIEW

In this session, you saw how data in a database differs from data in a flat file or in a collection of facts. You also read about the major components of SQL and how SQL is expanding to accommodate data types that have become increasingly important, such as graphical images and sound files. Additionally, this session revealed the following:

- The locations of the fields in flat files must be "hard coded" into the applications that access those files.

- A database contains not only data, but also metadata, which defines the database's structure.

- Relational databases store data in two-dimensional tables made up of columns and rows.
- SQL is not a general purpose language, but is specifically designed to deal with data in relational databases.
- Data types such as graphical images, movies, music and other sounds are not handled well by traditional relational database management systems.

QUIZ YOURSELF

1. Why are applications based on flat file systems hard to maintain? (See "Flat files.")
2. Why did database systems based on the relational model supercede those based on the hierarchical and the network models? (See "Relational Databases.")
3. What makes a relational database relational? (See "Relationships.")
4. What is the name of the internationally recognized standard language for dealing with data in relational databases? (See "SQL.")
5. What SQL statement is used to populate a relational database table with data? (See "Populating a database with data."
6. What kind of database management system can handle multimedia data types, but also understand SQL? (See "Object-relational database management systems (ORDBMS).")

Retrieving Data

✔ Retrieving data with a simple SELECT statement

✔ Using more complex retrievals

**30 Min.
To Go**

A *database* is a place where you keep valuable data that you care about. What makes the data valuable is the fact that you can selectively retrieve the particular data you want while leaving behind all the data that is not of current interest. This session shows you how to use the SELECT statement to make simple and then more advanced retrievals.

Retrieving Data with a Simple SELECT Statement

A relational database may consist of one or more tables. The database only has value to you if you retrieve data from it. In one instance, you may want to retrieve all the data in a table. In another instance, you may want only a specific subset of the data. SQL has only one command for data retrieval, the SELECT statement. However, optional clauses in the SELECT statement give you tremendous power to discriminate between the data you want and all the rest, retrieving only the data you want.

   To illustrate the use of the SELECT statement, consider an example. Imagine you are the CEO of a startup database application development company named Xanthic Systems. After doing some initial prospecting, you have compiled a list of prospective customers and have stored information about them in a database table named PROSPECTS. Each column in the table contains one of the prospects' attributes. Attributes are:

- Name
- Address1
- Address2
- City

- StateOrProvince
- PostalCode
- Country
- ContactName
- ContactPhone
- ContactFax
- ContactEmail
- Notes

The first eleven attributes are things you want to know about every prospect in your database. You can use the Notes attribute to record additional facts, such as a running contact log and a brief description of items discussed. Each attribute corresponds to a column in the PROSPECTS table. The rows of the table hold the individual records for each prospect.

Retrieving all the data in a table

The simplest retrieval is one in which you ask for all the data in a table. You can get it all with the following SELECT statement:

```
SELECT * FROM PROSPECTS;
```

This statement returns all the data in all the rows and columns of the PROSPECTS table. The asterisk (*) is a *wildcard* character that means "all attributes." It provides a handy shortcut when you want to retrieve the data in all of a table's columns, but you don't want to type all the attribute names.

It is much easier to type the short statement shown above than it is to type the following:

```
SELECT Name, Address1, Address2, City, StateOrProvince,
    PostalCode, Country, ContactName, ContactPhone, ContactFax,
    ContactEmail, Notes
FROM PROSPECTS;
```

It is handy to use the asterisk when entering an ad hoc query from the keyboard to minimize typing. However, if your SELECT statement is coded into a database application, it is better to explicitly specify each column. If after you write your application, the structure of a table changes, the meaning of "all attributes" may change, too, causing your query to produce unexpected results.

Notice in the two examples above that an SQL statement can be on one line or it can be spread over multiple lines. The semicolon is the statement termination character. The database engine keeps parsing a statement until it hits a semicolon. At that point it stops parsing and starts executing. Formatting doesn't matter to the parser, but indenting makes the code easier for humans to read.

How Do You Enter SQL Statements into an Access 2000 Database?

Access is not a full implementation of SQL, so although you can enter SELECT statements to query an existing database, you cannot easily create tables with SQL statements using Access. Full implementations such as SQL Server, Oracle, DB2, or PostgreSQL provide editors you can use to enter SQL statements. In SQL Server you can use the Query Analyzer. For others, consult their documentation.

You can enter SELECT and several other SQL statements into Access (including CREATE TABLE), but the path to doing so is obscure. After you open a database, select Queries from the Window displaying your database. Next, create a query in Design View or with a wizard. It doesn't matter what query you create. When the new query's name appears, double-click it to select it. Now you can select View ⇨ SQL View, which shows the SQL code of the query you entered. You can now erase that query and enter SQL Code for a new SQL statement. Execute your new statement by clicking on the exclamation point in the menu bar or by selecting Query ⇨ Run from the main menu.

Formatting may not matter to the parser, but it matters to people who try to read your code and make sense of it. Aside from indenting, there are other conventions that are commonly followed in the relational database community. One such convention is to capitalize reserved words. Another is to capitalize table names and to use mixed case for column names. I follow these conventions in this book.

The database engine that is at the core of all relational database management systems such as Oracle, SQL Server, PostgreSQL, or MySQL examines SQL statements one word at a time. The parser deduces the function of each word or symbol from its position in the statement and from its relationship to *commands* and other *reserved words*. In the previous example, SELECT is a command and FROM is a reserved word. It would confuse the parser if you were to use such reserved words as the names of columns or tables. Table 2-1 lists the SQL:1999 reserved words. Never use these reserved words in any way other than to serve their official function. I cover many of those official functions in later sessions. Many of the reserved words rarely come up in practice, and I do not discuss them. However, it is still important to avoid using them as column names or parameters because doing so can confuse your SQL language processor. Look carefully at the reserved word list; there are a lot of reserved words and it would be easy to unknowingly use one as a table or column name. Specific implementations of SQL may have additional reserved words. Consult the documentation for your DBMS to find what these are so that you do not inadvertently use them inappropriately.

Never use a reserved word for any purpose other than the one defined by SQL.

Table 2-1 *SQL:1999 Reserved Words*

ABSOLUTE	ACTION	ADD	ADMIN
AFTER	AGGREGATE	ALIAS	ALL
ALLOCATE	ALTER	AND	ANY
ARE	ARRAY	AS	ASC
ASSERTION	ASSERTIONS	AT	AUTHORIZATION
BEFORE	BEGIN	BINARY	BIT
BLOB	BOOLEAN	BOTH	BREADTH
BY	CALL	CASCADE	CASCADED
CASE	CAST	CATALOG	CHAR
CHARACTER	CHECK	CLASS	CLOB
CLOSE	COLLATE	COLLATION	COLUMN
COMMIT	COMPLETION	CONNECT	CONNECTION
CONSTRAINT	CONSTRAINTS	CONSTRUCTOR	CONTINUE
CORRESPONDING	CREATE	CROSS	CUBE
CURRENT	CURRENT_DATE	CURRENT_PATH	CURRENT_ROLE
CURRENT_TIME	CURRENT_TIMESTAMP	CURRENT_USER	CURSOR
CYCLE	DATA	DATE	DAY
DEALLOCATE	DEC	DECIMAL	DECLARE
DEFAULT	DEFERRABLE	DEFERRED	DELETE
DEPTH	DEREF	DESC	DESCRIBE
DESCRIPTOR	DESTROY	DESTRUCTOR	DETERMINISTIC
DIAGNOSTICS	DICTIONARY	DISCONNECT	DISTINCT
DOMAIN	DOUBLE	DROP	DYNAMIC
EACH	ELSE	EMBEDDED	END
END-EXEC	EQUALS	ESCAPE	EVERY
EXCEPT	EXCEPTION	EXEC	EXECUTE
EXTERNAL	FALSE	FETCH	FIRST
FLOAT	FOR	FOREIGN	FOUND

FREE	FROM	FULL	FUNCTION
GENERAL	GET	GLOBAL	GO
GOTO	GRANT	GROUP	GROUPING
HAVING	HOST	HOUR	IDENTITY
IGNORE	IMMEDIATE	IN	INDICATOR
INITIALIZE	INITIALLY	INNER	INOUT
INPUT	INSERT	INT	INTEGER
INTERSECT	INTERVAL	INTO	IS
ISOLATION	ITERATE	JOIN	KEY
LANGUAGE	LARGE	LAST	LATERAL
LEADING	LEFT	LESS	LEVEL
LIKE	LIMIT	LOCAL	LOCALTIME
LOCALTIMESTAMP	LOCATOR	MAP	MATCH
MINUTE	MODIFIERS	MODIFY	MODULE
MONTH	NAMES	NATIONAL	NATURAL
NCHAR	NCLOB	NEW	NEXT
NO	NONE	NOT	NULL
NUMERIC	OBJECT	OF	OFF
OLD	ON	ONLY	OPEN
OPERATION	OPTION	OR	ORDER
ORDINALITY	OUT	OUTER	OUTPUT
PAD	PARAMETER	PARAMETERS	PARTIAL
PATH	POSTFIX	PRECISION	PREFIX
PREORDER	PREPARE	PRESERVE	PRIMARY
PRIOR	PRIVILEGES	PUBLIC	READ
READS	REAP	RECURSIVE	REF
REFERENCES	REFERENCING	RELATIVE	RESTRICT
RESULT	RETURN	RETURNS	REVOKE

Continued

Table 2-1 *Continued*

RIGHT	ROLE	ROLLBACK	ROLLUP
ROUTINE	ROW	ROWS	SAVEPOINT
SCHEMA	SCROLL	SCOPE	SEARCH
SECOND	SECTION	SELECT	SEQUENCE
SESSION	SESSION_USER	SET	SETS
SIZE	SMALLINT	SOME	SPACE
SPECIFIC	SPECIFICTYPE	SQL	SQLEXCEPTION
SQLSTATE	SQLWARNING	START	TABLE
TEMPORARY	TERMINATE	THAN	THEN
TIME	TIMESTAMP	TIMEZONE_HOUR	TIMEZONE_MINUTE
TO	TRAILING	TRANSACTION	TRANSLATION
TREAT	TRIGGER	TRUE	UNDER
UNION	UNIQUE	UNKNOWN	UNNEST
UPDATE	USAGE	USER	USING
VALUE	VALUES	VARCHAR	VARIABLE
VARYING	VIEW	WHEN	WHENEVER
WHERE	WITH	WITHOUT	WORK
WRITE	YEAR	ZONE	

**20 Min.
To Go**

Getting only the attributes of interest

Most of the time, you are not going to want to retrieve the data in all the columns of a table. At different times, you may be interested in retrieving different attributes. For example, on one occasion, you may want to retrieve only Name, ContactName, and ContactEmail so you can send an electronic greeting to all your prospects. The following SELECT statement gives you what you want:

```
SELECT Name, ContactName, ContactEmail FROM PROSPECTS;
```

On another occasion, you may want to send your prospects a physical letter. To do that you would choose a different set of table columns.

```
SELECT Name, Address1, Address2, City, StateOrProvince,
    PostalCode, Country, ContactName
FROM PROSPECTS;
```

This produces a result set containing all the data needed to insert an internal address into a form letter and to print an envelope with each prospect's name and address. All you need to do is export the result set to a word processor; then use the word processor's mail merge capability to print the letters and envelopes.

Exporting to a word processor

Suppose you have a Microsoft Access database with a `PROSPECTS` table and you want to use it to send the prospects a snail mail letter. First produce a result set by executing the `SELECT` statement shown above. This produces the result set shown in Figure 2-1.

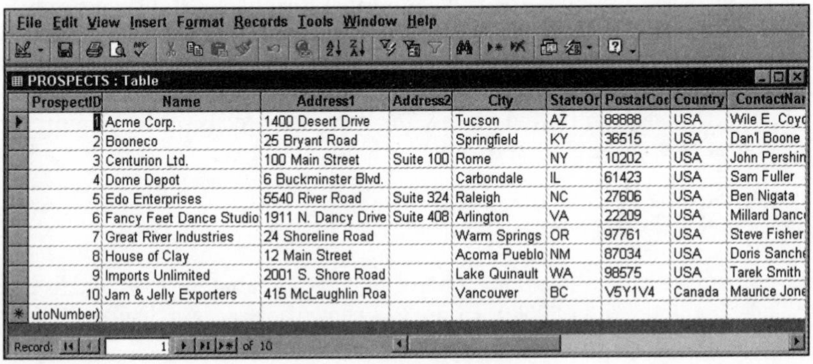

ProspectID	Name	Address1	Address2	City	StateOr	PostalCod	Country	ContactNar
1	Acme Corp.	1400 Desert Drive		Tucson	AZ	88888	USA	Wile E. Coyo
2	Booneco	25 Bryant Road		Springfield	KY	36515	USA	Dan'l Boone
3	Centurion Ltd.	100 Main Street	Suite 100	Rome	NY	10202	USA	John Pershin
4	Dome Depot	6 Buckminster Blvd.		Carbondale	IL	61423	USA	Sam Fuller
5	Edo Enterprises	5540 River Road	Suite 324	Raleigh	NC	27606	USA	Ben Nigata
6	Fancy Feet Dance Studio	1911 N. Dancy Drive	Suite 408	Arlington	VA	22209	USA	Millard Danc
7	Great River Industries	24 Shoreline Road		Warm Springs	OR	97761	USA	Steve Fisher
8	House of Clay	12 Main Street		Acoma Pueblo	NM	87034	USA	Doris Sanche
9	Imports Unlimited	2001 S. Shore Road		Lake Quinault	WA	98575	USA	Tarek Smith
10	Jam & Jelly Exporters	415 McLaughlin Roa		Vancouver	BC	V5Y1V4	Canada	Maurice Jone
utoNumber)								

Figure 2-1 *Result set from prospect address query*

You can now select File ➪ Export to send the result set to a Microsoft Word Merge file, which formats the data for a mail merge. Microsoft Word or some other word processor can now use the exported merge file to personalize your form letter. Figure 2-2 shows what the merge file looks like.

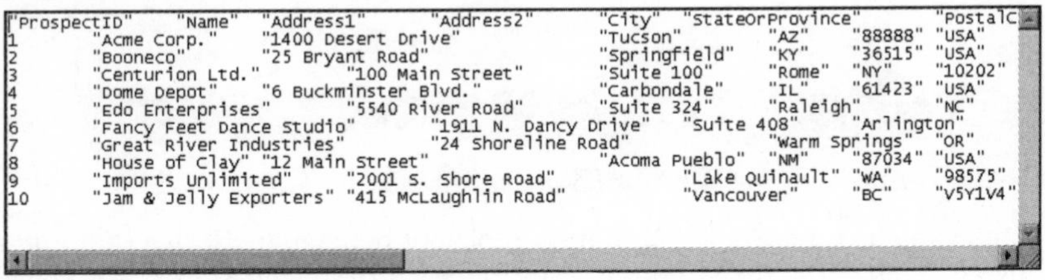

```
"ProspectID"    "Name"  "Address1"      "Address2"      "City"  "StateOrProvince"       "PostalC
1       "Acme Corp."    "1400 Desert Drive"             "Tucson"        "AZ"    "88888" "USA"
2       "Booneco"       "25 Bryant Road"                "Springfield"   "KY"    "36515" "USA"
3       "Centurion Ltd."        "100 Main Street"       "Suite 100"     "Rome"  "NY"    "10202"
4       "Dome Depot"    "6 Buckminster Blvd."           "Carbondale"    "IL"    "61423" "USA"
5       "Edo Enterprises"       "5540 River Road"       "Suite 324"     "Raleigh"       "NC"
6       "Fancy Feet Dance Studio"       "1911 N. Dancy Drive"   "Suite 408"     "Arlington"
7       "Great River Industries"        "24 Shoreline Road"             "Warm Springs"  "OR"
8       "House of Clay" "12 Main Street"                "Acoma Pueblo"  "NM"    "87034" "USA"
9       "Imports Unlimited"     "2001 S. Shore Road"            "Lake Quinault" "WA"    "98575"
10      "Jam & Jelly Exporters" "415 McLaughlin Road"           "Vancouver"     "BC"    "V5Y1V4"
```

Figure 2-2 *Exported prospect merge file*

Other DBMSs have a similar ability to export a result set to a text file suitable for mail merge, although the details of how you do it may differ.

Making More Highly Targeted Retrievals

It's great to be able to retrieve all, or even selected, attributes from a database table, but usually, you want to be more discriminating than that. Sometimes you want to retrieve data only from rows that meet certain conditions. Sometimes you want to retrieve data from two or more tables at the same time. SQL gives you a rich collection of tools to do those things. They are all contained in the `SELECT` toolbox.

Restricting retrievals to rows that meet a condition

Rather than retrieving all the data in a table all the time, you often want to retrieve only the data in certain rows. For example, the companies in Xanthic's constantly growing prospect table are scattered all across the United States and potentially may be located in other countries around the world. Suppose, as Xanthic's western regional marketing manager, you want to target a mailing at only the prospects with postal codes above 80000? These codes all lie in the western United States. You can easily focus on these prospects by adding a `WHERE` clause to your `SELECT` statement as follows:

```
SELECT * FROM PROSPECTS
   WHERE PostalCode > '80000';
```

This query returns data from all columns of the `PROSPECTS` table for rows where the value of PostalCode is greater than 80000. Figure 2-3 shows how Access displays the result of this query.

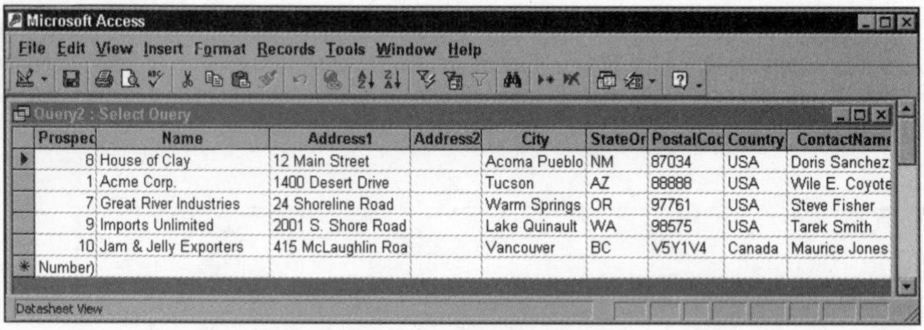

Prospec	Name	Address1	Address2	City	StateOr	PostalCoc	Country	ContactNam
8	House of Clay	12 Main Street		Acoma Pueblo	NM	87034	USA	Doris Sanchez
1	Acme Corp.	1400 Desert Drive		Tucson	AZ	88888	USA	Wile E. Coyote
7	Great River Industries	24 Shoreline Road		Warm Springs	OR	97761	USA	Steve Fisher
9	Imports Unlimited	2001 S. Shore Road		Lake Quinault	WA	98575	USA	Tarek Smith
10	Jam & Jelly Exporters	415 McLaughlin Roa		Vancouver	BC	V5Y1V4	Canada	Maurice Jones
Number)								

Figure 2-3 *Prospects in the Western US are retrieved*

This is a simple application of a `WHERE` clause, probably too simple. Notice that a prospect in Canada is listed along with all the prospects in the western United States. SQL considers V5Y1V4 to be greater than 80000 because V comes after 8 in the ASCII collating sequence. You are not interested in Canadian prospects at this time, so you need to refine the retrieval to include only U.S. prospects.

`WHERE` clauses can be much more complex than the one shown above, based on a wide variety of conditions. This added complexity, which is covered on Saturday, enables you to pull the proverbial needle of the data you want from the haystack of all the data in your database. For now, consider one small complexity that enables you to eliminate all prospects that are located outside the USA.

**10 Min.
To Go**

Refining a retrieval with multiple conditions

To satisfy your current requirement, you want to retrieve the records for all your prospects in the western United States. All such prospects have ZIP codes (stored in the PostalCode field) that are greater than 80000. Some foreign postal codes may also be greater than 80000, so to exclude them you need to specify an additional condition. You want to retrieve only records for prospects located in the United States. SQL enables you to do that easily and intuitively by adding to your WHERE clause.

```
SELECT * FROM PROSPECTS
WHERE PostalCode > '80000' AND Country = 'USA';
```

Executing this statement returns only those prospects that are located in the western United States. The AND operator is a *logical connective* and operates just the way you would expect it to. OR and NOT are additional logical connectives. Consider the following SQL statement:

```
SELECT * FROM PROSPECTS
WHERE PostalCode > '80000' AND NOT Country = 'USA';
```

This returns all prospects with postal codes greater than 80000 that are *not* located in the USA. If you want to retrieve the records for all your prospects in both the USA and Canada, but not the prospects in any other country, you can use the following code:

```
SELECT * FROM PROSPECTS
WHERE Country = 'Canada' OR Country = 'USA';
```

If a prospect is located in either Canada or the USA, this statement retrieves its record.

Retrieving data from two tables at once

In a relational database, related data is often spread across multiple tables, some of which change frequently. For example, Xanthic may have a PROSPECT table, a CUSTOMER table, a PRODUCT table, an EMPLOYEE table, a SERVICES table, and an INVOICE table. The PROSPECT table contains relatively static information about your prospects. The CUSTOMER table contains relatively static information about your customers. The PRODUCT table contains relatively static information about your standard products. The EMPLOYEE table contains relatively static information about your employees. The SERVICES table contains information about the services you normally provide. The INVOICE table contains information about sales transactions. Hopefully it is *not* static because you will go out of business rather quickly if you stop making sales.

Suppose a question arises about a specific sales transaction. You can retrieve the corresponding invoice data from the INVOICE table, but that may not be enough. It probably contains the customer number of the customer who made the purchase, but no additional information about the customer. Similarly, it probably contains only the employee ID of the person who made the sale. Additional information about the sales person, such as his or her name, would not be in the INVOICE table.

To deal with the situation, you have to draw data from multiple tables. There are several ways to do this. One is to use a JOIN operator to combine tables.

I cover joins in Session 12. A method that may be more appropriate in other situations uses the relational operators that Session 11 discusses. Session 13 covers nested SELECTs, which provide a third means of retrieving data from multiple tables.

A fourth method of retrieving data from multiple tables is the *view*. A view is a virtual table that is composed of selected columns from one or more tables. It is called a virtual table because it is just a definition, not a real table with real data in it. The DBMS pulls data from the real tables that underlie the view and displays it as if it had been retrieved from the view. Figure 2-4 is a schematic representation of a view pulled from the CUSTOMER table and the INVOICE table. It shows that the TRANSACTION view pulls customer names from the CUSTOMER table, and transaction details from the INVOICE table.

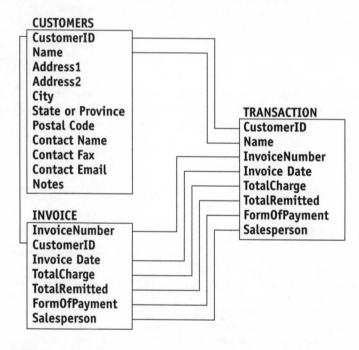

Figure 2-4 *The* TRANSACTION *view draws columns from the* CUSTOMER *table and the* INVOICE *table.*

Session 20 describes how to create a view.

Done!

REVIEW

In this session, you have just started to see how to use SQL to retrieve useful information from a relational database. However, it is already clear that SQL is a powerful, yet intuitive tool for dealing with large amounts of data. This session also covered the following:

- The SELECT statement is the only command SQL uses to retrieve data from a database.
- The asterisk (*) is a wildcard character that means "all attributes."
- SQL doesn't care how you format your statements, as long as they are syntactically correct. Indenting and the use of multiple lines in an SQL statement make it more readable to humans.
- Never use a reserved word for any purpose other than the one defined by SQL.
- Use logical connectives (AND, OR, NOT) to test for multiple conditions within a WHERE clause.
- In a relational database, related data is often spread across multiple tables, some of which may change frequently.
- A view is a virtual table composed of selected columns from one or more tables.

QUIZ YOURSELF

1. What aspect of a database table corresponds to the attributes of the entity that the table describes? (See "Retrieving Data with a Simple SELECT Statement.")
2. When is it not advisable to use the asterisk wildcard symbol in a SELECT statement? (See "Retrieving Data with a Simple SELECT Statement.")
3. Why is it important to avoid using reserved words when naming tables or attributes? (See "Retrieving Data with a Simple SELECT Statement.")
4. How should you construct a SELECT statement so that only the rows you want are retrieved? (See "Making More Highly Targeted Retrievals.")
5. What is a view, and when would you want to use one? (See "Making More Highly Targeted Retrievals.")

Data Types

Session Checklist

✔ The exact numeric data types

✔ The approximate numeric data types

✔ The character string types

✔ The bit string types

✔ The boolean types

✔ The datetime types

✔ The interval types

✔ The ROW types

✔ The ARRAY types

✔ The REF types

✔ Build your own user-defined types

✔ The distinct types

✔ Non-standard types

✔ Converting data types with CAST

**30 Min.
To Go**

Databases deal with data. In the early days, life was simple. Data came in essentially two forms, numbers and text characters. Now, as applications have grown more sophisticated, and particularly with the rise in importance of multimedia, the number of different types of data maintained in databases has expanded dramatically.

Every general-purpose computer language, such as C, Java, Visual Basic, or Fortran, has a set of data types that it recognizes and can use. The data types defined for any one of these languages are not designed to be compatible with the data types of any of the other languages. The designers of each one of these languages defined data types based on what they felt would be most appropriate for their target audience. Similarly, ANSI/ISO Standard SQL also has a defined set of data types, which are not compatible with the data types of any of the general-purpose languages. This incompatibility creates some challenges when SQL statements are embedded in applications written in a host language. In Session 10, I cover how to overcome those challenges.

The release of the SQL:1999 specification was the occasion of a major expansion of the number of data types supported by SQL. I discuss them all, although it may be some time before several of the new types are fully implemented in production database management systems. On the other hand, production database management systems, such as SQL Server and PostgreSQL implement data types that are not included in the SQL:1999 specification. I cover some of these extensions to the data type list also.

Exact Numeric Types

SQL:1999 defines four exact numeric types. As the name implies, each of these types can represent a number exactly, with no error, no fuzziness, and no plus or minus tolerance. These types are:

- INTEGER
- SMALLINT
- NUMERIC
- DECIMAL

INTEGER

The INTEGER data type holds numbers that have no fractional part (whole numbers). In SQL, the *precision* of a number is defined as the maximum number of digits that it may hold. The precision of the INTEGER type is not defined by SQL:1999, and thus may vary from one implementation to another.

SMALLINT

The SMALLINT type is very similar to the INTEGER type. The only difference is that its precision must be equal to or less than the precision of the INTEGER type of the same implementation. If you know that a column of a table you are defining will never exceed the precision of the SMALLINT type, you should use it rather than the INTEGER type. Either one works, but the SMALLINT type will probably use less memory. Some implementations don't offer the SMALLINT type, opting for simplicity at the expense of some inefficiency in memory usage and disk storage.

NUMERIC

The NUMERIC type is for numbers that do have a fractional part, digits to the right of the decimal point. With the NUMERIC type, you can specify both the precision and the scale of a number. The scale of a number is the number of digits to the right of the decimal point. Clearly, the scale of a number cannot exceed its precision; nor can it be negative. You can accept the default precision and scale of your implementation's NUMERIC type, or you can specify the precision and scale you want. To accept the default precision and scale when defining columns in a table, merely specify type as NUMERIC. To specify a non-default precision, specify NUMERIC *(p)* where *p* is the number of digits you want the precision to be. To specify both a non-default precision and a non-default scale, specify NUMERIC *(p,s)*. Table 3-1 gives some examples of the largest numbers that can be accommodated with various combinations of precision and scale.

Table 3-1 *Examples of Precision and Scale for NUMERIC Data Type (Assuming Default Precision = 12, Default Scale = 6)*

Type Specification	Largest number displayable
NUMERIC	999,999.999999
NUMERIC (10)	9,999.999999
NUMERIC (10,2)	99,999,999.99
NUMERIC (12,12)	.999999999999

You can also see from the last line of Table 3-1 that the smallest number of NUMERIC type that this system can handle is .000000000001. This may seem like a pretty small number, but for many scientific applications, it is not nearly small enough. To represent numbers that are smaller than this, you must resort to one of the approximate numeric types covered later in this session.

DECIMAL

The DECIMAL type is almost identical to the NUMERIC type, with one small difference. With the NUMERIC type, you always get exactly what you ask for. With the DECIMAL type, you may get more than you ask for. If you specify, for example, NUMERIC (10), SQL allows data up to 10 digits in length and disallows any data with more than 10 digits. However, if you specify DECIMAL (10), SQL does not necessarily reject numbers of more than 10 digits. If your implementation allows a precision of 12, SQL accepts values up to 12 digits in length, even though you specified a precision of 10. This can be helpful if you inadvertently set too low a precision value, but it can also cause problems because the system doesn't act the way you expect it to.

If you think you may want to migrate your database to another platform at some time in the future, use the NUMERIC type throughout rather than using DECIMAL. That way you can be sure that the same data is always treated the same way, regardless of what platform is hosting your database.

Approximate Numeric Types

Some numbers are either too large or too small to be represented with one of the exact numeric types. There are three approximate numeric types that you can use for such numbers:

- REAL
- DOUBLE PRECISION
- FLOAT

Numbers stored as approximate numeric types take up more space in memory than do the same numbers stored as exact numeric types. If you can be sure that the values in a table column will never exceed the capacity of your system's exact numeric types, then use an exact numeric type, which conserves memory and disk storage, and enhances performance. However, if there is any possibility that a column value may exceed the capacity of an exact type, then specify an approximate numeric type. Performance may suffer, but that is better than generating an error.

REAL

The REAL data type stores a single precision floating point number. The precision is implementation-dependent. In general, the more bits a machine's registers can hold, the higher the precision. A machine with 64-bit registers is able to store numbers with a higher precision than a 32-bit machine can handle.

A floating point number is one in which the decimal point can float around rather than be restricted to a fixed scale. Thus, 2.7182, 27.82, and 2,718,281.828 are all examples of floating point numbers. You would not, however, use the REAL data type to represent such numbers, which are all "medium sized" and fit in the registers of any modern computer.

The REAL type is appropriate for a very large number such as Avogadro's number, which is 6.02252E23 (6.02252 times 10 raised to the 23rd power). The REAL type can also be used for very small numbers such as the Planck constant, 6.6256E-34.

DOUBLE PRECISION

Numbers of the DOUBLE PRECISION type are similar to those of the REAL type but, for any given implementation, have more digits of precision in the mantissa (the 6.6256 part) than the REAL type. The DOUBLE PRECISION type of some implementations also supports a larger absolute value of exponent (the E-34 part) than does the same implementation's REAL type.

Check the documentation for your system to see exactly how it defines DOUBLE PRECISION. Because numbers of the DOUBLE PRECISION type take up more memory than do numbers of the REAL type, use the REAL type in preference to DOUBLE PRECISION whenever you can.

FLOAT

With the FLOAT data type, you can specify the precision rather than having to accept whatever default precision your system has for the REAL and DOUBLE PRECISION data types. Specifying FLOAT (6) gives you six digits of precision regardless of your system defaults. If the system can give you six digits of precision with its single precision circuitry, it does so. If not, it automatically uses its double precision circuitry instead.

If you think you may ever want to migrate your database to a different system that may have different default precision values, use the FLOAT type rather than either REAL or DOUBLE PRECISION, and explicitly specify precision. That way when your data is transferred to the new system you can be sure it will not be altered.

Character Strings

20 Min.
To Go

SQL:1999 recognizes six different data types for text characters. They are as follows:

- CHARACTER (CHAR): Holds a text string with a fixed length. If the data entered into a field of this type is shorter than the fixed length, the remaining positions are filled in with blank characters.
- CHARACTER VARYING (VARCHAR): Holds a text string of variable length. Whatever the length of the data entered, that is the length of the field. There is no filling with blanks.
- CHARACTER LARGE OBJECT (CLOB): Used for very long character strings that are beyond the capacity of the CHARACTER type.
- NATIONAL CHARACTER (NCHAR), NATIONAL CHARACTER VARYING (NVARCHAR), NATIONAL CHARACTER LARGE OBJECT (NCLOB): Like the corresponding regular CHARACTER types except for a different character set, such as Greek, Russian, or Kanji.

With NATIONAL CHARACTER types, you can create a table that uses one character set for one column and a different character set for another column. That's real flexibility, but it's likely most people will not want to do that. More likely would be to use one national character set in one table and a second national character set in another table, or create an entire database in a character set other than the standard English character set.

Bit Strings

The bit types — BIT, BIT VARYING, and BINARY LARGE OBJECT — are analogous to the corresponding character types, except they hold binary digits (0 or 1) rather than ASCII characters. A specification of BIT (8) declares a field with a maximum length of 8 bits.

Booleans

Columns of the BOOLEAN data type can hold any one of three values: TRUE, FALSE, or UNKNOWN. The BOOLEAN data type is named for the 19th century mathematician George Boole, who conceived of the two-valued logic that we now call Boolean logic and invented the rules for manipulating that logic, now called Boolean algebra. All digital computers in use today operate according to Boolean logic.

Datetimes

Five different datetime types are defined by SQL:1999. They are as follows:

- DATE: Contains no time data
- TIME WITHOUT TIMEZONE: Contains no date data
- TIMESTAMP WITHOUT TIMEZONE: Contains both time and date data
- TIME WITH TIMEZONE: Contains no date data
- TIMESTAMP WITH TIMEZONE: Contains both time and date data

 Many implementations of SQL do not support all five of these data types. When you migrate a database from one platform to another, check to see that the datetime types supported on the new system match the types your data uses. If there is an incompatibility, you have to do a type conversion.

Intervals

There are two INTERVAL types, which measure the difference between two datetime values. One type measures an interval in terms of years and months and the other type measures an interval in terms of days and time. One INTERVAL type does not work across the board because some months consist of 28 days, some consist of 29 days, some consist of 30 days, and some consist of 31 days. You can specify an interval of seven years as INTERVAL "7" YEAR, while an interval of fifteen days is specified as INTERVAL "15" DAY. In the first case the year/month INTERVAL type is used and in the second case, the day/time INTERVAL type is used.

ROW Type

The ROW type is a new feature introduced in SQL:1999. It enables you to nest an entire row of data within a single field of a table row. Many implementations do not yet support the ROW type.

The ROW type violates First Normal Form, which I describe in Session 22. If you are not fully aware of what you are doing with ROW type data, you may introduce inconsistencies into your data. If you can do without it, perhaps it is better to avoid using the ROW type. People got by without it for many years.

ARRAY Type

With the ARRAY type, you can put an array, consisting of multiple elements, into a single field of a table.

The ARRAY type is a new feature of SQL:1999; it violates First Normal Form. (See Session 22.)

REF Types

The reference (REF) type is not really a type, but rather is a pointer to a data item, ROW type, or abstract data type. It was introduced with SQL:1999 as part of the object-oriented features of that international standard.

The REF type is not a part of core SQL, which means that a vendor can claim compatibility with SQL:1999 even if they have not implemented the REF type. Object-oriented programming, and thus the usage of the REF type, is beyond the scope of this book.

User-Defined Types

A very powerful new feature introduced in SQL:1999 is the user-defined type. If the implementation you are using does not support a data type you need, you can create it yourself. A big benefit of user-defined types is the fact that you can create data types that match the data types of the host language, such as C or C++, that your database application is written in.

**10 Min.
To Go**

Implementations that do not support user-defined types have a problem when the host language recognizes different types from the ones supported by SQL. In such cases you must perform a conversion using the CAST command, which is covered in Session 10.

Distinct Types

Distinct types are a simple form of user-defined type. For example, many people want to keep track of currency data. Now, with international business more prevalent than ever before, more organizations must deal with multiple currencies. SQL's FLOAT type works for currencies but may get them mixed up. To overcome that problem, you can use the FLOAT type as the base for the definition of a DOLLAR type. You can then use the FLOAT type again as the basis for a EURO type. You could use it a third time as the basis for a YEN type. Although the DOLLAR, EURO, and YEN types are all derived from the FLOAT type, they are all distinct from each other and SQL does not allow them to be mixed.

Non-Standard Types

Every implementation of SQL, for reasons that its developers feel are good and sufficient, offers types that differ from the SQL:1999 standard types to a greater or lesser extent. Table 3-2 compares SQL:1999 types with the closest comparable data types available on several popular database management systems.

Table 3-2 *Comparison of Data Types Available on Popular DBMS Products*

SQL:1999	MS Access	MS SQL Server	Oracle	PostgreSQL
N/A*	N/A	BigInt	N/A	Int8
Integer	Long Integer	Int	Pls_Integer	Integer
Smallint	Integer	SmallInt	Pls_Integer	Int2
N/A	N/A	TinyInt	N/A	N/A
Numeric	Currency	Numeric	Number	Numeric
Decimal	Decimal	Decimal	Number	Numeric
N/A	N/A	Small Money	N/A	N/A
N/A	Currency	Money	N/A	N/A
Real	Single	Real	Number	Float4
Double precision	Double	Double Precision	Number	Float
Float	Double	Float	Number	Float
Character	Text	Char	Char	Char
Varchar	Text	VarChar	Varchar2	Varchar
N/A	N/A	N/A	Long	N/A
Clob	Memo	Text	Clob	Text
Nchar	Text	NChar	Nchar	N/A

SQL:1999	MS Access	MS SQL Server	Oracle	PostgreSQL
Nvarchar	Text	NVarChar	Nvarchar2	N/A
Nclob	Memo	Ntext	Nclob	N/A
N/A	N/A	N/A	Bfile	N/A
Bit	Byte	Binary	N/A	N/A
Bit varying	Byte	VarBinary	N/A	N/A
N/A	N/A	N/A	Binary Integer	N/A
N/A	N/A	N/A	Long Raw	N/A
Blob	OLE Object	Image	Blob	N/A
Boolean	Yes/No	Bit	Boolean	Bool
N/A	N/A	Small DateTime	N/A	N/A
Date	Long Date	DateTime	Date	Date
Time w/o timezone	Long Time	DateTime	N/A	Time
Timestamp without timezone	Long Time	TimeStamp	Timestamp	Timestamp
Time with timezone	Long Time	DateTime	N/A	Time
Timestamp with timezone	Long Time	TimeStamp	Timestamp	Timestamp
Interval	N/A	N/A	N/A	Interval
N/A	N/A	N/A	N/A	Point
N/A	N/A	N/A	N/A	Lseg
N/A	N/A	N/A	N/A	Path
N/A	N/A	N/A	N/A	Box
N/A	N/A	N/A	N/A	Circle
N/A	N/A	N/A	N/A	Polygon
N/A	N/A	N/A	N/A	Inet
N/A	N/A	N/A	N/A	Cidr
N/A	N/A	N/A	N/A	Macaddr

(N/A means Not Available)

Table 3-2 shows that none of the platforms listed offers all of the SQL:1999 data types, and furthermore, each offers at least one type that is not included among the SQL:1999 types. Access extends the standard with a Currency type. SQL Server has BigInt, TinyInt, Small Money, Money, and Small DateTime. Oracle has Long, Binary Integer, Bfile, and Long Raw. PostgreSQL extends the standard with Int8, the geometric types Point, Lseg, Path, Circle, and Polygon, and the network types Inet, Cidr, and Macaddr.

The differences in types offered reflect the histories of the various DBMSs and the types of applications they typically address.

If you think you may ever migrate a database from one DBMS platform to another, don't use any of the types that are extensions beyond those defined by the SQL:1999 standard. Even then you may have problems because the DBMS you are porting to may not support a SQL:1999 standard type that you are using.

CAST Data Type Conversions

As shown in Table 3-2, some data type incompatibilities exist among the various popular implementations of SQL. Those are not the only incompatibilities. When SQL statements are embedded in programs written in host languages such as C++, Java, or Visual Basic, they must be able to receive data from their host program and send results back to the host program. If the host language uses different data types than the particular SQL implementation that it encloses, the incompatibility can make data transfer difficult or impossible.

A data type problem can arise even when using standard SQL data types. You may have, for example, date data in a column of the DATE type in one table and date data in a column of the CHARACTER type in another table. You cannot combine data from these two table columns due to the type incompatibility.

The CAST expression addresses these problems. It converts data of one type to another type. Naturally there are restrictions on the conversions that you can make. The actual data being converted must be compatible with the type it is being converted to. For example, you may have a character string "2001-12-31" (type CHAR(10)) that you want to convert to DATE type data. CAST can handle such a conversion for you. But, if you have a CHAR(10) string such as "hyperspace" CAST cannot convert it to the DATE type.

Suppose you had two tables, APPLICANTS and EMPLOYEES. APPLICANTS holds records of job applicants with each person's social security number in a CHAR(9) field named SSN. The EMPLOYEES table holds records of current employees with each person's social security number in an INTEGER field named SSN. You want to see if any employees are still listed in the APPLICANTS tables. If SSN in both tables was of the INTEGER type, you could answer that question with the following query:

```
SELECT * FROM EMPLOYEES
    WHERE EMPLOYEES.SSN = APPLICANTS.SSN ;
```

The result set would be a list of records of people who appear in both tables. However, because the data types of the two SSN columns are different, the above query would not work. You cannot make a comparison of two incompatible data types. You can, however,

CAST the data type of the APPLICANTS column to INTEGER, which allows the comparison to be made. This takes the following form:

```
SELECT * FROM EMPLOYEES
  WHERE EMPLOYEES.SSN =
      CAST(APPLICANTS.SSN AS INTEGER);
```

This returns the same result set that would have been returned if APPLICANTS.SSN had been of the INTEGER type in the first place.

You can use CAST the same way when converting data passed to SQL by a host language in a host variable. Sometimes one or more input values for an SQL statement may not be known until runtime. In such cases, the host language program that the SQL is embedded within passes the needed input values to the SQL statement using host variables. As long as the actual data being passed is compatible with the target SQL data type, SQL accepts the CASTed data coming from the host program.

Done!

REVIEW

Programming languages and database management systems deal with data of a variety of types. There is no agreement on what these types should be, although DBMS vendors try to offer the types defined by the SQL:1999 specification. These types do not agree very well with the types used by the most popular programming languages.

The core SQL:1999 specification defines several exact numeric types, approximate numeric types, character string types, bit string types, and date and time types, as well as the Boolean type, ROW type, and ARRAY type. In addition, with user-defined types, you can create your own data types.

In order to secure a competitive advantage, database management systems often offer data types that are not included in the SQL:1999 specification. Use of these proprietary types compromises the portability of databases that employ them.

QUIZ YOURSELF

1. What is the advantage of using the SMALLINT type rather than the INTEGER type? (See "Exact Numeric Types.")

2. Why may you *not* want to use the SMALLINT type? (See "Exact Numeric Types.")

3. What should you do if you want to store text strings that may be longer than the CHARACTER type can handle? (See "Character Strings.")

4. A DBMS that covers several of the SQL:1999 numeric data types with a single type, such as Oracle's NUMBER type, is trading off what features for implementation simplicity? (See "Exact Numeric Types.")

Representing Data Values

Session Checklist

✔ Row values are not atomic

✔ Literal values are exactly what they appear to be

✔ Use variables to temporarily hold values

✔ Column references identify table columns

✔ Functions perform operations and return a value

✔ Simple value expressions perform operations and change operands

Clearly, the most important single element of a database system is the data it contains. Without the data, there is no point to any of the rest. The values contained in the tables' fields are what you want. In this session, I discuss the different ways of referring to and retrieving the data values in a database.

30 Min. To Go

In Session 3, I describe the various types of data that SQL supports. You can retrieve that data in a variety of ways.

Cross-Ref

Row Values

Normally, when we speak of a *value,* we are referring to a single number, text string, date, or other unit of data. A *field* contains such a value in a particular column of a table for a particular row of that table. This type of value is called a *scalar* or *atomic* value because it cannot be broken down into smaller parts. A *row value,* however, is a composite of all the individual values in a row of a table. It is a collection of atomic values, but the collection is also considered to be a value.

Literal Values

The value in a database table field could be a variable or a constant. As the names imply, the value of a variable can change but the value of a constant cannot. A literal value is a constant for which the value is literally the constant itself. Table 4-1 shows example literal values for the SQL data types.

Table 4-1   *Example Literal Values for SQL Data Types*

Data Type	Example Literal Value
INTEGER	31415926
SMALLINT	31415
NUMERIC	314159.26
DECIMAL	314159.26
REAL	3.14159E15
DOUBLE PRECISION	3.14159265359E15
FLOAT	3.14159E15
CHARACTER (15)	'Electronic '
VARCHAR	'Electronic'
NATIONAL CHARACTER (15)	'_____ '
NVARCHAR	'_____'
BIT (12)	B'011100010100'
BIT VARYING (16)	B'011100010100'
DATE	'2001-06-14'
TIME	'22:39:54:11'
TIMESTAMP	TIMESTAMP '2001-06-14-22:39:54:110000'
TIME WITH TIMEZONE	TIME '22:39:54:1100-08:00'
TIMESTAMP WITH TIMEZONE	TIMESTAMP '2001-06-14-22:39:54:1100+01:00'
INTERVAL DAY	INTERVAL '10' DAY

In a database query, you may use a literal value to retrieve a row from a table. You can do so by asking to retrieve the row where the value in a particular column is equal to a literal value. An example of such a usage is:

```
SELECT *
FROM INVOICE
WHERE InvoiceDate = '2001-07-15';
```

Variables

In the code example in the previous section, using a literal value to retrieve invoice records from July 15, 2001 is appropriate if the sales from that date are the only ones you care about. But what if you also care about the sales on July 16, 17, and so on? Rewriting the query with a new date every time can become tedious.

If you want the same type of information over and over again but for a different date every time, it makes sense to write a program to retrieve that information and use a variable to specify the date. You can embed an SQL query within the program and retrieve a whole series of records. Your program in pseudocode, where pseudocode is shown in italics, may look something like this:

```
Solicit start date for retrieval into variable DateOfSale
Solicit last date for retrieval into variable EndDate
Loop label

EXEC SQL SELECT *
        FROM INVOICE
        WHERE InvoiceDate = :DateOfSale;

Increment DateOfSale
Loop Until DateOfSale = EndDate
```

Write the procedural code, such as accepting input from the user and setting up a loop, in a language such as Visual Basic or C++. EXEC SQL is a directive to the procedural language compiler that the current statement is an embedded SQL statement. Rather than trying to execute the SQL, the program passes it to the DBMS for execution and then accepts the result that the DBMS passes back.

Column References

In most cases, you are interested in only some of the information in a table rather than all of it. You want to retrieve the information in some columns, but not others.

In Session 2, you learned that you can select from a table only the data that currently interests you by specifying the columns that contain that data. For example:

```
SELECT Name, Address1, Address2, City, StateOrProvince,
    PostalCode, Country, ContactName

FROM PROSPECTS;
```

This retrieves only the address information from the PROSPECTS table. Name, Address1, and so on are the names of columns in the PROSPECTS table, and are called *column references*. Because PROSPECTS is the only table involved in the SELECT statement, it is clear that these column references refer to columns in the PROSPECTS table. Sometimes however, a statement may deal with more than one table.

Suppose you have a CUSTOMERS table that holds the names of organizations that have already bought something from you. Suppose further that the columns in the CUSTOMERS table have the same names as the columns in the PROSPECTS table and that you would like to see if any companies are in both tables. You can find what you want with a query on both tables that uses fully qualified column references. A fully qualified column reference explicitly states which table a column is from. One such use may be:

```
SELECT CUSTOMERS.Name, CUSTOMERS.City
FROM PROSPECTS, CUSTOMERS
WHERE CUSTOMERS.NAME = PROSPECTS.Name;
```

If there are any records in the CUSTOMERS table where the value in the Name field is equal to the value in the Name field of the PROSPECTS table, those records are retrieved. The City retrieved is the one from the CUSTOMERS table. The value of the City field in the corresponding PROSPECTS record is not retrieved.

Functions

**20 Min.
To Go**

SQL includes several functions that perform common operations within an SQL statement. There are two main categories of functions: aggregate functions and value functions.

Aggregate functions

Aggregate functions, also called *set functions,* operate on sets of rows rather than individual rows. They return results having to do with the whole set of rows. To illustrate how the aggregate functions work, consider Xanthic's INVOICE table, shown in Figure 4-1.

InvoiceNumbe	CustomerID	InvoiceDate	TotalCharge	TotalRemitted	FormOfPayme	Salesperso
273	3141	12/17/2001	$120.00	$120.00	cash	Warren
274	5347	12/17/2001	$2,880.00	$2,880.00	check	Schneider
275	1440	12/18/2001	$960.00	$480.00	Visa	Peters
276	2339	12/19/2001	$240.00	$240.00	American Expre	Peters
277	3141	12/20/2001	$10,540.00	$1,054.00	check	Warren
278	2339	12/21/2001	$6,750.00	$3,375.00	check	Peters
279	4772	12/21/2001	$180.00	$180.00	Visa	Schneider
280	5771	12/24/2001	$2,350.00	$2,350.00	check	Schneider
281	8333	12/24/2001	$4,500.00	$2,250.00	check	Warren

Figure 4-1 The Xanthic Systems INVOICE *table*

There aren't many records in this sample table, but imagine that there are hundreds of records. The sales manager probably has many questions that can't be answered by simply looking at the display of the table rows. The following sections examine the possible questions.

COUNT

One question the sales manager may ask is, "How many sales were made altogether?" You can answer this question using the COUNT aggregate function.

```
SELECT COUNT (*)
FROM INVOICE;
```

SQL returns the result "9" in this case, which is the number of rows in the table.

AVG

Another likely question is, "What was the average sale?" Answer this using the AVG aggregate function.

```
SELECT AVG (TotalCharge)
FROM INVOICE;
```

The result, $3,168.89, gives the sales manager an idea about how his sales team is doing.

MAX

One question that may arise is, "What is the largest sale in the table?" This is a job for the MAX aggregate function.

```
SELECT MAX (TotalCharge)
FROM INVOICE;
```

This returns $10,540.00, the value of Warren's sale to the customer with ID = 3141.

MIN

Just as there are occasions when you want to know the maximum value in a column, there are other occasions when you want to know the minimum value. There is an aggregate function for that, too.

```
SELECT MIN (TotalCharge)
FROM INVOICE;
```

This query yields an answer of $120.00, which is the value of Warren's first sale to customer 3141. That's interesting. A small initial purchase led to a large one later. It pays to treat even the smallest customer well.

SUM

Perhaps the one fact the sales manager would want to know more than any other is, "What were the total sales?" The SUM function gives the answer to that question.

```
SELECT SUM (TotalCharge)
FROM INVOICE;
```

The result, $28,520.00, should make the sales manager happy. That's not bad for a week's sales.

Value functions

Any modern database management system gives you an array of value functions to help you manipulate character strings, numbers, dates, or other types of data. ANSI/ISO standard SQL offers a relatively small set. Any DBMS that you are likely to use probably offers the SQL value functions plus more. Here I briefly describe the SQL value functions. Consult the documentation for your particular DBMS to see what non-standard functions it offers. The standard SQL value functions fall into three categories: string value functions, numeric value functions, and datetime value functions.

String value functions

SQL has six value functions that operate on character strings. They are:

- SUBSTRING
- UPPER
- LOWER
- TRIM
- TRANSLATE
- CONVERT

SUBSTRING

The SUBSTRING value function enables you to extract a string of consecutive characters from within a larger string. Usage of this function takes the following form:

```
SUBSTRING (SourceString FROM Start FOR Length)
```

Suppose for example that the Xanthic Systems marketing manager, wondering about the geographic distribution of prospects, wants to extract the area code from the phone numbers in the PROSPECTS table. The phone numbers are stored in the form '(aaa) xxx-xxxx' so the area code is comprised of the second, third, and fourth characters. You can use the SUBSTRING value function in a SELECT statement to retrieve the area codes from the PROSPECTS table. The function call looks like this:

```
SUBSTRING (ContactPhone FROM 2 FOR 3)
```

ContactPhone is the column reference that contains the whole phone number. The function starts at character position 2 and collects three characters, neatly extracting the area code from the rest of the characters in the ContactPhone column.

Both PostgreSQL 7.1 and MySQL 4.0 support SQL:1999 syntax as shown here. SQL Server and Oracle 9i offer the same functionality but with non-standard syntax.

UPPER

The UPPER value function, when applied to a character string, converts all the characters in the string to uppercase. It does not affect any characters that are already in uppercase. For example:

```
UPPER (Weekend Crash Course) → WEEKEND CRASH COURSE
```

LOWER

The LOWER value function has the reverse effect of the UPPER function. It converts all the characters in the string to lowercase. It has no effect on characters that are already in lowercase. So:

```
LOWER (Weekend Crash Course) → weekend crash course
```

TRIM

The TRIM value function trims unwanted characters off the leading and trailing ends of a character string. Here are a few examples:

```
TRIM (LEADING ' ' FROM ' Weekend ') → 'Weekend '
TRIM (TRAILING ' ' FROM ' Weekend ') → ' Weekend'
TRIM (BOTH ' ' FROM ' Weekend ') → 'Weekend'
TRIM (TRAILING 'O' FROM 'CONCERTO') → 'CONCERT'
```

In the first example, the leading blank is trimmed off. In the second example, the trailing blank is removed. The third example shows both leading and trailing blanks have been trimmed. The fourth example demonstrates that you can trim off any character, not just blanks. However, the blank character is the default for the trim value function, so the following is also a valid use:

```
TRIM (BOTH FROM ' Weekend ') → 'Weekend'
```

TRANSLATE and CONVERT

The TRANSLATE and CONVERT value functions do similar things. They either translate a string from one character set to the same string in a different character set or convert a string from one form of use to another form of use. So for example, you could translate a string from the English character set to the Kanji character set. This does not, however, translate the meaning; it only substitutes a Kanji character for the equivalent English character. The result probably won't make much sense. Another use is to translate from one coding scheme to another, such as ASCII to EBCDIC. Translations and conversions are product specific and vary from one DBMS to another.

Numeric value functions

There are five numeric value functions:

10 Min. To Go

- POSITION
- CHARACTER_LENGTH
- OCTET_LENGTH
- BIT_LENGTH
- EXTRACT

The important thing to remember about numeric value functions is that the output of the function is always a number. The input can be data of a non-numeric type.

POSITION

The POSITION value function operates on character strings. It searches for the target sub-string you specify within a source string and returns the character position of the first character of the target string. The syntax is:

```
POSITION (target IN source)
```

Some examples:

```
POSITION ('312' IN ContactPhone) → 2
```

312 is the area code in the ContactPhone column of the PROSPECTS table. The numeral 3 is in character position 2 of '(312) 555-4444' because character position 1 holds a left parenthesis. Looking at the same table row, another example would be:

```
POSITION ('44' IN ContactPhone) → 11
```

The first numeral 4 is at character position 11.

If the target string does not occur in the source string, the result is 0:

```
POSITION ('banana' IN ContactPhone) → 0
```

CHARACTER_LENGTH

The CHARACTER_LENGTH value function returns the number of characters in the source string, so, for example, when applied to ContactPhone for the row with '(312) 555-4444', it returns 14.

```
CHARACTER_LENGTH (ContactPhone) → 14
```

OCTET_LENGTH

Computers use eight bits to encode a single character from the character set of an alphabetic written language such as English, Spanish, German, or French. Eight bits is sufficient to represent up to 256 different alphabetic characters, including upper and lower case letters, numerals, and punctuation. Those eight bits have traditionally been called a *byte*. SQL however, prefers the more specific word *octet*, which implies "eightness." An English word that is six characters long, such as *banana*, takes up six octets of memory. Some languages, such as Chinese, have so many different characters that eight bits is not sufficient to represent them all. For such languages each character is encoded into two octets. This allows the representation of 65,536 different characters, which is enough for ideographic languages such as Chinese.

The OCTET_LENGTH value function is similar to the CHARACTER_LENGTH value function, except it counts octets rather than characters. When you are dealing with an alphabetic language such as English, OCTET_LENGTH and CHARACTER_LENGTH both return the same result. When you are dealing with an ideographic language such as CHINESE, the number of octets returned by OCTET_LENGTH is twice the number of characters in the string.

BIT_LENGTH

BIT_LENGTH is similar to OCTET_LENGTH and CHARACTER_LENGTH but measures the number of bits in a bit string rather than the number of octets or characters in a character string. For example:

```
BIT_LENGTH (B'011100010100') → 12
```

The B indicates that the following string is a bit string. The string contains 12 bits, so that is the result returned by the BIT_LENGTH value function.

EXTRACT

The EXTRACT value function reaches into a datetime or interval and pulls out a specified component:

```
EXTRACT (DAY FROM InvoiceDate) → 17
```

For the selected row, the date in the InvoiceDate column is 12/17/2001. The EXTRACT value function returned the DAY portion of the datetime value.

Datetime value functions

There are three datetime value functions:

- CURRENT_DATE
- CURRENT_TIME
- CURRENT_TIMESTAMP

CURRENT_DATE does not take an argument, but both CURRENT_TIME and CURRENT_TIMESTAMP take a single argument that specifies the precision of the fractional part of the seconds. Here is an example of the usage of each:

```
CURRENT_DATE → 2001-12-31
CURRENT_TIME (2) → 09:37:25.23
CURRENT_TIMESTAMP (1) → 2001-12-31:09:37:25.2
```

The date and time information is retrieved from the computer's system clock.

Simple Value Expressions

SQL expressions are called value expressions because regardless of what type of data they deal with, they must reduce to a single value. Some of the SQL value expressions are relatively straightforward and others are quite complex. Here I talk only about the simple ones, which are the ones you are most likely to encounter anyway. There are four kinds of simple value expressions:

- String
- Numeric
- Datetime
- Interval

String value expressions

A string value expression can include any character string or multiple character strings combined by the concatenation operator (||). Here are some examples:

```
ContactName                    → 'Wile E. Coyote'
'Wile E. Coyote'               → 'Wile E. Coyote'
'Mr. ' || ContactName          → 'Mr. Wile E. Coyote'
```

ContactName is a column reference, and in the selected row of the PROSPECTS table, the customer's contact is named Wile E. Coyote. A string value expression can also be a concatenation of a literal value and a column reference, as shown in the third example above.

Numeric value expressions

Numeric value expressions deal with data of any of the numeric types. Four operators (addition, subtraction, multiplication, and division) are valid for the numeric value expressions. Here are some examples of valid numeric value expressions:

```
56
56 + 76
TotalCharge - TotalRemitted
TotalCharge - (TotalCharge * DiscountPercent)
TotalCharge/10
```

Numeric value expressions are evaluated according to an order of precedence. The order in which an expression is evaluated follows these rules:

- **Operations in parentheses are performed first.**

- **Exponentiation operations are performed next.**

- **Multiplication and Division are performed next, starting with the leftmost such operator.**

- **Addition and subtraction are performed last, starting with the leftmost such operator.**

Datetime value expressions

Datetime value expressions operate on date and time data, which can be of the DATE, TIME, TIMESTAMP, or INTERVAL types. For example, if you want to specify tomorrow's date you can use

```
CURRENT_DATE + INTERVAL '1' DAY
```

You can specify a time in your local time zone with:

```
TIME (2) '22:24:22.24' AT LOCAL
```

Interval value expressions

If you subtract one datetime from another, you get an *interval*. You can also multiply or divide an interval by a numeric constant. Remember that there are two types of interval, the year-month interval and the day-time interval. They must be treated separately because months are not all made up of the same number of days. If you want to know how old you are, you can have SQL compute it for you with:

```
(CURRENT_DATE - BIRTHDATE) YEAR TO MONTH
```

If you want to know how slow your customers are in paying their bills you can use

```
(PaymentReceived - InvoiceDate) DAY
```

Done!

REVIEW

SQL deals with both constants and variables. You can use literal values in a query when you don't plan to ask for similar information in the future. If you *do* plan to make similar queries, you can save time and effort by defining a variable for the desired quantity. That way you don't have to reconstruct the entire query each time. You only have to change the value of the variable, and then run the original query again.

Aggregate functions give you information about characteristics of sets of table rows that you specify. With value functions you can operate on the values contained in fields of database tables. With simple value expressions, you can perform operations on a column's values that are appropriate for the column's data type.

QUIZ YOURSELF

1. You can retrieve rows from a table with a SELECT statement that compares the contents of a column to a literal value. How would you retrieve all the rows from the PROSPECTS table where the StateOrProvince column contains the value "Canada"? (See "Literal Values.")
2. What is a fully qualified column reference? (See "Column References.")
3. What function would you use to retrieve the number of rows in a table? (See "Aggregate functions.")
4. What would be the result of the following value function? (See "Value functions.") UPPER (TRIM (Both 's' FROM 'spin the wheels'))
5. What value would be returned by the following value expression? (See "Simple Value Expressions.")

   (15 + 45) / 6

PART

I

Friday Evening
Part Review

1. What is a flat file composed of?
2. What is a big negative factor in using flat files from the point of view of the application program that accesses them?
3. What is metadata?
4. What kind of structure is the relational model based upon?
5. What is SQL?
6. Type an SQL statement that retrieves the contents of the ContactName and ContactPhone fields from the PROSPECTS table.
7. Type an SQL statement that retrieves the contents of the ContactName and ContactPhone fields from the PROSPECTS table, only for those prospects who live in Canada.
8. In SQL, what is the precision of a number?
9. When is it appropriate to use the REAL data type rather than the NUMERIC data type?
10. What values might you find in a field of the BOOLEAN data type?
11. What is the problem with using a proprietary data type that is not included in the SQL:1999 specification?
12. What provision does SQL give a DBMS for dealing with data that is not of a type that the DBMS recognizes?
13. What is a fully qualified column reference?
14. Type an SQL statement that returns the number of rows in the PROSPECTS table.
15. Type an SQL statement that retrieves all the rows in the PROSPECTS table where the value in the Country field starts with the letter "U."
16. What must a value expression reduce to?

☑ Friday

☑ Saturday

☐ Sunday

Part II — Saturday Morning

Part III — Saturday Afternoon

Part IV — Saturday Evening

PART

II

Saturday Morning

Retrieving Specific Data

Session Checklist

✔ Using comparison predicates to establish relationships

✔ Reasoning with three-valued logic rather than two-valued logic

✔ Performing complex queries by combining conditions with logical connectives

✔ Locating a value with BETWEEN and NOT BETWEEN

✔ Determining set membership with IN and NOT IN

**30 Min.
To Go**

In this session, you add some of SQL's most useful retrieval tools to your repertoire. In Session 2, I introduced the use of WHERE clauses as a way of restricting the rows returned by a query to those rows that satisfied a stated condition. In this session, I give a thorough treatment of comparison predicates such as the one used in Session 2, as well as several additional ways to make sure you get the records you want and only the records you want.

Using Comparison Predicates

The following statement (from Session 2) retrieved all the rows in the PROSPECTS table where the value in the PostalCode Column was greater than 80,000.

```
SELECT * FROM PROSPECTS
    WHERE PostalCode > '80000';
```

This is an example of the use of a comparison predicate. The predicate compares the value in the PostalCode column to the literal value 80,000. For each row where the condition was satisfied, that row was selected. SQL has six comparison operators that are used in comparison predicates, as shown in Table 5-1.

Table 5-1 *SQL's Comparison Operators*

Comparison	Symbol
Equal	=
Not equal	<>
Less than	<
Less than or equal	<=
Greater than	>
Greater than or equal	>=

The Equal predicate is the one that sees the most use, but all the others are fairly common, too. Here are a few more examples of their use:

The following retrieves all records from the PROSPECTS table where the prospect is located in California:

```
SELECT * FROM PROSPECTS
    WHERE StateOrProvince = 'CA';
```

This following retrieves all records from the INVOICE table where the total charge was greater than or equal to $1,000:

```
SELECT * FROM INVOICE
    WHERE TotalCharge >= 1000;
```

This following retrieves all records from the PROSPECTS table where the prospect is located outside the United States:

```
SELECT * FROM PROSPECTS
    WHERE Country <> 'USA';
```

Reasoning with Three-Valued Logic

Just about any computer language you are liable to come across uses two-valued logic. Two and only two logical states are allowed, true and false. For example, either a prospect's country is equal to USA or it is not. SQL differs from all those other computer languages in that it uses three-valued logic. The three values are true, false, and unknown. If an operand in a predicate has a NULL value, that means the value of the operand is unknown. It may be true; it may be false; we just don't know.

The possibility of NULL values for an operand in a predicate affects what rows are retrieved by SELECT statements. Consider the retrieval:

```
SELECT * FROM PROSPECTS
    WHERE Country <> 'USA';
```

As SQL moves through the rows of the PROSPECTS table there are three cases it may encounter:

- The Country field could contain 'USA'
- The Country field could contain a definite value other than 'USA'
- The Country field could contain a NULL value

If the Country field of a row contains 'USA,' that row is not selected. If the Country field of a row contains a definite value other than 'USA,' that row is selected. If the Country field contains a NULL value, that row is not selected. Because SQL does not know whether the row satisfies the condition, it assumes it does not.

If the table column you are testing with a comparison predicate may contain NULL values, be sure you state your query so that the results you get are the results you want. If you want to retrieve rows with an unknown truth value as well as the rows that clearly satisfy the condition, you can include them by adding another comparison using the OR logical connective (see following section).

Combining Conditions with Logical Connectives

Frequently, people want to make retrievals based on multiple conditions, rather than on just one. Multiple conditions can be combined in a single query using the logical connectives AND, OR, and NOT.

AND

Sometimes you want several conditions to all be simultaneously satisfied before you retrieve a row from a table. For example, you may want to retrieve all rows from Xanthic Systems' INVOICE table where TotalCharge is greater than $1,000 and the Salesperson is Schneider. You can do this with the AND logical connective.

```
SELECT * FROM INVOICE
    WHERE TotalCharge > 1000
        AND Salesperson = 'Schneider';
```

All rows that satisfy both conditions are retrieved. Rows that satisfy only one of the two conditions, or neither of them, are not retrieved. You can connect as many conditions as you like in the same way. You are not restricted to two. So, for example, the following query retrieves all rows for sales made by Schneider that fall within a range.

```
SELECT * FROM INVOICE
    WHERE TotalCharge > 1000
        AND TotalCharge < 2500
        AND Salesperson = 'Schneider';
```

Note that if Schneider had made a sale for exactly $1,000 or $2,500, it would not be included in the retrieval. Because "Greater than" and "Less than" operators are used, the endpoints of the range are not included.

OR

Sometimes you want to select a row if any one of several conditions is true. These are jobs for the OR logical connective. You can use it to connect as many predicates as you want to. If at least one of the predicates evaluates to a TRUE value, the row is retrieved. Consider the following query:

```
SELECT * FROM PROSPECTS
    WHERE StateOrProvince = 'NY'
      OR StateOrProvince = 'KY'
      OR StateOrProvince = 'VA';
```

The rows for all prospects located in the states of New York, Kentucky, or Virginia are retrieved. Prospects located anywhere else are excluded.

The OR logical connective provides a means of retrieving rows where you don't know whether they satisfy a given condition or not. The following query retrieves rows that have a NULL value in the condition column as well as rows that clearly satisfy the stated condition.

```
SELECT * FROM PROSPECTS
    WHERE Country <> 'USA'
    OR Country IS NULL;
```

NOT

The NOT logical connective, which doesn't really connect anything, negates the truth value of a predicate. If a predicate evaluates to TRUE, putting a NOT in front of it flips the evaluation to FALSE. Conversely, if a predicate evaluates to FALSE, preceding it with NOT converts its evaluation to TRUE. We can use the NOT connective in a retrieval from the INVOICE table to find all the sales made by salespeople other than Schneider.

```
SELECT * FROM INVOICE
    WHERE NOT (Salesperson = 'Schneider');
```

In this case, you get exactly the same result that you would get with the following query:

```
SELECT * FROM INVOICE
    WHERE Salesperson <> 'Schneider';
```

However, the NOT connective comes in handy when you want to negate predicates other than the comparison predicates.

Mixing logical connectives

You can make rather complex retrievals with multiple predicates connected by different logical connectives. The AND, OR, and NOT connectives can all appear in the same WHERE clause. I can illustrate this situation with the following query.

```
SELECT * FROM INVOICE
    WHERE ((TotalCharge > 1000
        AND TotalCharge < 7000)
        OR CustomerID = 3141)
        AND NOT (Salesperson = 'Schneider');
```

The parentheses in the WHERE clause are there to ensure that the predicates are evaluated in the correct order. Innermost parentheses are evaluated first from left to right. This statement first retrieves all rows where Total charge was greater than $1,000 and less than $7,000. Then it retrieves all rows where Customer ID is 3141, regardless of the value of TotalSale. Finally it eliminates from the retrieval all rows where Salesperson is Schneider, returning all the qualifying rows for salespeople other than Schneider.

**20 Min.
To Go**

Using BETWEEN and NOT BETWEEN to Locate a Value

Earlier in this session you saw how to select rows from a table based on whether the value in a field falls within a specified range:

```
SELECT * FROM INVOICE
    WHERE TotalCharge > 1000
        AND TotalCharge < 2500;
```

This statement, using two predicates and the AND logical connective, retrieves all rows where TotalCharge is greater than $1,000 and less than $2,500. The endpoints of $1,000 and $2,500 are not included in the range. If you want to include the endpoints in the range, you can do so with a slight modification of the query to:

```
SELECT * FROM INVOICE
    WHERE TotalCharge >= 1000
        AND TotalCharge <= 2500;
```

A third way to specify a range in a predicate is to use the BETWEEN operator. If the value of a field falls between two specified endpoints, it satisfies the retrieval condition and its row is retrieved. Such a query looks similar to this:

```
SELECT * FROM INVOICE
    WHERE TotalCharge
        BETWEEN 1000 AND 2500;
```

When you use the BETWEEN operator, the endpoints of the specified range are included in the selection. In the above statement, if there were a field in the table where TotalCharge equaled $1,000 or $2,500, its row would be selected. The BETWEEN operator gives the same results as are given by a selection using the greater than or equal and less than or equal comparison operators connected by the AND logical connector. The two immediately previous SELECT statements produce the same set of rows as a result.

The NOT BETWEEN operator works just as you would expect. If a predicate using the BETWEEN operator returns a TRUE value, the same predicate using the NOT BETWEEN operator returns a FALSE value. If a predicate using the BETWEEN operator returns a FALSE value, the same predicate using the NOT BETWEEN operator returns a TRUE value. If a predicate using the BETWEEN operator returns an UNKNOWN value, the same predicate using the NOT BETWEEN operator also returns an UNKNOWN value.

One thing to watch out for with the BETWEEN predicate is that the order of the operands matters, unlike sloppy old illogical English, where the order of operands doesn't matter. In English, if I say that a number is between 2500 and 1000, most people consider that to be equivalent to saying that the number is between 1000 and 2500. SQL is neither so sloppy; nor is it so forgiving. If a column contains the number 2000, for example, the predicate "BETWEEN 1000 AND 2500'" retrieves it, but the predicate "BETWEEN 2500 and 1000" does not. When you use the BETWEEN predicate, always make sure that the operand on the left is smaller than the operand on the right.

Using IN and NOT IN to Determine Set Membership

**10 Min.
To Go**

The IN and NOT IN operators are used in predicates that test whether or not specified values are contained within a given set of values. For example, Xanthic's Regional Sales Manager for the southwestern United States may want to see all the records in the PROSPECTS table for organizations located in New Mexico, Arizona, California, Nevada, or Utah. The following query can retrieve those records:

```
SELECT * FROM PROSPECTS
   WHERE StateOrProvince IN ('NM','AZ','CA','NV','UT');
```

For any given row in the PROSPECTS table, if the value in the StateOrProvince field is included in the list, SQL returns a TRUE value and the row is selected. If the row contains a value that is not included in the list, SQL returns a FALSE value and the row is not selected. If the row contains a NULL value, SQL returns an UNKNOWN value and the row is not selected.

The NOT IN operator works the same way as the IN operator, only it retrieves records that are not in the given set of values. Xanthic's National Sales Manager is responsible for business throughout the world, except in the territory of the Southwestern Regional Sales Manager. You can retrieve all the prospects that are not in the Southwestern territory with the following query:

```
SELECT * FROM PROSPECTS
   WHERE StateOrProvince NOT IN ('NM','AZ','CA','NV','UT');
```

With SQL there is often more than one way to perform any desired function. For example, the query shown above using the IN operator can also be done using comparison operators and logical connectives. It looks like this:

```
SELECT * FROM PROSPECTS
    WHERE StateOrProvince = 'NM'
       OR StateOrProvince = 'AZ'
       OR StateOrProvince = 'CA'
       OR StateOrProvince = 'NV'
       OR StateOrProvince = 'UT';
```

This formulation gets the same answer as the formulation using IN, but requires somewhat more typing. The function of the NOT IN operator could be formulated similarly to give the National Sales Manager the desired data:

```
SELECT * FROM PROSPECTS
    WHERE StateOrProvince <> 'NM'
      AND StateOrProvince <> 'AZ'
      AND StateOrProvince <> 'CA'
      AND StateOrProvince <> 'NV'
      AND StateOrProvince <> 'UT';
```

Using the IN and NOT IN operators is faster to type, easier to understand, and less prone to logic errors.

Whenever there is more than one way to perform a function, the DBMS optimizer generates alternative execution plans. It then evaluates those plans and selects the one that it deems the best. So, if you write an SQL statement that uses the IN operator, and for that particular DBMS in that particular situation the use of comparison predicates and logical connectors would be faster, the DBMS chooses the execution plan that uses comparison predicates and logical connectors. You don't have to worry about which formulation will execute the fastest. Let the optimizer worry about that. Just formulate your query in the way that is easiest for you.

Done!

REVIEW

To restrict the rows retrieved by queries, you can add WHERE clauses that use predicates to apply conditions to table rows. Only rows that satisfy the conditions are retrieved. You can specify single or multiple predicates. Use the AND and OR logical connectives to combine predicates into a more restrictive retrieval condition. Use the NOT logical connective to negate the action of whatever predicate it is applied to.

Use the BETWEEN operator to create predicates that retrieve records that lie within a range of values. Such predicates are generally shorter and easier to understand than equivalent predicates using comparison operators and logical connectives. The IN and NOT IN operators form the basis for predicates that test for membership in a set of values.

QUIZ YOURSELF

1. Using one of the comparison operators, code an SQL statement that retrieves the values in the City column of the PROSPECTS table from the rows where the value of StateOrProvince is either 'IL' or 'WA'. (See "Using Comparison Predicates.")

2. Using the IN operator, code an SQL statement that retrieves the values in the City column of the PROSPECTS table from the rows where the value of StateOrProvince is either 'IL' or 'WA'. (See "Using IN and NOT IN to Determine Set Membership.")

3. Code an SQL statement that retrieves the values in the City column of the PROSPECTS table from the rows where the value of StateOrProvince is neither 'IL' nor 'WA'. (See "Using IN and NOT IN to Determine Set Membership.")

4. Code an SQL statement that uses the BETWEEN operator to retrieve the names of all the prospects whose names fall between Dome Depot and Imports Unlimited. (See "Using BETWEEN and NOT BETWEEN to Locate a Value.")

5. Code an SQL statement that retrieves all rows of the INVOICE table where the value in the FormOfPayment column is neither cash nor check. (See "Combining Conditions with Logical Connectives.")

Retrieving Not-So-Specific Data

Session Checklist

✔ Determining similarity using LIKE and NOT LIKE

✔ Using NULL and NOT NULL to specify whether a value is unknown or known

✔ Using quantifiers to seek the truth

**30 Min.
To Go**

Session 5 describes predicates that help you retrieve the data you want from a database when you have a clear idea of what you want. There are times, however, when you want something but do not know how to describe it exactly. If you can describe it approximately, you may still be able to retrieve it with predicates based on some additional operators. For example, the LIKE operator is one you can use when you have only partial knowledge of your search target.

Using LIKE and NOT LIKE to Determine Similarity

Use the LIKE operator in predicates that compare a target character string in the database against a test string that (hopefully) matches part of the target string. Build the test string using characters you know are in the target string, supplemented by wildcard characters that represent the parts of the target string that you don't know.

The SQL:1999 standard specifies two wildcard characters, the underscore (_) and the percent sign (%). The underscore can stand for any single character in the target string. The percent sign can stand for a string of characters of any length, from zero up to the full length of the target string.

Microsoft Access, uses the asterisk (*) as the multi-character wildcard character, rather than the percent sign. Neither the percent sign nor the underscore work as wildcard characters in Access.

Following are some examples of queries that use wildcard characters in a predicate:

```
SELECT Address1
FROM PROSPECTS
    WHERE Address1 LIKE '% Drive';
```

Produces this result:

```
1400 Desert Drive
1911 N. Dancy Drive
```

All addresses having "Drive" as the last five characters are retrieved. Another example is:

```
SELECT Address1
FROM PROSPECTS
    WHERE Address1 LIKE '%Shore%';
```

This formulation, with wildcards on both ends of the test string, retrieves:

```
24 Shoreline Road
2001 S. Shore Road
```

To show the use of the single character wildcard, consider the following query:

```
SELECT City
FROM PROSPECTS
    WHERE City LIKE 'W_rm%';
```

This retrieves:
```
Warm Springs
```

If there had been a city named "Worm Springs" in the PROSPECTS table, it would have been returned also. However, if there had been a city named "Wheatfarm Springs," it would not have been retrieved because the underscore can substitute for one and only one character in the target string.

If the comparison field of the row you are testing contains a NULL value, the comparison returns an UNKNOWN result and the row is not selected.

You can use the NOT operator to negate the effect of the LIKE operator. If a query with a predicate incorporating the LIKE operator retrieves a set of rows from a table, the same query using the NOT LIKE operator retrieves all the rows that were not retrieved by the first query. The one exception to this statement is that neither query retrieves rows that have a NULL value in the comparison field. Consider the following query:

```
SELECT * FROM PROSPECTS
    WHERE Country NOT LIKE 'U%';
```

This retrieves all of your customers who are not located in the USA, the UK, Uganda, Uruguay, Uzbekistan, or any other country starting with the letter *U*.

Specifying Whether a Value Is Unknown or Known with NULL and NOT NULL

A database table field that does not contain any value is said to have a *NULL* value. A NULL is not the same as a numeric zero. Zero is a definite value. A NULL is not the same as a blank character. A blank character is a definite value. A field in a newly created table contains a NULL value until someone enters a definite value into it. A field may be left with a NULL value if, when the data for a row is entered, the value for that field is not known. It may also be left with a NULL value if, for that row, no definite value exists.

To say that a field in a table has a NULL value is the same as saying that the value of the field is unknown.

With the NULL operator in a predicate, you can retrieve rows based on whether the value in a specified field is NULL. Similarly, you can retrieve rows from a table using the NOT NULL operator, based on whether the value in a specified field is not NULL.

Suppose, for example, that you want to retrieve all rows from the PROSPECTS table where the Address2 field has a NULL value. Either you don't know the suite number that extends the street address, or there is no suite number. Find all the rows in the table where the contents of the second address field is unknown with the following query:

```
SELECT * FROM PROSPECTS
    WHERE Address2 IS NULL;
```

Similarly, retrieve all the records where there *is* a value in the Address2 field with the statement that follows:

```
SELECT * FROM PROSPECTS
    WHERE Address2 IS NOT NULL;
```

Never make a query like the following:

```
SELECT * FROM PROSPECTS
    WHERE Address2 = NULL;
```

Because NULL means unknown, it is not possible for any value to be equal to an unknown value. Two fields that both contain NULL values are not considered to be equal to each other. Because both values are unknown, they may be equal to each other or they may not.

Seeking Truth with the ALL, SOME, and ANY Quantifiers

The ALL, SOME, and ANY operators act like the quantifiers in symbolic logic. A couple of thousand years ago, Aristotle had a lot to say about the Greek equivalents of ALL, SOME and ANY. He invented the syllogism as a method of finding new truths based on things that he already knew to be true. A syllogism can take the following form:

> *All penguins are birds.*
> *All birds have feathers.*
> *Therefore, all penguins have feathers.*

The first two statements, called *premises,* are assumed to be true. If they are indeed true, then the third statement, the conclusion, must also be true. Even though penguins do not appear to have feathers, we can be confident that they do, if we accept the two premises. Another form of syllogism is illustrated by the next example:

> *Some birds are ostriches.*
> *All ostriches are flightless.*
> *Therefore, some birds cannot fly.*

In this case, the first statement makes an assertion only about some birds, not all birds. Thus, even though the second statement makes an assertion about all ostriches, we can only draw the weak conclusion that some birds cannot fly. We cannot make a strong statement regarding the flying capability of all birds.

In SQL the ANY operator is considered to be a synonym of SOME. I can paraphrase the syllogism above to say, "If any birds are ostriches and all ostriches are flightless, then some birds cannot fly."

The ALL, SOME, **and** ANY **operators are used in nested queries, which I discuss in Session 13.**

For now, we can look at several examples of this use. Suppose the Xanthic Systems sales manager is interested in retrieving records for large sales that have not been paid in full. The sales with the largest inflationary effect on accounts receivable are those sales where the TotalCharge is greater than the largest TotalRemitted in the table. You can find these records with the following nested query:

```
SELECT * FROM INVOICE
    WHERE TotalCharge > ALL (SELECT TotalRemitted FROM INVOICE);
```

**10 Min.
To Go**

The inner SELECT (within the parentheses) is going to retrieve all the values in the TotalRemitted column of the INVOICE table. The WHERE clause in the outer SELECT retrieves all rows from the INVOICE table where the value of TotalCharge is greater than all the values retrieved by the inner SELECT. The result of this retrieval is shown in Figure 6-1.

InvoiceNumbe	CustomerID	InvoiceDate	TotalCharge	TotalRemitted	FormOfPayme	Salesperson
277	3141	12/20/2001	$10,540.00	$1,054.00	check	Warren
278	2339	12/21/2001	$6,750.00	$3,375.00	check	Peters
281	8333	12/24/2001	$4,500.00	$2,250.00	check	Warren

Figure 6-1 Records retrieved by nested select, using the ALL operator

The records retrieved have values in the TotalCharge column that are greater than the values in all the rows of the TotalRemitted column.

If we ran the same query with the SOME operator, the result would be quite different.

```
SELECT * FROM INVOICE
   WHERE TotalCharge > SOME (SELECT TotalRemitted FROM INVOICE);
```

In this case, the only records that would not be retrieved are those where the value in the TotalCharge column is less than or equal to the smallest value in the TotalRemitted column. Assuming nobody is going to remit more than they are charged, the only records left out of this retrieval will be those containing the smallest value in the TotalCharge field, which are those paid in full. If you replace the SOME operator with the ANY operator, you get exactly the same result. All rows are retrieved where the value in the TotalCharge column is greater than the value in the TotalRemitted column of any row in the INVOICE table.

Whether you use the SOME operator or the ANY operator is a matter of personal preference because they both produce the same result. I personally prefer to use the SOME operator because there is some ambiguity involved with the ANY operator. In English, if I say that the value of a particular sale is greater than the value of ANY field in the TotalRemitted column, you may interpret that to mean that there are no values in the TotalRemitted column that are greater than the sale value. That is not the way SQL interprets it. There is no confusion if I say that the value of a particular sale is greater than the value of SOME field in the TotalRemitted column. If the value is greater than the smallest value in the TotalRemitted column, the condition is satisfied and SQL retrieves the row for that value.

Done!

REVIEW

We can retrieve records from tables using the LIKE and NOT LIKE operators if we have partial knowledge of the contents of one or more fields. We can retrieve records from tables using the NULL and NOT NULL operators if we know that a field either does not or does contain a definite value. We can retrieve records from one table if a value in that table is greater than, less than, or equal to SOME or ALL of the values in a column of either the same or a different table. Taken together, these operators comprise a powerful toolbox for retrieval of records when you cannot completely specify what you want to retrieve.

QUIZ YOURSELF

1. Write a SELECT statement that retrieves a PROSPECT record when all you know is that the prospect's NAME includes the words "Dance Studio." (See "Using LIKE and NOT LIKE to Determine Similarity.")

2. Write a SELECT statement that retrieves all records from the PROSPECT table where there is no entry in the ContactPhone field. (See "Specifying Whether a Value is Unknown or Known with NULL and NOT NULL.")

3. If all marsupials carry their young in pouches, and all species of kangaroo are marsupials, what can you conclude about kangaroos and pouches? (See "Seeking Truth with the ALL, SOME, and ANY Quantifiers.")

4. What will the following SQL statement retrieve? (See "Seeking Truth with the ALL, SOME, and ANY Quantifiers.")

```
SELECT * FROM PROSPECTS
    WHERE PostalCode > SOME (SELECT PostalCode FROM PROSPECTS);
```

Retrieving Data Based on What Exists

Session Checklist

✔ Retrieving one thing based on whether another thing EXISTS

✔ Retrieving something based on whether it is UNIQUE

✔ Testing two values to see if they are DISTINCT

**30 Min.
To Go**

Thereare times when you will want to retrieve rows from one table based on whether rows in another table satisfy a specified condition. A retrieval from the second table based on that specified condition will return a result set. The contents of the result set will determine what is retrieved from the first table. If this sounds confusing, let's clarify matters by looking at an example using the EXISTS operator.

Retrieving One Thing Only If Something Else EXISTS

Suppose the sales manager of Xanthic Systems wants to obtain a list of customers who have bought more than $1,000 worth of product on a single invoice. He would like to target these customers with a special promotion. He can retrieve the list he wants with a nested SELECT that uses an EXISTS operator.

```
SELECT * FROM CUSTOMERS
   WHERE EXISTS
      (SELECT DISTINCT CustomerID FROM INVOICE
         WHERE INVOICE.CustomerID = CUSTOMERS.CustomerID
         AND TotalCharge > 1000) ;
```

This query returns the result set shown in Figure 7-1. All the rows returned are for customers who bought more than $1,000 worth of product on a single invoice.

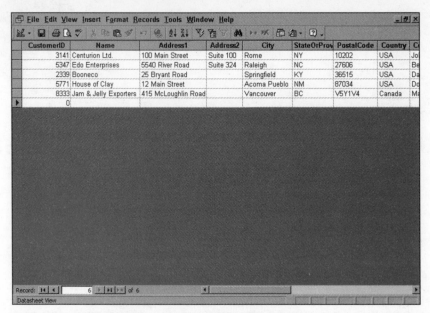

Figure 7-1   *Result set from query with* EXISTS *operator*

Because the INVOICE table may record multiple high-dollar sales to the same customer, I use the SELECT DISTINCT syntax to eliminate duplicate CustomerID records in the record set returned. The WHERE clause links a record having a particular CustomerID in the CUS-TOMER table with all the records having the same CustomerID in the INVOICE table. It also specifies that only records having a value in TotalCharge that is greater than $1,000 will be retrieved.

The inner SELECT, on the INVOICE table, returns the CustomerIDs of all the customers who have bought more than $1,000 worth of product on a single invoice. The outer SELECT on the CUSTOMERS table then returns the name and address information on those customers from the CUSTOMERS table.

If none of the records in the INVOICE table is for a sale that exceeds $1,000, the inner SELECT returns an empty record set. The EXISTS operator handles the empty record set by aborting the outer SELECT. No address records are displayed because none of the customers qualify.

To further illustrate the point I made in Session 5 while discussing the IN and NOT IN operators — that there is usually more than one way to obtain a given result — next consider how to obtain the same result without using an EXISTS operator, but by using a correlated subquery with one of the aggregate functions instead (Session 4).

A correlated subquery first finds the table and row specified by the outer SELECT and then executes the inner SELECT on the row in the inner SELECT's table that correlates with the current row of the outer SELECT's table.

```
SELECT * FROM CUSTOMERS
    WHERE 0 <>
        (SELECT COUNT (*) FROM INVOICE
            WHERE INVOICE.CustomerID = CUSTOMERS.CustomerID
            AND TotalCharge > 1000) ;
```

This query returns the result set shown in Figure 7-2. The result set is identical to the one shown in Figure 7-1. This is one example of the fact that there are usually multiple ways to make a desired retrieval. If your version of SQL does not support one method, it may well support another one that is equivalent.

CustomerID	Name	Address1	Address2	City	StateOrProv	PostalCode	Country	C
3141	Centurion Ltd.	100 Main Street	Suite 100	Rome	NY	10202	USA	Jo
5347	Edo Enterprises	5540 River Road	Suite 324	Raleigh	NC	27606	USA	Be
2339	Booneco	25 Bryant Road		Springfield	KY	36515	USA	Da
5771	House of Clay	12 Main Street		Acoma Pueblo	NM	87034	USA	Do
8333	Jam & Jelly Exporters	415 McLoughlin Road		Vancouver	BC	V5Y1V4	Canada	Ma
0								

Figure 7-2   *Result set from query with correlated subquery*

With this formulation, the inner SELECT's WHERE clause is the same as in the previous case. For each customer in turn, the inner SELECT is executed. The inner SELECT returns the number of rows in the INVOICE table that satisfy the conditions in the WHERE clause. If no rows satisfy the conditions, the inner SELECT returns a zero and the outer SELECT is not performed. If one or more rows do satisfy the conditions of the inner SELECT statement (one or more sales to the current customer are for amounts over $1,000), the WHERE clause of the outer SELECT statement is satisfied. Execution loops through all the records in the CUSTOMERS table, and the outer SELECT returns to the user the rows from the CUSTOMERS table that describe customers who have bought more that $1,000 worth of products on a single invoice.

Suppose Xanthic's sales manager next wants to know the names and addresses of all customers who have bought something, but have not bought as much as $1,000 worth of product on any single invoice. These are the customers who tend to buy low cost items. For this retrieval, he can use almost the same query as the first one above, but with the NOT EXISTS operator replacing the EXISTS operator.

The NOT EXISTS operator gives the opposite result that the EXISTS operator gives. For a given row of the outer SELECT's table, if the inner SELECT retrieves one or more records, the NOT EXISTS operator returns a FALSE value to the outer SELECT, and the outer SELECT statement is not executed. If the inner SELECT retrieves an empty record set, the NOT EXISTS operator returns a TRUE value to the outer SELECT, and the outer SELECT statement is executed. This action is repeated for every row in the table specified in the outer SELECT statement. Figure 7-3 shows the result set for the following query:

```
SELECT * FROM CUSTOMERS
    WHERE NOT EXISTS
        (SELECT DISTINCT CustomerID FROM INVOICE
            WHERE INVOICE.CustomerID = CUSTOMERS.CustomerID
            AND TotalCharge > 1000) ;
```

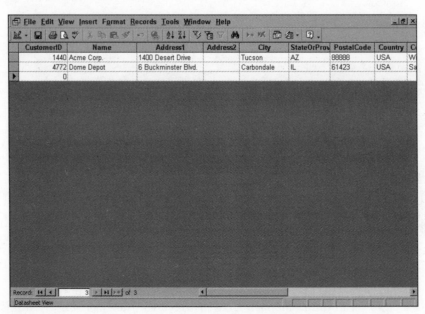

Figure 7-3   *Result set from query with NOT EXISTS operator*

The rows returned in the result set give the names and addresses of all customers who have not bought as much as $1,000 worth of product on a single invoice.

With the EXISTS and NOT EXISTS operators, there is no possibility of an UNKNOWN result. The only possibilities are TRUE and FALSE. The inner SELECT either returns a non-zero number of rows or it doesn't return any. Thus the EXISTS or NOT EXISTS operators generate either a TRUE value or a FALSE value as the only possibilities.

Retrieving Something Only If It Is UNIQUE

You use the UNIQUE operator, like the EXISTS operator, with subqueries. Whereas the EXISTS subquery evaluates to TRUE if the inner SELECT returns at least one row, the UNIQUE subquery evaluates to TRUE if none of the returned rows are duplicated. So, the UNIQUE operator returns a TRUE value if:

- The inner SELECT returns no rows
- The inner SELECT returns only one row.
- The inner SELECT returns multiple rows, with no duplicates among them.

What if the result set from the inner SELECT contains two null rows, but otherwise qualifies as UNIQUE? Do those two NULL rows destroy the set's uniqueness? No. The UNIQUE operator ignores NULL values and returns a TRUE value.

Because the inner SELECT returns either a result set that is free of duplicates or a set containing duplicates, the UNIQUE operator returns either a TRUE or FALSE value. There is no other possibility. Consider this example:

```
SELECT * FROM CUSTOMERS
    WHERE UNIQUE
        (SELECT CustomerID FROM INVOICE
            WHERE INVOICE.CustomerID = CUSTOMERS.CustomerID
            AND TotalCharge > 1000) ;
```

This statement returns the records for all customers who have made one and only one purchase that exceeds $1,000. Customers who have made more than one purchase larger than $1,000 are excluded by the UNIQUE operator. Using the Xanthic database, the result is as shown in Figure 7-4.

CustomerID	Name	Address1	Address2	City	StateOrProv	PostalCode	Country
3141	Centurion Ltd.	100 Main Street	Suite 100	Rome	NY	10202	USA
5347	Edo Enterprises	5540 River Road	Suite 324	Raleigh	NC	27606	USA
2339	Booneco	25 Bryant Road		Springfield	KY	36515	USA
5771	House of Clay	12 Main Street		Acoma Pueblo	NM	87034	USA
8333	Jam & Jelly Exporters	415 McLoughlin Road		Vancouver	BC	V5Y1V4	Canada
0							

Figure 7-4 *Result set from query with the UNIQUE operator*

Conversely, consider the following example:

```
SELECT * FROM CUSTOMERS
    WHERE NOT UNIQUE
```

```
(SELECT CustomerID FROM INVOICE
    WHERE INVOICE.CustomerID = CUSTOMERS.CustomerID
    AND TotalCharge > 1000) ;
```

This statement returns records for all customers who have made more than one purchase exceeding $1,000. These high-value repeat customers are likely targets for a sales promotion effort. Unfortunately, in the Xanthic database, there are no customers who have bought over $1,000 on two or more invoices as shown in Figure 7-5, which is the result set returned by the above NOT UNIQUE query.

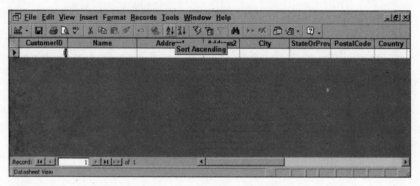

Figure 7-5   *Result set from query with the NOT UNIQUE operator*

The UNIQUE operator is not a part of core SQL and is not currently implemented by all database management systems. The above examples do not work consistently in Microsoft Access 2000 and do not work at all in Microsoft SQL Server 2000, Oracle 9i, PostgreSQL, or MySQL. If you want to use the UNIQUE operator, be sure your DBMS supports it and that you will not want to migrate your application to another DBMS at a later time.

As was the case with the EXISTS operator, you can achieve the result of the UNIQUE operator by other means. Here is a query that returns the same result as the one above that includes the UNIQUE operator.

```
SELECT * FROM CUSTOMERS
    WHERE 1 =
        (SELECT COUNT (*) FROM INVOICE
            WHERE INVOICE.CustomerID = CUSTOMERS.CustomerID
            AND TotalCharge > 1000) ;
```

This query, incorporating a correlated subquery, returns exactly the same result set as the above query with the UNIQUE operator. For every row in the outer SELECT on the CUSTOMERS table, the inner SELECT is performed, and the count of occurrences is compared to one. Whenever one and only one row is counted, the corresponding row in the CUSTOMERS table is added to the result set.

Similarly, you can use a correlated subquery in place of the NOT UNIQUE operator. Here is a query, using a correlated subquery, that is equivalent to the query above that uses the NOT UNIQUE operator.

```
SELECT * FROM CUSTOMERS
    WHERE 1 <
        (SELECT COUNT (*) FROM INVOICE
            WHERE INVOICE.CustomerID = CUSTOMERS.CustomerID
            AND TotalCharge > 1000) ;
```

Because the Xanthic database contains no customers who have bought over $1,000 worth of merchandise on more than one invoice, this query returns an empty result set, just as the one with the NOT UNIQUE operator did.

**10 Min.
To Go**

Determining Whether Two Values Are DISTINCT

The DISTINCT predicate is new in SQL:1999. It tests whether two values are distinct from each other. If they are, it returns a TRUE value; otherwise it returns a FALSE value. The DISTINCT operator acts almost exactly like the <> (does not equal) comparison operator. The only difference is in the way null values are treated.

If either or both of the values being compared contains a NULL value, the <> operator returns a value of UNKNOWN. In contrast, the DISTINCT predicate can only return one of two possible values, TRUE or FALSE. If two NULL values are compared, the DISTINCT predicate returns a FALSE value. Two NULL values are not considered to be distinct from each other. On the other hand, if a NULL value is compared with any definite value, the DISTINCT predicate returns a TRUE value. A NULL value is considered to be distinct from all non-NULL values. Table 7-1 shows some example DISTINCT predicates and their results.

Table 7-1 *Example* DISTINCT *Predicates and Their Results*

Operator	Result
17 IS DISTINCT FROM 47	TRUE
17 IS DISTINCT FROM 17	FALSE
NULL IS DISTINCT FROM 47	TRUE
17 IS DISTINCT FROM NULL	TRUE
NULL IS DISTINCT FROM NULL	FALSE

You may wonder why the standards committee decided to provide the DISTINCT operator when it essentially duplicates the function of the <> operator, except in the way it handles NULL values (especially because the way it handles NULL values is less intuitive than the way the <> operator handles them). The answer is that situations arise where you do not want to return an UNKNOWN result. There are occasions where you may want to consider two NULL values to be the same. On those occasions, where you cannot use the <> operator, you can use the DISTINCT operator.

Here is an example of the use of the DISTINCT predicate in a query:

```
SELECT * FROM INVOICE
    WHERE Salesperson IS DISTINCT FROM 'Warren' ;
```

This query retrieves all rows where the value in the Salesperson column is something other than 'Warren.' If any of the rows in the INVOICE table have a NULL value in the Salesperson column, this query retrieves them also because a NULL value is considered to be distinct from the value 'Warren.'

To achieve the same result without the DISTINCT operator would take a somewhat more complex query:

```
SELECT * FROM INVOICE
    WHERE Salesperson <> 'Warren'
    OR Salesperson IS NULL ;
```

Another example rounds out the picture:

```
SELECT * FROM INVOICE
    WHERE Salesperson IS DISTINCT FROM NULL ;
```

This query retrieves all rows from the INVOICE table that have non-NULL values in the Salesperson column. Rows having a NULL value in the Salesperson column are not retrieved. The above query is equivalent to the following query, which is shorter and well supported on practically all relational database platforms.

```
SELECT * FROM INVOICE
    WHERE Salesperson IS NOT NULL ;
```

Don't confuse the DISTINCT operator with the keyword DISTINCT that SQL uses to eliminate duplicate records from a retrieval. They are two entirely different things that serve two entirely different purposes. The DISTINCT operator always appears in the form "IS DISTINCT FROM" while the ordinary use of the DISTINCT keyword does not.

The DISTINCT predicate was just introduced into SQL with the SQL:1999 specification and is not a part of core SQL. It has not been incorporated into all database management systems yet. For example, Access 2000, SQL Server 2000, Oracle 9i, PostgreSQL 7.1, and MySQL 4.0 do not support the DISTINCT predicate. Make sure your DBMS supports the DISTINCT predicate before you try to use it.

REVIEW

Retrievals of one piece of data from a database can be based not only on the properties of that data, but also on whether certain other data exists elsewhere in the database. The EXISTS and NOT EXISTS operators return a TRUE or FALSE value to a query based on whether anything is retrieved by its subquery. The UNIQUE and NOT UNIQUE operators return a TRUE or FALSE value to a query based on whether any rows retrieved by its subquery are duplicated. The DISTINCT predicate returns a TRUE or FALSE value to a query based on whether the values retrieved by the query are distinct from the value of a search condition.

QUIZ YOURSELF

1. What does the following statement do? (See "Retrieving One Thing Only if Something Else EXISTS.")

    SELECT Name FROM CUSTOMERS

      WHERE EXISTS

        (SELECT DISTINCT CustomerID FROM INVOICE

         WHERE INVOICE.CustomerID = CUSTOMERS.CustomerID

         AND FormOfPayment = 'check') ;

2. What does the following statement do, assuming your DBMS supports the UNIQUE operator? (See "Retrieving Something Only If It Is UNIQUE.")

    SELECT Name FROM CUSTOMERS

      WHERE NOT UNIQUE

        (SELECT DISTINCT CustomerID FROM INVOICE

         WHERE INVOICE.CustomerID = CUSTOMERS.CustomerID

         AND TotalCharge > 100) ;

3. What value is returned by the following predicate? (See "Determining Whether Two Values Are DISTINCT.")

    0 IS DISTINCT FROM NULL

4. What query that uses a correlated subquery is equivalent to the following query? (See "Retrieving Something Only If It Is UNIQUE.")

    SELECT Name FROM CUSTOMERS

      WHERE NOT UNIQUE

        (SELECT DISTINCT CustomerID FROM INVOICE

         WHERE INVOICE.CustomerID = CUSTOMERS.CustomerID

         AND TotalCharge > 100) ;

Retrieving Data Based on How It Matches Other Data

Session Checklist

✔ Looking at time intervals with the OVERLAPS predicate

✔ Finding rows that MATCH the value of an expression

✔ Evaluating a text string for similarity to an expression

**30 Min.
To Go**

S QL has a wide variety of predicates that compare one data element to another, looking for commonalities. Some of these, such as LIKE, IN, EXISTS, UNIQUE, and DISTINCT have been covered in previous sessions. In this session, the OVERLAPS predicate specifically addresses comparisons of dates and times, the MATCH predicate compares multiple fields in the rows of a result set to a set of target values, and the SIMILAR predicate finds partial matches when comparing two character strings.

Comparing Time Intervals with the OVERLAPS Predicate

Data containing times and dates is important in many applications. In some cases, this data is used to determine when some action or event started and when it finished. The duration between such a start and its associated finish is an *interval of time*. Often for scheduling purposes and to avoid conflicts, it is important to know whether the interval associated with one action or event overlaps the interval associated with a second action or event. If the start and finish of both actions or events are known, SQL's OVERLAPS predicate can determine whether the two overlap in time. The OVERLAPS predicate can handle temporal data expressed as either dates, times, or timestamps.

The OVERLAPS predicate is not a part of core SQL. This means that some database management systems that (rightly) claim to be SQL:1999-compliant may not implement it. Microsoft Access 2000 , SQL Server 2000, Oracle 9i, PostgreSQL 7.1, and MySQL 4.0 do not support the OVERLAPS predicate.

The OVERLAPS predicate returns a TRUE value if there is any overlap between the two specified time intervals; it returns a FALSE value if there is no overlap. You can express an interval either by specifying a start time and an end time or by specifying a start time and an interval. Each possibility is discussed in the following sections.

Date to date

You can test for overlap of data of the Date type by specifying the start date and end date of both intervals you want to compare. For example:

```
(DATE '2001-12-17', DATE '2001-12-21')
OVERLAPS
(DATE '2001-12-19', DATE '2001-12-20');
```

The first interval runs from December 17, 2001 to December 21, 2001. The second interval runs from December 19, 2001 to December 20, 2001. These two intervals overlap, so the OVERLAPS predicate returns a TRUE value.

Xanthic Systems may use this form of the predicate to see which employees were at the company during the company's tenth anniversary year, as follows:

```
SELECT FirstName, LastName FROM EMPLOYEES
    WHERE (HireDate, TerminationDate)
        OVERLAPS ('1987-07-08', '1988-07-07') ;
```

This statement returns the names of all employees who were on staff between July 8, 1987 and July 7, 1988.

If an employee who was hired during the interval from July 8, 1987 to July 7, 1988 is still with the company, his or her TerminationDate field contains a NULL value. Nonetheless, the OVERLAPS predicate returns a TRUE value, because there must clearly be some overlap. However, if the employee were hired before July 8, 1987, the predicate returns an UNKNOWN value, because the person may have been terminated before July 8, 1987, but the fact was not recorded.

Date and Interval

You can specify the time intervals in an OVERLAPS predicate using a start date and an interval rather than a start date and an end date. You can also use the start/end form in one of the predicate's operands and the start/interval form in the other operand. Here is an example that returns the same result as that returned by the example in the previous section:

```
SELECT FirstName, LastName FROM EMPLOYEES
    WHERE (HireDate, TerminationDate)
        OVERLAPS ('1987-07-08', INTERVAL '1' YEAR) ;
```

Time to time

The OVERLAPS predicate works exactly the same way on times as it does on dates. Here is an example of a test of two time intervals:

```
(TIME '3:09:00', TIME '3:16:00')
OVERLAPS
(TIME '3:16:01', TIME '3:30:00')
```

This predicate returns a FALSE value because even though the two time intervals are contiguous, they are not overlapping. Here is another example:

```
(TIME '3:09:00', TIME '3:16:00')
OVERLAPS
(TIME '3:15:59', TIME '3:30:00')
```

This predicate returns a TRUE value because there is a one second overlap between the first time interval and the second.

Time and interval

A test for overlapping time intervals can use the start/interval form as well as the start/end form, as shown in the following example:

```
(TIME '3:09:00', INTERVAL '7' MINUTE)
OVERLAPS
(TIME '3:15:59', INTERVAL '1' HOUR)
```

This predicate returns a TRUE value because the second interval starts before the first one ends, overlapping by one second.

Timestamp to timestamp

The OVERLAPS predicate also works with timestamp data the same way it works with date and time data. Here is an example using timestamps for both the start and the end of the time intervals being compared:

```
(TIMESTAMP '2001-12-17 3:09:00.000000', TIMESTAMP '2001-12-17 3:16:00.000000')
OVERLAPS
(TIMESTAMP '2001-12-17 3:15:59.999999', TIMESTAMP '2001-12-17 3:30:00.000000')
```

This predicate returns a TRUE value because there is an overlap of one millionth of a second.

Timestamp and interval

As is the case with date and time type data, you can use the OVERLAPS predicate with timestamp data, specifying the intervals with a start timestamp and an interval rather than a pair of timestamps. An example would be:

```
(TIMESTAMP '2001-12-17 3:09:00.000000', INTERVAL '7' MINUTES)
OVERLAPS
(TIMESTAMP '2001-12-17 3:15:59.999999', INTERVAL '32' SECONDS)
```

This predicate returns a TRUE value because of the one-millionth of a second overlap between the two intervals.

Date flipping

If you specify a time interval, but the first date given is later than the second date given, SQL switches the two before evaluating the predicate so when you enter a predicate such as the following:

```
(TIME '3:29:00', TIME '3:16:00')
OVERLAPS
(TIME '3:16:01', TIME '3:30:00')
```

SQL actually evaluates the predicate:

```
(TIME '3:16:00', TIME '3:29:00')
OVERLAPS
(TIME '3:16:01', TIME '3:30:00')
```

This predicate returns a TRUE value because the two intervals overlap.

Handling NULL dates and times

If an interval includes a NULL value, the OVERLAPS predicate comparing it to another interval may return either a TRUE or an UNKNOWN value, depending on the other operands. For example:

```
(DATE '2001-12-17', NULL)
OVERLAPS
(DATE '2001-12-19', DATE '2001-12-20');
```

This returns a value of UNKNOWN because the first interval may have ended before December 19, 2001, or it may have extended beyond that date. Another example is:

```
(DATE '2001-12-17', DATE '2001-12-21')
OVERLAPS
(NULL, DATE '2001-12-20');
```

In this case the predicate returns a TRUE value because regardless of what the NULL value may actually be, December 20, 2001 falls within the interval specified by the first operand.

**20 Min.
To Go**

Looking for Rows that MATCH the Value of an Expression

The MATCH predicate differs from others you have seen in that it deals with entire table rows rather than just a single field. It is used to compare an expression that evaluates to a single row against the rows in a table. In general, the MATCH predicate returns a TRUE value if its two operands match and a FALSE value otherwise. However, there are several different kinds of matches, and there is a different form of the MATCH predicate for each case. They are:

```
RowExpression MATCH <Table subquery>
RowExpression MATCH SIMPLE <Table subquery>
RowExpression MATCH UNIQUE <Table subquery>
RowExpression MATCH UNIQUE SIMPLE <Table subquery>
RowExpression MATCH PARTIAL <Table subquery>
RowExpression MATCH UNIQUE PARTIAL <Table subquery>
RowExpression MATCH FULL <Table subquery>
RowExpression MATCH UNIQUE FULL <Table subquery>
```

The MATCH predicate is not a part of core SQL and is not supported by Microsoft Access 2000, Microsoft SQL Server 2000, Oracle 9i, PostgreSQL 7.1, or MySQL 4.0.

The row expression can be any expression that evaluates to a single table row. The table subquery must produce a result set with the same number of rows as the row produced by the row expression, and the data types of the result set columns must be the same as the data types of the corresponding fields in the row produced by the row expression.

MATCH SIMPLE is the default form of this predicate, so a MATCH predicate and a MATCH SIMPLE predicate produce the same result when used with the same operands. Similarly, MATCH UNIQUE and MATCH UNIQUE SIMPLE produce the same result.

MATCH and MATCH SIMPLE produce a TRUE value in two cases:

- The row expression contains at least one NULL.
- The row expression contains no NULLs and is equal to at least one row of the table subquery's result set.

MATCH UNIQUE and MATCH UNIQUE SIMPLE produce a TRUE value in two cases:

- The row expression contains at least one NULL.
- The row expression contains no NULLs and is equal to one and only one row of the table subquery's result set.

MATCH PARTIAL produces a TRUE value in two cases:

- The row expression contains only NULL values.
- The table subquery returns at least one row whose non-NULL values match the values of the corresponding fields in the row expression.

MATCH UNIQUE PARTIAL produces a TRUE value in two cases:

- The row expression contains only NULL values.
- The table subquery returns one and only one row whose non-NULL values match the values of the corresponding fields in the row expression.

MATCH FULL produces a TRUE value in two cases:

- The row expression contains only NULL values.
- The row expression contains no NULLs, and the table subquery returns at least one row that is equal to the row expression.

MATCH UNIQUE FULL produces a TRUE value in two cases:

- The row expression contains only NULL values.
- The row expression contains no NULLs, and the table subquery returns one and only one row that is equal to the row expression.

To see how these predicates work, consider the results of a retrieval from the Xanthic Systems CUSTOMERS table, shown in Figure 8-1.

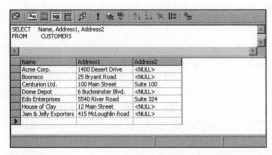

Name	Address1	Address2
Acme Corp.	1400 Desert Drive	<NULL>
Booneco	25 Bryant Road	<NULL>
Centurion Ltd.	100 Main Street	Suite 100
Dome Depot	6 Buckminster Blvd.	<NULL>
Edo Enterprises	5540 River Road	Suite 324
House of Clay	12 Main Street	<NULL>
Jam & Jelly Exporters	415 McLoughlin Road	<NULL>

Figure 8-1 *Retrieval from Xanthic's CUSTOMERS table, as shown by SQL Server*

The following MATCH predicates all evaluate to TRUE.

```
ROW(Centurion Ltd.,NULL,Suite 100)
MATCH SIMPLE
(SELECT Name, Address1, Address2 FROM CUSTOMERS);

ROW(Centurion Ltd.,100 Main Street,Suite 100)
MATCH SIMPLE
(SELECT Name, Address1, Address2 FROM CUSTOMERS);

ROW(Centurion Ltd.,100 Main Street,Suite 100)
MATCH UNIQUE SIMPLE
(SELECT Name, Address1, Address2 FROM CUSTOMERS);

ROW(NULL,100 Main Street,Suite 100)
MATCH UNIQUE PARTIAL
(SELECT Name, Address1, Address2 FROM CUSTOMERS);

ROW(Centurion Ltd.,100 Main Street,Suite 100)
MATCH UNIQUE FULL
(SELECT Name, Address1, Address2 FROM CUSTOMERS);
```

Testing a Text String for Similarity to an Expression

The SIMILAR predicate is a more general relative of the LIKE predicate. Where the LIKE predicate compares a character string in a database table field to a test text string, the

SIMILAR predicate compares a character string in a database table field to a regular expression. A regular expression is a sequence of ordinary characters, possibly combined with some metacharacters. The metacharacters are:

- Underscore _
- Percent sign %
- Asterisk *
- Plus sign +
- Vertical bar |
- Concatenation character ||
- Left parenthesis (
- Right parenthesis)
- Left bracket [
- Right bracket]
- Circumflex ^
- Hyphen -
- Colon :

 The SIMILAR **predicate, first introduced in the SQL:1999 specification is not a part of core SQL and is not widely implemented. Microsoft Access 2000, Microsoft SQL Server 2000, Oracle 9i, PostgreSQL 7.1, and MySQL 4.0, do not support it.**

Each one of the metacharacters has a different special meaning. For example, the asterisk means multiplication, the plus sign means addition, the hyphen means negation or subtraction. The underscore and percent sign have the same wildcard meaning in a SIMILAR predicate that they have in a comparison predicate. Consider the following example from Xanthic's CUSTOMERS table:

```
Name SIMILAR TO '%oneco'
```

This returns a TRUE value when accessing the row of the CUSTOMERS table that has Booneco in the Name column because the % metacharacter can substitute for zero or more characters in a text string.

The vertical bar metacharacter acts like a logical OR. The bar separates a list of choices. If any one of the choices provides a match to the test text string, the predicate returns a TRUE value. Here's an example:

```
SELECT * FROM COMPUTER
    WHERE OperatingSystem SIMILAR TO
      '('Windows ' ('3.1'|'95'|'98'|'ME'|'CE'|'NT'|'2000'))' ;
```

The WHERE clause returns a TRUE value if the OperatingSystem column in the COMPUTER table contains 'Windows 3.1', 'Windows 95', or any of the other choices.

REVIEW

The predicates covered in this session, OVERLAPS, MATCH, and SIMILAR, although described in the SQL:1999 specification, are not part of core SQL and have not been implemented by most of the database management systems available today. Use them only if you are sure that your DBMS supports them.

The OVERLAPS predicate compares two date, time, or datetime intervals and returns a TRUE value if there is a temporal overlap. The MATCH predicate compares a row expression against the result set of a query, returning a TRUE value if a match is found. The meaning of the word *match* varies, depending on whether any of the fields in the row expression contains a NULL value. The SIMILAR predicate compares the value in a table field against a string that may contain metacharacters.

QUIZ YOURSELF

1. What result is returned by the following predicate? (See "Comparing Time Intervals with the OVERLAPS Predicate.")

   ```
   (TIMESTAMP '2001-05-26 4:55:00.000000', TIMESTAMP '2001-09-16
   1:01:00.000000')
   OVERLAPS
   (TIMESTAMP '2001-04-23 1:01:00.000000', INTERVAL '33' DAY)
   ```

2. What result is returned by the following predicate? (See "Comparing Time Intervals with the OVERLAPS Predicate.")

   ```
   (TIMESTAMP '2001-05-26 4:55:00.000000', TIMESTAMP '2001-09-16
   1:01:00.000000')
   OVERLAPS
   (TIMESTAMP '2001-04-23 1:01:00.000000', NULL)
   ```

3. Produce a table row that causes the following predicate to return a TRUE result. (See "Looking for Rows that MATCH the Value of an Expression.")

   ```
   ROW(1492, Spanish, 56.941)
   MATCH PARTIAL
   (Date, Language, Weight)
   ```

4. Produce a table row that causes the following predicate to return a FALSE result. (See "Looking for Rows that MATCH the Value of an Expression.")

   ```
   ROW(1492, Spanish, 56.941)
   MATCH PARTIAL
   (Date, Language, Weight)
   ```

Advanced Value Expressions

Session Checklist

✔ Using CASE conditional expressions to perform alternative actions

✔ Applying ROW value constructors to multiple columns

**30 Min.
To Go**

Session 4 covers simple value expressions, such as string value expressions, numeric value expressions, datetime value expressions, and interval value expressions. They all share the characteristic that regardless of data type, the expression reduces to a single value. In this session, I discuss more complicated value expressions. The CASE conditional expressions also reduce to a single value, but are considerably more complex than the simple value expressions discussed in Session 4. The ROW value constructors do not reduce to a single value, but rather reduce to a list of data values.

Performing Alternative Actions Using CASE Conditional Expressions

Every complete computer language has some sort of conditional structure that performs a test, and based on the outcome, directs program execution to follow one path or another. SQL is not a complete computer language and in its original form did not have any sort of conditional structure. SQL-92 introduced the CASE conditional expression and SQL:1999 introduced the CASE statement. The CASE conditional expression does not affect flow of execution, but it does perform a test, and depending on the outcome, selects one of multiple values to return.

I cover the CASE statement and other flow of execution structures in Session 16.

Searching a table with a CASE expression

You can use the CASE expression two different ways. In the first way, you can work through a table until you find a row where one of a set of specified search conditions is TRUE. When the CASE expression finds such a row, it terminates, returning the value associated with the successful search condition. The CASE expression takes the following form:

```
CASE
    WHEN condition1 THEN result1
    WHEN condition2 THEN result2
    ...
    WHEN conditionN THEN resultN
    ELSE resultX
END
```

The entire CASE structure, being a value expression, reduces to a value. In the above example, if *condition1* is true, then *result1* is the value returned. If *condition1* is false, but *condition2* is true, then *result2* is the value returned. This pattern continues for as many conditions as are specified. If none of the conditions are satisfied, then the ELSE clause is executed and *resultX* is the value returned. If none of the conditions are satisfied and the optional ELSE clause is omitted, a NULL value is returned.

 Microsoft Access 2000 does not support the CASE **expression; neither does MySQL 4.0. Microsoft SQL Server 2000 and PostgreSQL 7.1 do support the** CASE **expression, as does Oracle 9i.**

A not-so-smart use of a CASE expression

The CASE expression can either be valuable or not so valuable in a SELECT statement, depending on how you use it. Let's look at a not-so-valuable use first. You may use it on the PROSPECTS table to retrieve the name of the city where a prospect is located. It can take the form:

```
SELECT CASE
          WHEN Name = 'Booneco' THEN City
          ELSE 'N/A'
       END
    AS City
FROM PROSPECTS ;
```

This returns a list with as many rows as the PROSPECTS table has. The list consists entirely of 'N/A' values, except for one row that holds 'Springfield,' the city where Booneco is located. For a table with a large number of rows, such a result is not very helpful, especially because Booneco's city can be retrieved more easily with the following statement:

```
SELECT City FROM PROSPECTS
    WHERE Name = 'Booneco' ;
```

This formulation has the additional advantage of returning only one row, containing the city where Booneco is located.

The CASE expression is more valuable when used in an UPDATE statement than when used in a SELECT statement. The UPDATE statement is SQL's tool for changing the values of data in a database table. I describe it thoroughly in Session 22. For now, let's look at how Xanthic may use it along with a CASE expression to change the data in one of their tables.

A smarter use of a CASE expression

Suppose Xanthic wants to recognize people who have been with the company a long time. With a CASE expression, you can output a list of employee names and any significant service milestones that they have achieved. Consider the statement and its result shown in Figure 9-1.

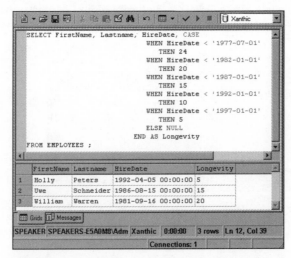

Figure 9-1 *CASE expression used in a search, as implemented by Microsoft SQL Server*

The service milestones achieved by the employees are displayed as Longevity.

Comparing fields in a table to a specified value expression with a CASE expression

20 Min. To Go

In the previous section, you saw that you can use the CASE expression to see if records in a table satisfy one of a set of conditions, returning one of a set of specified values if they do. You can also use the CASE expression to compare a test value expression against a set of value expressions rather than a set of conditions, returning one of a set of specified values if they are equal. This version of the CASE expression takes the form:

```
CASE value_expressionT
    WHEN value_expression1 THEN result1
    WHEN value_expression2 THEN result2
    ...
    WHEN value_expressionN THEN resultN
    ELSE resultX
END
```

If value_expression1 equals value_expressionT, then the CASE expression returns result1. If value_expression1 does not equal value_expressionT, but value_expression2 does equal value_expressionT, then the CASE expression returns result2, and so on down the line. If none of the WHEN clauses produces a match, the ELSE clause executes and returns resultX. The ELSE clause is optional. If it is omitted and none of the WHEN clauses produces a match, the CASE expression returns a NULL value.

An example of this form of the CASE expression shows how you may use it with Xanthic's CUSTOMER table to output the e-mail addresses and native languages of all customers, based on their country of residence. Figure 9-2 shows the query that includes the CASE expression and the result of executing the query.

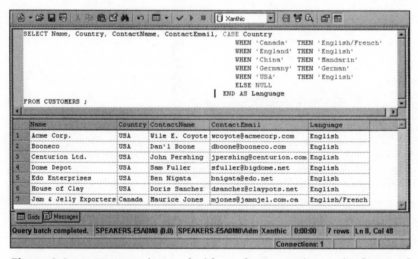

Figure 9-2   *CASE expression used with a value expression, as implemented by Microsoft SQL Server*

The NULLIF expression

I have mentioned that although SQL uses the NULL value to represent an unknown value, host languages often used with SQL — such as Java or Visual Basic — do not support the NULL value. Data collected by a program written in such a host language will typically represent an unknown value in some arbitrary way, such as "–1", "?", "***", or "N/A". To use such data with SQL, you must find some way to convert these various representations of unknown data to NULL values that SQL understands. One way to do this is with a CASE expression. After importing foreign data containing unknown values represented by "–1" into an SQL table, convert those "–1" values to NULL values with an UPDATE statement that contains a CASE expression.

 The UPDATE **statement is covered in detail in Session 22.**

The following statement is an example of such a use.

```
UPDATE CUSTOMERS
    SET ContactFax = CASE ContactFax
                    WHEN -1 THEN NULL
                    ELSE ContactFax
                END ;
```

Any records in the CUSTOMERS table that have a "–1" in the ContactFax field change the value to NULL. All other records are unaffected.

The above method works fine, but SQL provides a shortcut for accomplishing the same thing, the NULLIF expression. The NULLIF expression is nothing but a restricted case of the CASE expression, but it is shorter, and perhaps a little easier to understand. Here is the same conversion given above, but using the NULLIF expression.

```
UPDATE CUSTOMERS
    SET ContactFax = NULLIF (ContactFax, -1) ;
```

You can read this statement as, "Update the CUSTOMERS table by setting column ContactFax to NULL if the existing value of ContactFax is –1. Make no change for all other existing values of ContactFax."

The COALESCE expression

Like NULLIF, COALESCE is a shortcut version of the CASE expression that deals with NULL values. However, instead of converting a specific value to a NULL value, it sifts a specific value out of a list of values that contains NULL values. Suppose you have a list of values, some of which are NULL. The COALESCE expression works through the list until it finds the first non-NULL value, which it returns as its result. If all the values in the list are NULL, COALESCE returns a NULL value.

You can do the same thing that COALESCE does with a CASE expression, as shown in the following code:

```
CASE
    WHEN value1 IS NOT NULL
        THEN value1
    WHEN value2 IS NOT NULL
        THEN value2
    ...
    WHEN valueN IS NOT NULL
        THEN valueN
    ELSE NULL
END
```

This code checks the first value in the list. If that value is non-NULL, the CASE expression returns that value and terminates. If value1 is NULL, the CASE expression tests value2 in the same way. It continues until it finds and returns a non-NULL value. If all the values in the list are NULL, the ELSE clause executes, returning a NULL value and terminating the expression. You can achieve the same result with the following COALESCE expression:

```
COALESCE(value1, value2, ..., valueN)
```

Value1, value2, ..., and valueN are value expressions that reduce to a single value. If that single value is the NULL value, the COALESCE expression skips over it and moves to the next value expression. As soon as COALESCE finds a non-NULL value, it returns that value. COALESCE is most valuable when you have a list that you know contains only one non-NULL value. It is also valuable if any non-NULL value in the list satisfies your purposes, or if you know the first one in the list is the one you want.

Operating on Multiple Columns with Row Value Constructors

**10 Min.
To Go**

Unlike the value expressions discussed so far, which return a single value, you can use a row value constructor to return an entire row of values or a selected portion of a row. A row value constructor is a list of values enclosed in parentheses and separated by commas. For example, to use a row value constructor to return all the rows in Xanthic's PROSPECTS table that duplicate rows in their CUSTOMERS table, use the following syntax:

```
SELECT * FROM PROSPECTS
    WHERE (PROSPECTS.Name, PROSPECTS.Address1, PROSPECTS.Address2, PROSPECTS.City)
      =
          (CUSTOMERS.Name, CUSTOMERS.Address1, CUSTOMERS.Address2, CUSTOMERS.City) ;
```

This query returns all the rows from the PROSPECTS table where the name and address information match the name and address information in a row of the CUSTOMERS table. You may want to eliminate this data duplication by deleting the retrieved rows from the PROSPECTS table, as shown below:

```
DELETE FROM PROSPECTS
    WHERE (PROSPECTS.Name, PROSPECTS.Address1, PROSPECTS.Address2, PROSPECTS.City)
      =
          (CUSTOMERS.Name, CUSTOMERS.Address1, CUSTOMERS.Address2, CUSTOMERS.City) ;
```

Row value constructors are not implemented in Microsoft Access 2000, Microsoft SQL Server 2000, Oracle 9i, PostgreSQL 7.1, or MySQL 4.0.

Because row value constructors are not widely implemented, you may be better off using a more common form that produces the same result. You can do the deletion given above as follows:

```
DELETE FROM PROSPECTS
  WHERE PROSPECTS.Name = CUSTOMERS.Name
    AND PROSPECTS.Address1 = CUSTOMERS.Address1
    AND PROSPECTS.Address2 - CUSTOMERS.Address2
    AND PROSPECTS.City = CUSTOMERS.City ;
```

Done!

REVIEW

The CASE value expression is a good tool for searching a table for rows that satisfy one of a series of condtions. It evaluates a condition for each row in the table. If the evaluation produces a TRUE result, the result associated with that condition is returned and the CASE value expression terminated. If the first condition is not satisfied by a row, CASE tries the second condition. It keeps trying to find a condition that evaluates to a TRUE value until either it succeeds or runs out of conditions. If none of the conditions evaluates to TRUE, an optional ELSE clause is executed. If the ELSE is absent, the CASE expression returns a NULL value.

The NULLIF and COALESCE value expressions are special cases of the CASE expression. NULLIF returns a NULL value if its specified condition is met. COALESCE returns the first non-NULL value it finds in a list of values. If all the values in the list are NULL, COALESCE returns a NULL value.

The row value constructor operates on lists of values, making it fundamentally different from value expressions, which reduce to a single value. It compares one set of values, possibly a table row, possibly part of a table row, against a set of values that corresponds in number and in data type. When the comparands are equal, the row value constructor returns a TRUE value. When the comparands are not equal, it returns a FALSE value.

QUIZ YOURSELF

1. How many values does a CASE expression return just before terminating its execution? (See "Searching a table with a CASE expression.")

2. What does the NULLIF expression do? (See "The NULLIF expression.")

3. What value does the following expression return? (See "The COALESCE expression.")

   COALESCE (NULL, NULL, 0, -0-, NULL, "ice cream")

4. Assuming all the columns in the PROSPECTS table correspond to columns in the CUSTOMERS table, and that the two tables have some records in common, write an SQL query that retrieves the Name and the City columns of those matching rows. (See "Operating on Multiple Columns with Row Value Constructors.")

Grouping and Ordering of Retrieved Data

Session Checklist

✔ Grouping related records with the GROUP BY clause.

✔ Restricting groups retrieved with the HAVING clause.

✔ Sorting groups with the ORDER BY clause

**30 Min.
To Go**

When you retrieve data from a database table using the SELECT statement, the data is returned in the order that the rows happened to have been entered into the table. In most cases this order is not the most helpful. The data would probably be a lot more useful if it were sorted according to whatever is of most interest to you right now. SQL provides three clauses that you can add to your SELECT statements to provide that sorted output: GROUP BY, HAVING, and ORDER BY.

To show the effect of these clauses on retrievals, consider the data in Xanthic's INVOICE table. The INVOICE table has the structure shown in Figure 10-1. The table is filled with records of recent sales transactions, as shown in Figure 10-2.

In this example, there are only a few records, so it is relatively easy to extract useful information without extensive study. However, in a typical business context, there will probably be hundreds of thousands of records in such a table. In such a case, merely looking at the data will not tell you much.

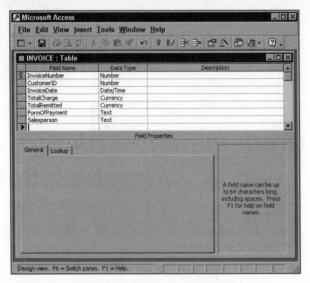

Figure 10-1 *Structure of* INVOICE *table*

InvoiceNumber	CustomerID	InvoiceDate	TotalCharge	TotalRemitted	FormOfPayment	Salesperson
273	3141	12/17/2001	$120.00	$120.00	cash	Warren
274	5347	12/17/2001	$2,880.00	$2,880.00	check	Schneider
275	1440	12/18/2001	$960.00	$480.00	Visa	Peters
276	2339	12/19/2001	$240.00	$240.00	American Express	Peters
277	3141	12/20/2001	$10,540.00	$1,054.00	check	Warren
278	2339	12/21/2001	$6,750.00	$3,375.00	check	Peters
279	4772	12/21/2001	$180.00	$180.00	Visa	Schneider
280	5771	12/24/2001	$2,350.00	$2,350.00	check	Schneider
281	8333	12/24/2001	$4,500.00	$2,250.00	check	Warren
0	0		$0.00	$0.00		

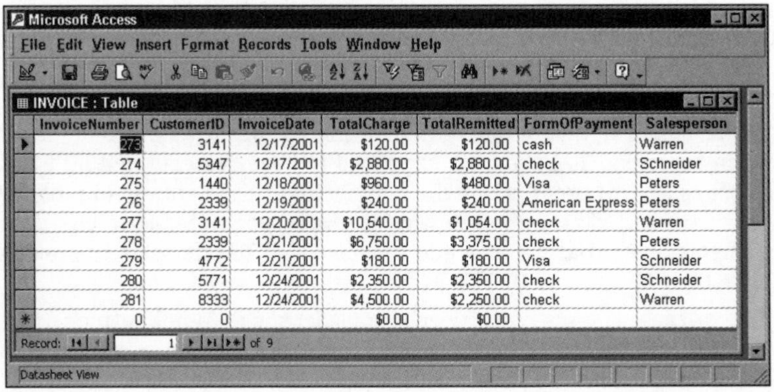

Figure 10-2 *Data in the* INVOICE *table*

Grouping Related Records with the GROUP BY Clause

A manager may want to get an overview of salesperson performance. Because the records in the INVOICE table are in the order that they were entered into the database, it is not easy to tell who is selling more and who is selling less. By grouping invoice records by salesperson, the desired information becomes much more visible. Use the GROUP BY clause in conjunction with one of the aggregate functions, such as SUM. The manager can sort the records into groups with the following SELECT statement:

```
SELECT Salesperson, SUM(TotalCharge)
FROM INVOICE
GROUP BY Salesperson ;
```

This produces the result set shown in Figure 10-3.

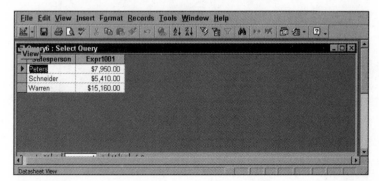

Figure 10-3 *Invoice totals are grouped by salesperson, sorted alphabetically*

The GROUP BY clause sorts retrieved records alphabetically, based on the columns listed in the GROUP BY clause. All of Peters's sales are shown first, then all of Schneider's, followed by all of Warren's sales. From this we can see that for the time period studied, these three salespeople were selling successfully. If Xanthic has additional salespeople not present in this record set, they apparently sold nothing and perhaps are candidates for a training session.

SQL enables you to group records by multiple attributes. For example, if you want to look at the daily production of each salesperson, you can group records first by Salesperson and second by InvoiceDate. The code would be:

```
SELECT Salesperson, InvoiceDate, SUM(TotalCharge)
FROM INVOICE
GROUP BY Salesperson, InvoiceDate ;
```

Figure 10-4 shows the result.

This query shows all of Peters's sales for the first date she sold something, followed by all of her sales for the second date and so on. After all of Peters's sales are listed, all of Schneider's sales for the first day he sold something are listed, and so on. This sequence carries on until all the retrieved records have been displayed in the desired groups.

A SELECT **statement that contains a** GROUP BY **clause may reference only columns that are contained in the** GROUP BY **clause. Any column not included in the** GROUP BY **clause cannot be retrieved by the** SELECT **statement. The** SELECT **statement can, however, also contain aggregate functions such as SUM, MIN, MAX, AVG, COUNT, and so on.**

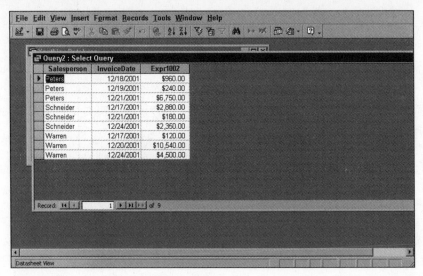

Figure 10-4   *Retrieved records are grouped by InvoiceDate within each Salesperson group*

Restricting Groups Retrieved with the HAVING Clause

**20 Min.
To Go**

The GROUP BY clause is great as long as you want to see all the records in all the groups. Perhaps, however, you are interested in only some of the groups. In that case you can restrict the groups retrieved to the ones you want. Suppose you want to look only at the records having to do with sales made by Warren. You can selectively retrieve only those rows by adding a HAVING clause to the GROUP BY clause in your SELECT statement. The following code has that effect.

```
SELECT Salesperson, InvoiceDate, SUM(TotalCharge)
FROM INVOICE
GROUP BY Salesperson, InvoiceDate
HAVING Salesperson = 'Warren';
```

Figure 10-5 shows the result of this code.

If you are interested in the results of two salespeople appropriately grouped, you can do that too, by adding a compound HAVING clause such as the following:

```
SELECT Salesperson, InvoiceDate, SUM(TotalCharge)
FROM INVOICE
GROUP BY Salesperson, InvoiceDate
HAVING Salesperson = 'Warren'
   OR Salesperson = 'Peters';
```

Figure 10-6 shows what adding another condition to the HAVING clause does to the retrieval.

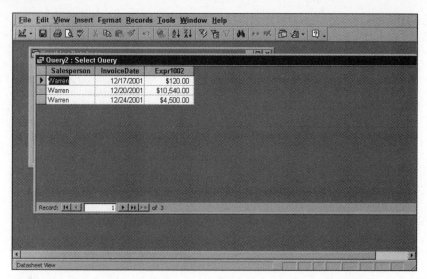

Figure 10-5   *Records returned are restricted to those where Salesperson is Warren*

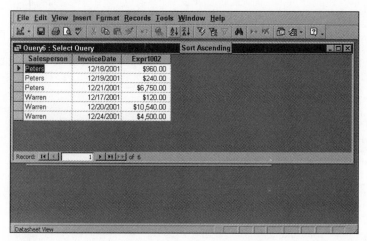

Figure 10-6   *Sales information from both Warren and Peters is retrieved*

This returns records of all of Peters's sales in chronological order, followed by all of Warren's sales, making it easy to compare their performance. If you want to select out the records of sales of three salespeople or four, you can do so by adding additional OR sub-clauses. This feature is useful if you have dozens or hundreds of salespeople.

Sorting Groups with the ORDER BY Clause

10 Min.
To Go

While the GROUP BY clause enables you to sort records into groups in conjunction with such aggregate operators as SUM, MAX, and MIN, the ORDER BY clause gives you a straight sort of table records, sorted by the fields you specify in either ascending or descending order.

Different database management systems have different conventions for storing data. Even if you enter the data into a table in exactly the order in which you will want to retrieve it, if the database gets reorganized, the order of items may change. What worked before may not work now. You can specify the order in which you want the records to be displayed by adding an `ORDER BY` clause. The `ORDER BY` clause must not appear ahead of any `GROUP BY` clause. In fact, it must be the last clause in the `SELECT` statement. Putting an `ORDER BY` clause anywhere but at the end of a `SELECT` statement could lead to unexpected results. To sort records within a group by invoice date, use something similar to the following code:

```
SELECT *
FROM INVOICE
ORDER BY Salesperson, InvoiceDate;
```

SQL displays records for each salesperson in date order, with the earliest dates first.

The default sort order imposed by the `ORDER BY` clause is ascending, meaning from smallest to largest or earliest to latest. You can also sort in descending order, from largest to smallest or latest to earliest. Suppose, for example, you wanted to display the records within each salesperson's group, showing the largest sale first, then the next largest, descending down to the smallest sale. Do it with the following code:

```
SELECT *
FROM INVOICE
ORDER BY Salesperson, TotalCharge DESC;
```

The `DESC` keyword specifies a descending sort based on the TotalCharge field. It produces the result shown in Figure 10-7.

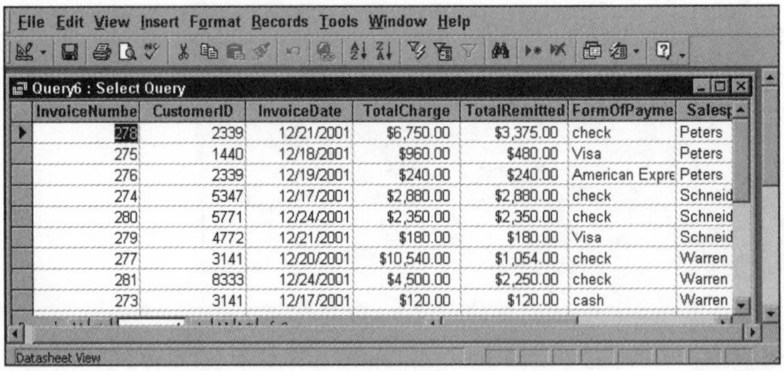

InvoiceNumbe	CustomerID	InvoiceDate	TotalCharge	TotalRemitted	FormOfPayme	Salesp
278	2339	12/21/2001	$6,750.00	$3,375.00	check	Peters
275	1440	12/18/2001	$960.00	$480.00	Visa	Peters
276	2339	12/19/2001	$240.00	$240.00	American Expre	Peters
274	5347	12/17/2001	$2,880.00	$2,880.00	check	Schneid
280	5771	12/24/2001	$2,350.00	$2,350.00	check	Schneid
279	4772	12/21/2001	$180.00	$180.00	Visa	Schneid
277	3141	12/20/2001	$10,540.00	$1,054.00	check	Warren
281	8333	12/24/2001	$4,500.00	$2,250.00	check	Warren
273	3141	12/17/2001	$120.00	$120.00	cash	Warren

Figure 10-7 `INVOICE` *records ordered first by Salesperson and then by TotalCharge, in descending order.*

Done!

REVIEW

You can control the order in which query results are displayed using the GROUP BY, HAVING and ORDER BY clauses. Use the GROUP BY clause with such aggregate operators as SUM, AVG, MAX, and MIN to combine information from multiple records into meaningful groups for display. Use the HAVING clause to restrict retrieval to the specific groups of records that are of current interest to you. Use the ORDER BY clause to perform sorts on the data retrieved. Sorts can be based on one or more columns and may be either ascending or descending. You can perform an ascending sort on one column and a descending sort on another.

QUIZ YOURSELF

1. Write an SQL query that pulls all the salespeople's names and their average sales figures from the INVOICE table and displays the result. (See "Grouping Related Records with the GROUP BY Clause.")

2. Write an SQL query that pulls only Schneider's and Peters's names and their highest invoice total charge from the INVOICE table and displays the result. (See "Restricting Groups Retrieved with the HAVING Clause.")

3. Write an SQL query that displays all the records in the INVOICE table, sorted by total remitted, with the highest amounts shown first. (See "Sorting Groups with the ORDER BY Clause.")

PART

II

Saturday Morning
Part Review

1. Type an SQL query that retrieves all rows from the INVOICE table where the value stored in the TotalRemitted column is at least $200.

2. Type an SQL query that retrieves all rows from the CUSTOMERS table where the customer is not located in the USA and there is no entry in the ContactFax field.

3. Type an efficient SQL query that retrieves all rows from the PROSPECTS table where the prospect does not live in any of the following countries: USA, Canada, UK, Germany, China.

4. Type an SQL query that retrieves all rows from the PROSPECTS table where the Address1 field contains the word *brook* somewhere within it.

5. What is wrong with the following query?

```
SELECT * FROM CUSTOMERS
  WHERE ContactFax = NULL ;
```

6. In what type of queries are the ALL, SOME, and ANY operators used?

7. When used to introduce a subquery in a nested query, what does the EXISTS operator do?

8. Under what circumstances does a UNIQUE operator that introduces a sub-query return a FALSE value?

9. What value does a DISTINCT predicate return when it compares 12 to a NULL value?

10. What value does the OVERLAPS predicate below return?

```
(TIME '3:09:00', TIME '3:16:00')
OVERLAPS
(TIME '3:16:00', TIME '3:23:00')
```

11. What kind of MATCH predicate should you use if you want to see if a specific row expression which contains no NULL values matches one and only one row in a table?

12. In what way is the SIMILAR operator more general than the LIKE operator?

13. What does the CASE conditional expression do?

14. What does the following statement do?

```
UPDATE PROSPECTS
    SET Country = NULLIF (Country, 'USSR') ;
```

15. What does the COALESCE expression do?

16. How does a row value constructor differ from a value expression?

17. Type an SQL query that retrieves all CustomerIDs and the number of occurrences of each in the INVOICE table, grouped by CustomerID.

18. Type an SQL query that retrieves all CustomerIDs and the number of occurrences of each in the INVOICE table, grouped by CustomerID, where only groups with CustomerIDs less that 2000 are included.

19. Type an SQL query that returns all the records in the INVOICE table, sorted by TotalCharge, with the highest values listed first.

Retrieving Data from Multiple Tables with Relational Operators

Session Checklist

✔ Retrieving data items that occur in either one of two tables

✔ Retrieving all data items that occur in both of two tables

✔ Retrieving data items that occur in one of two tables but not the other

**30 Min.
To Go**

S QL is the standard language for dealing with relational databases. In Session 1, I talk about what makes a relational database relational. Generally, the tables in a database are related to each other in some fashion. So far this weekend, we have not delved into how they may be related. In this session, we look at a variety of ways you can pull information from multiple related tables to answer questions you may have. In well-designed relational databases, the answers to typical questions can rarely be found in a single table. Multiple table queries are the rule rather than the exception.

SQL has a number of relational operators whose job it is to draw information from multiple source tables. Three of these, UNION, INTERSECT, and EXCEPT are implementations of the principal operators of the mathematical field called relational algebra. In addition, SQL includes a large number of join operators, each one a little different from the others in terms of what it retrieves from the source tables. In Session 12, I discuss these operators and give examples of how you can use them.

Retrieving All Rows That Occur in Either of Two Tables

The UNION operator works in the special case where you have multiple tables that all have the same structure. It combines all the records from all the tables, deleting any duplicates. Tables have the same structure when they all have the same number of columns, and the data type and size specified for each column of the first table is the same as the corresponding column in the other tables. Corresponding columns need not have the same names, but they must have the same types and sizes. Tables that satisfy these criteria are called *union-compatible*.

Suppose Xanthic Systems has two operating divisions, one in North America and the other in Europe. Both perform similar services for similar customers, but there are some differences based on geography and culture. In both cases, a division consists of several departments. Each department has a manager and a staffing level.

Xanthic's top management needs to keep up to date on worldwide staffing. The company's database includes the NASTAFF table with staffing information for the North American division, and the EUROSTAFF table with staffing information for the European division. Using Microsoft SQL Server 2000, Figure 11-1 shows the data in NASTAFF and Figure 11-2 shows the data in EUROSTAFF.

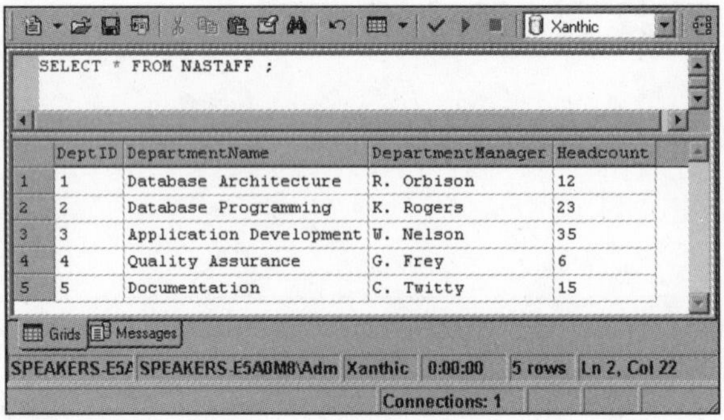

```
SELECT * FROM NASTAFF ;
```

	DeptID	DepartmentName	DepartmentManager	Headcount
1	1	Database Architecture	R. Orbison	12
2	2	Database Programming	K. Rogers	23
3	3	Application Development	W. Nelson	35
4	4	Quality Assurance	G. Frey	6
5	5	Documentation	C. Twitty	15

Figure 11-1 *Retrieval of all records from the NASTAFF table*

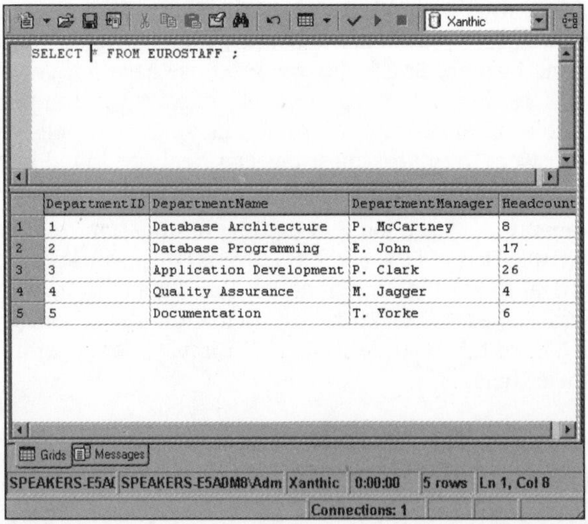

```
SELECT * FROM EUROSTAFF ;
```

	DepartmentID	DepartmentName	DepartmentManager	Headcount
1	1	Database Architecture	P. McCartney	8
2	2	Database Programming	E. John	17
3	3	Application Development	P. Clark	26
4	4	Quality Assurance	M. Jagger	4
5	5	Documentation	T. Yorke	6

Figure 11-2 *Retrieval of all records from the EUROSTAFF table*

Because NASTAFF and EUROSTAFF are `UNION`-compatible, using the `UNION` operator on them retrieves all the records from both tables, as shown in Figure 11-3.

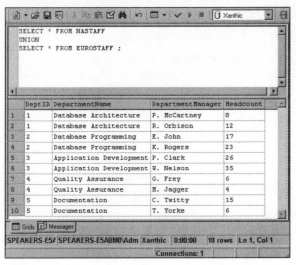

Figure 11-3 *Retrieval of all records from both NASTAFF and EUROSTAFF*

This retrieval puts all of Xanthic's staffing information in one easy-to-comprehend display. With it, corporate management can make sure that staffing stays consistent with productivity and profitability. Notice that in the one case where a column name in NASTAFF differed from the name of the corresponding column in EUROSTAFF, SQL Server 2000 took the column name from NASTAFF to identify the corresponding column in the result set.

If you want to perform a UNION operation without deleting duplicates, you can do so with the UNION ALL operator. The code for the same retrieval illustrated in Figure 11-3, but retaining duplicates, is shown below:

```
SELECT * FROM NASTAFF
UNION ALL
SELECT * FROM EUROSTAFF ;
```

In Microsoft Access 2000, this query produces the result set shown in Figure 11-4.

There are a couple of things to note here. First, because none of the records in NASTAFF are duplicated in EUROSTAFF, the same records that were returned by UNION were also returned by UNION ALL. The second thing to notice is that the UNION ALL operation retrieved the records in a different order than the UNION operation retrieved them in Figure 11-3. This shows that the order in which records are retrieved is sensitive to whether you use UNION or UNION ALL, even if the exact same rows are returned.

If only some of the columns of two tables are union compatible, you can still perform a UNION as long as it only involves those columns that are union compatible. For this usage, the UNION CORRESPONDING form of the UNION operator must be used.

Access 2000, SQL Server 2000, PostgreSQL 7.1, MySQL 4.0 and Oracle 9i do not support the UNION CORRESPONDING **syntax.**

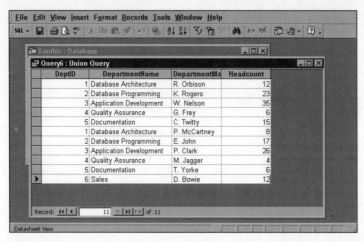

Figure 11-4 *Retrieval of all records from both NASTAFF and EUROSTAFF without deleting duplicates*

Retrieving All Rows That Occur in Both of Two Tables

**20 Min.
To Go**

When you perform the UNION operation on two union-compatible tables, the result includes all qualifying rows from the first table plus all qualifying rows from the second table, but only one copy of any duplicate rows that occur in both tables. In contrast, the INTERSECT operation returns only one copy of any duplicate rows that occur in both tables, and no rows that do not occur in both tables. If I use the same example table that I used to illustrate the UNION operation in the previous section, I would get an empty result set because none of the rows in NASTAFF are duplicated in EUROSTAFF. The following code returns an empty result set, as shown in Figure 11-5:

```
SELECT * FROM NASTAFF
INTERSECT
SELECT * FROM EUROSTAFF ;
```

Figure 11-5 depicts the INTERSECT operation as implemented by Oracle SQL*Plus.

```
SQL>
SQL>
SQL> SELECT * FROM NASTAFF
  2  INTERSECT
  3  SELECT * FROM EUROSTAFF ;

no rows selected

SQL>
```

Figure 11-5 INTERSECT *of NASTAFF and EUROSTAFF shows that they have no common rows.*

Microsoft Access 2000, Microsoft SQL Server 2000 and MySQL 4.0 do not support the INTERSECT set operator.

If Xanthic had two EMPLOYEES tables, perhaps named NAEMPS and EUROEMPS, and some globetrotting employees appeared in both, assuming their records in both tables were identical, their records could be retrieved using the INTERSECT set operator as follows:

```
SELECT * FROM NAEMPS
INTERSECT
SELECT * FROM EUROEMPS ;
```

Figure 11-6 shows the result of this INTERSECT operation after an employee named A. Bocelli has been added to both NAEMPS and EUROEMPS.

```
SQL> SELECT * FROM NAEMPS
  2   INTERSECT
  3   SELECT * FROM EUROEMPS ;

  DEPTID DEPARTMENTNAME          DEPARTMENTMANAGER     HEADCOUNT
--------- --------------------   --------------------  ---------
        6 Worldwide Marketing    A. Bocelli                    1

SQL>
```

Figure 11-6   INTERSECT *of NAEMPS and EUROEMPS returns A. Bocelli as the only employee common to both tables.*

Retrieving All Rows That Occur in One of Two Tables but Not the Other

**10 Min.
To Go**

When you use the UNION set operator on two tables, it returns all rows that appear in either table, excluding duplicates. When you use the INTERSECT set operator on two tables, it returns only the rows that appear in both tables. When you use the EXCEPT set operator on two tables, it returns all rows that appear in the first table that do not appear in the second table. To say it another way, this operation returns all rows from the first table, minus any rows that also appear in the second table.

 Oracle 9i supports this function, but calls it MINUS rather than EXCEPT. MySQL 4.0 does not support the EXCEPT set operator, nor does Access 2000 or SQL Server 2000. PostgreSQL 7.1 does support EXCEPT.

The following code retrieves all North American employees who do not also work in Europe.

```
SELECT * FROM NAEMPS
EXCEPT
SELECT * FROM EUROEMPS ;
```

In Oracle 9i, the same retrieval looks like the following:

```
SELECT * FROM NAEMPS
MINUS
SELECT * FROM EUROEMPS ;
```

This gives the result shown in Figure 11-7. All the employees in NAEMPS are returned except A. Bocelli, who also appears in EUROEMPS.

```
SQL> SELECT * FROM NAEMPS
  2  MINUS
  3  SELECT * FROM EUROEMPS ;

  DEPTID DEPARTMENTNAME            DEPARTMENTMANAGER    HEADCOUNT
-------- ------------------------ -------------------- ---------
       1 Database Architecture    R. Orbison                  12
       2 Database Programming     K. Rogers                   23
       3 Application Development   W. Nelson                   35
       4 Quality Assurance        G. Frey                      6
       5 Documentation            C. Twitty                   15

SQL> |
```

Figure 11-7   *The Oracle* MINUS *operation on NAEMPS and EUROEMPS returns all North America employees except A. Bocelli.*

Done!

REVIEW

Useful data retrieved from a database is usually taken from multiple tables rather than just one. To perform such retrievals, you must use one of the relational or join operators. The relational operators UNION, INTERSECT, and EXCEPT apply only to union-compatible tables, which have matching table structures. UNION retrieves all the requested data from both tables regardless of whether the data in the two tables match, eliminating duplicates from the result. INTERSECT retrieves only the data that is common to both of the source tables. EXCEPT retrieves all the data from the first table, except the data that the first table shares with the second table.

The relational operators covered in this session are valuable in a variety of circumstances. Because support for them varies greatly, you may want to consider such support when you are choosing a relational database management system. None of the database management products covered in this book support the UNION CORRESPONDING operator. Oracle 9i and PostgreSQL 7.1 support the INTERSECT and EXCEPT (MINUS) operators, but MySQL 4.0, Access 2000 and SQL Server 2000 do not.

QUIZ YOURSELF

1. What are the two criteria for union-compatibility? (See "Retrieving All Rows That Occur in Either of Two Tables.")
2. What should you do if you want the UNION of two tables to include any duplicates rather than discard them? (See "Retrieving All Rows That Occur in Either of Two Tables.")
3. What does the EXCEPT operator do? (See "Retrieving All Rows That Occur in One of Two Tables but Not the Other.")
4. When does the INTERSECT operator return an empty result set? (See "Retrieving All Rows That Occur in Both of Two Tables.")

Retrieving Data from Multiple Tables Using Joins

Session Checklist

✔ Pulling data from two tables with the cross join

✔ Getting specific with the equi-join

✔ Joining tables with multiple matching columns with the natural join

✔ Joining tables based on conditions other than equality with the condition join

✔ Joining tables whose columns have matching names with the column name join

✔ Retrieving non-matching columns with outer joins

**30 Min.
To Go**

The UNION, INTERSECT, and EXCEPT set operators operate on two or more tables only if the tables are union-compatible. *Union-compatible* tables have corresponding columns of the same types and sizes, but the columns do not necessarily have the same names. Frequently, you will want to draw data from multiple tables that are not union-compatible. Use the various kinds of join operator to perform such operations. The simplest of these is the cross join. The other joins build on the foundation of the cross join to enable you to pull the exact information you want from multiple tables, even if those tables have very little in common.

The Cross Join

The cross join takes every row of the first table and associates every row of the second table to it. This produces a result set holding the number of rows in the first table multiplied by the number of rows in the second table. This operation can produce a table with a lot of rows very quickly, and most of those rows are probably worthless to you.

Suppose Xanthic's sales manager wants some insight into what customers are buying and who is selling to them. A cross join delivers that information, but it is buried within a huge amount of irrelevant information. Consider the query shown in Figure 12-1.

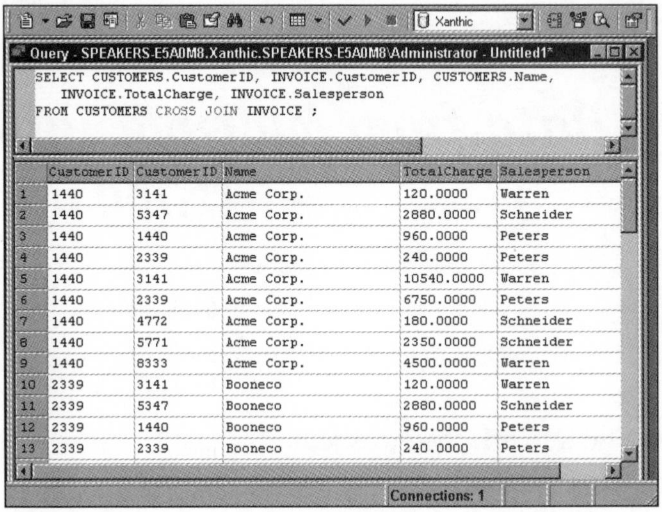

Figure 12-1   *Cross join of Xanthic's* CUSTOMERS *table and* INVOICE *table*

Just the first few of the 63 rows returned are shown in Figure 12-1. Because there are seven customers in the CUSTOMER table and nine sales recorded in the INVOICE table, the cross product (also called Cartesian product) of the operation is 7 X 9 = 63 rows.

The result of this retrieval is confusing and misleading because the first customer in the CUSTOMER table, Acme Corp., is associated not only with its own purchases, but also with all the purchases made by all the other customers. This is not usually what you want.

Although the cross join generally does not give you the data you want in a form that is easy to understand, it does serve as a first step toward giving you something useful.

The Equi-Join

The equi-join builds on the basic cross join by adding a WHERE clause that restricts the rows retrieved. Using an equi-join in the example from the previous section rather than a cross join returns only nine rows, all of which are relevant, rather than nine relevant rows buried among 54 irrelevant rows. Figure 12-2 shows the query and the result.

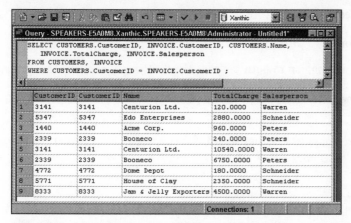

Figure 12-2 *Equi-join of Xanthic's* CUSTOMERS *table and* INVOICE *table*

As you can see, in all nine rows retrieved, the CustomerID from the CUSTOMERS table matches the CustomerID from the INVOICE table. Each row associates a single purchase with the customer who made it.

It can become tedious typing long SQL statements such as this one:

```
SELECT CUSTOMERS.CustomerID, INVOICE.CustomerID, CUSTOMERS.Name,
    INVOICE.TotalCharge, INVOICE.Salesperson
FROM CUSTOMERS, INVOICE
WHERE CUSTOMERS.CustomerID = INVOICE.CustomerID ;
```

To alleviate some of the boredom and give some rest to the fingers, you can use aliases for table names. Specify the alias in the FROM clause and use it instead of the table name everywhere else. To use aliases with the above code, do this:

```
SELECT C.CustomerID, I.CustomerID, C.Name,
    I.TotalCharge, I.Salesperson
FROM CUSTOMERS C, INVOICE I
WHERE C.CustomerID = I.CustomerID ;
```

C is the alias for CUSTOMERS, and *I* is the alias for INVOICE. If you decide to use aliases, be sure to use them exclusively within any SQL statement. If you mix usage of an alias for a table name with the table name itself, SQL gets confused.

**20 Min.
To Go**

The Natural Join

The natural join is a kind of equi-join. In a two-column join, it acts like a series of WHERE clauses that compare all the columns in the second table whose names match the names of columns in the first table. If you were to apply a natural join to the example in the previous section, the code would look like this:

```
SELECT C.CustomerID, I.CustomerID, C.Name,
    I.TotalCharge, I.Salesperson
FROM CUSTOMERS C NATURAL JOIN INVOICE I ;
```

The only column that is common to both tables is the CustomerID column. This column is tested for equality, and the result is exactly the same as it was in the previous section; nine rows are returned, each one recording a single purchase by the customer who made the purchase.

 Oracle 9i, PostgreSQL 7.1, and MySQL 4.0 support the NATURAL JOIN **syntax. SQL Server 2000 does not.**

The Condition Join

The condition join is just like the equi-join except the condition being tested does not have to be equality; it can be any well-formed predicate. If the condition being tested evaluates to TRUE, the corresponding rows become part of the result set. Syntax is a little different from what it is for other joins. The condition is contained in an ON clause rather than a WHERE clause.

Figure 12-3 shows the result of a condition join query.

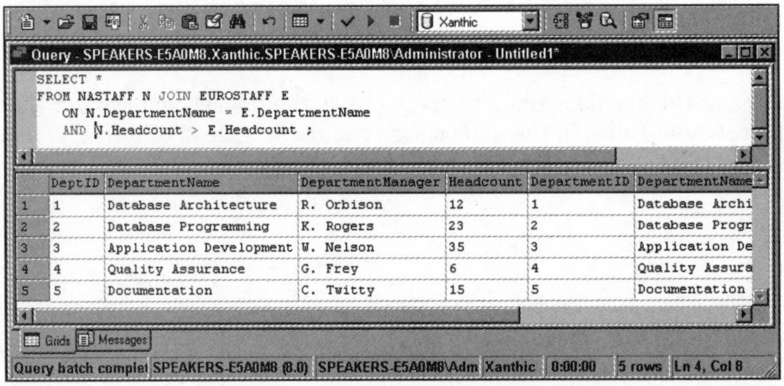

Figure 12-3   Condition join of NASTAFF to EUROSTAFF

This query returns a row for every case where a department in the North American region has a larger staff than the corresponding department in the European region. If the greater than sign (>) had been turned around into a less than sign (<), no rows would have been returned because in every case, the staffing level of the European departments is lower than the staffing levels of the corresponding North American departments.

The Column Name Join

10 Min. To Go

The column name join is like a natural join, but is more flexible. The natural join selects all the rows from the two source tables where there are matches in all the columns whose names match the names of columns in the second table. The column name join permits you to select a subset of the matching column names. This capability is valuable if the source tables have some common column names that may not contain matching data for corresponding rows.

Three of the four columns of the NASTAFF table have the same names as the corresponding three columns of the EUROSTAFF table. However, the content of the DepartmentManager column from the NASTAFF table never matches the content of the DepartmentManager column from the EUROSTAFF table. The content of the Headcount column of the NASTAFF table match the corresponding column of the EUROSTAFF table only by coincidence. To do a meaningful condition name join on these two tables, you need to exclude both the DepartmentManager column and the Headcount column. The following condition name join does the job:

```
SELECT *
FROM NASTAFF JOIN EUROSTAFF
USING (DepartmentName) ;
```

 MySQL 4.0 and PostgreSQL 7.1 support the ANSI standard column name JOIN **syntax given here. SQL Server 2000, and Oracle 9i do not.**

For those implementations that do not support the column name join syntax, you can use the following syntax to achieve the same objective.

```
SELECT *
FROM NASTAFF N JOIN EUROSTAFF E
WHERE N.DepartmentName = E.DepartmentName ;
```

This code, using standard equi-join syntax, does the same job as the above column name join syntax on platforms that do not support column name joins.

Outer Joins

All the joins discussed so far (except the cross join) are *inner joins*. They return only rows where some condition (usually equality) is satisfied by both source tables. The outer joins, in addition to the rows returned by inner joins, also return rows that do not satisfy the stated condition. There are three types of outer joins, the left outer join, the right outer join, and the full outer join.

Left outer join

When coding a left outer join, one table is written to the left of the JOIN keyword and a second table is written to the right. The left outer join returns all rows that meet the condition in the WHERE clause, plus all the rows in the left table that do not meet the condition in the WHERE clause. The rows in the right table that do not meet the condition in the WHERE clause are excluded. To understand this concept a little better, Xanthic can provide us with an example.

Xanthic Systems currently has operations in North America and Europe and has just opened development facilities in Asia and Australia. To keep track of their far-flung empire, they have added REGION, DIVISION, and MANAGERS tables to their database, structured as follows:

REGION table

RegionID	RegionName	Location
1	North America	Portland
2	Europe	Dublin
3	Asia	Hong Kong
4	Australia	Perth

DIVISIONS table

DivisionID	DivisionName	RegionID
1	HQ	1
2	Development, NA	1
3	Sales, NA	1
4	Development, EU	2
5	Sales, EU	2
6	Development, AS	3
7	Research	NULL

MANAGERS table

ManagerID	ManagerName	DivisionID	DepartmentName
1	R. Orbison	2	Database Architecture
2	P. McCartney	4	Database Architecture
3	H. Peters	3	Sales
4	U. Schneider	5	Sales
5	K. Rogers	2	Database Programming
6	W. Nelson	2	Application Development
7	G. Frey	2	Quality Assurance
8	C. Twitty	2	Documentation
9	E. John	4	Database Programming
10	P. Clark	4	Application Development
11	M. Jagger	4	Quality Assurance
12	T. Yorke	4	Documentation

The DIVISION table is related to the REGION table by the inclusion of RegionID as a foreign key. The MANAGERS table is related to the DIVISION table by the inclusion of DivisionID as a foreign key.

I can demonstrate a left outer join, and as a bonus make it a three-table join. Here's the code:

```
SELECT *
FROM REGION R LEFT OUTER JOIN DIVISION D
   ON (R.RegionID = D.RegionID)
LEFT OUTER JOIN MANAGERS M
   ON (D.DivisionID = M.DivisionID) ;
```

This statement selects all the columns from all three tables, REGION, DIVISION, and MAN-AGERS. First it performs a left outer join on REGION and DIVISION where the RegionID in DIVISION matches the RegionID in REGION. Next it performs a left outer join on the result of the previous join and the MANAGERS table where DivisionID in the MANAGERS table matches DivisionID in the result set of the first left outer join. The result set includes:

- All records from the REGION table
- All records from the DIVISION table where D.RegionID matches R.RegionID
- All records from the MANAGERS table where M.DivisionID matches the DivisionID field in the result set of the first left outer join

Figure 12-4 shows the result.

RegionID	RegionName	Location	DivisionID	DivisionName	RegionID	ManagerID	ManagerName	DivisionID	DepartmentName
1	North America	Portland	1	HQ	1	NULL	NULL	NULL	NULL
1	North America	Portland	2	Development, NA	1	1	R. Orbison	2	Database Architecture
1	North America	Portland	2	Development, NA	1	5	K. Rogers	2	Database Programming
1	North America	Portland	2	Development, NA	1	6	W. Nelson	2	Application Development
1	North America	Portland	2	Development, NA	1	7	G. Frey	2	Quality Assurance
1	North America	Portland	2	Development, NA	1	8	C. Twitty	2	Documentation
1	North America	Portland	3	Sales, NA	1	3	H. Peters	3	Sales
2	Europe	Dublin	4	Development, EU	2	2	P. McCartney	4	Database Architecture
2	Europe	Dublin	4	Development, EU	2	9	E. John	4	Database Programming
2	Europe	Dublin	4	Development, EU	2	10	P. Clark	4	Application Development
2	Europe	Dublin	4	Development, EU	2	11	M. Jagger	4	Quality Assurance
2	Europe	Dublin	4	Development, EU	2	12	T. Yorke	4	Documentation
2	Europe	Dublin	5	Sales, EU	2	4	U. Schneider	5	Sales
3	Asia	Hong Kong	6	Development, AS	3	NULL	NULL	NULL	NULL
4	Australia	Perth	NULL	NULL	NULL	NULL	NULL	NULL	NULL

Figure 12-4   *Result of left outer join of* REGION*,* DIVISION*, and* MANAGERS *tables*

There is a record in the result set corresponding to every row in the REGION table, includ-ing the Australia row, which does not match any row in the DIVISION table. There is no row in the result set corresponding to the Research row in the DIVISION table because that row does not have a RegionID that matches any row in the REGION table. Because no manager has been named for either the HQ division or the Asian development division, the rows from the MANAGERS table corresponding to those positions contain nothing but NULL values.

The result set of this example explicitly shows the results of a three table left outer join.

- All records of the leftmost source table are represented.
- All records of the second source table that match records of the leftmost table are represented.
- All records of the third source table that match records of the first left outer join are represented.
- Unmatched records from the leftmost table of a left outer join are filled out with NULL values in the fields taken from the source tables to the right.

MySQL 4.0 supports the left outer join and the right outer join, but does not support full outer joins. SQL Server 2000, PostgreSQL 7.1, and Oracle 9i support all three outer join operators.

Right outer join

The right outer join works exactly like the left outer join, but in reverse. The right outer join returns all rows that meet the condition in the WHERE clause, plus all the rows in the right table that do not meet the condition in the WHERE clause. The rows in the left table that do not meet the condition in the WHERE clause are excluded. Because you as the programmer can control which source table you put on the left and which you put on the right, the right outer join is somewhat redundant. Anything you can do with a right outer join, you can also do with a left outer join by switching the positions of the source tables.

Full outer join

The full outer join works like a combination of the left outer join and the right outer join. It returns all rows that meet the condition in the WHERE clause, plus all the rows in the left table that do not meet the condition in the WHERE clause, plus all the rows in the right table that do not meet the condition of the WHERE clause. This covers all the bases. If you were to do a full outer join on the REGION, DIVISION, and MANAGERS tables in the above example you would get all the following:

- All rows for every region, whether that region had any divisions or not
- All rows for every manager, whether she or he was assigned to a division or not
- All rows for every division, whether it was assigned to a region or not, or whether it had any assigned managers or not

Done!

REVIEW

The various join operators can combine information from tables that do not have matching structures. Not all of the relational and join operators specified by the ANSI/ISO standard (SQL:1999) are supported by all the most popular database management systems. Make sure your system supports a particular syntax before you try to use it.

QUIZ YOURSELF

1. Why is the result set of a cross join so large? (See "The Cross Join.")
2. What is the difference between an equi-join and a natural join? (See "The Natural Join.")
3. When might you want to use a left outer join rather than one of the inner joins? (See "Left outer join.")
4. Write an SQL query that retrieves the names from all records in the CUSTOMERS table that do not match any of the names in the PROSPECTS table. (See "The Condition Join.")

Nested Queries

Session Checklist

✔ Examining what a nested query does

✔ Taking a look at nested queries that return a single value

✔ Putting the ALL, SOME, and ANY quantifiers to work

✔ Using nested queries as existence tests

✔ Going over other correlated subqueries

30 Min.
To Go

Pulling data from multiple tables to produce some meaningful synthesis is one of the most common uses of a relational database. In the previous session, I cover how to do this with relational operators, such as UNION, INTERSECT, and EXCEPT, as well as with the various flavors of the JOIN operator. SQL provides another very powerful mechanism for drawing data from multiple tables to produce a desired result, known as the *nested query*.

What a Nested Query Does

An SQL nested query consists of an outer enclosing statement that contains within it a subquery. The subquery may enclose another subquery, which could enclose another, analogous to nesting bowls or Russian dolls. There is no theoretical limit to the number of levels of nesting, but each different implementation has a practical limit.

Each level of a nested query can pull data from a different table than that accessed by the other levels. On the other hand, multiple levels can access the same table. What you do in this regard depends on what you want to achieve. All the subqueries of the outermost query must be SELECT statements. The outermost statement itself can be a SELECT statement, or it can be an UPDATE, INSERT, or DELETE statement.

I cover UPDATE, INSERT, and DELETE in Session 14.

Cross-Ref

An example can demonstrate how to use a nested query to pull data from two related tables. Suppose the sales manager wants a list of all customers who have bought more than $1,000 worth of product on a single invoice. You can retrieve this information with a nested query such as the following:

```
SELECT * FROM CUSTOMERS
   WHERE CustomerID IN (SELECT CustomerID FROM INVOICE
                        WHERE (TotalCharge) > 1000) ;
```

The inner SELECT, on the INVOICE table, returns the CustomerIDs of all customers who have at least one invoice with a total charge greater than $1,000. The outer SELECT, on the CUSTOMERS table, returns a row for every CustomerID in the CUSTOMERS table that matches one of the CustomerID fields returned by the inner SELECT. Figure 13-1 shows how this query works on the Xanthic Systems database.

	CustomerID	Name	Address1	Address2	City	StateOrProv
1	2339	Booneco	25 Bryant Road	NULL	Springfield	KY
2	3141	Centurion Ltd.	100 Main Street	Suite 100	Rome	NY
3	5347	Edo Enterprises	5540 River Road	Suite 324	Raleigh	NC
4	5771	House of Clay	12 Main Street	NULL	Acoma Pueblo	NM
5	8333	Jam & Jelly Exporters	415 McLoughlin Road	NULL	Vancouver	BC

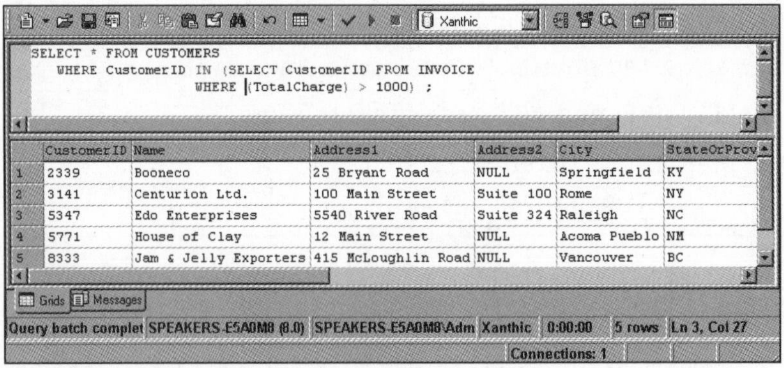

Figure 13-1 *Nested query retrieves Xanthic's high value customers.*

The IN keyword used in the above query is explained in the following section.

MySQL 4.0 does not support nested queries.

Note

The IN conditional operator in a nested query

There are several forms of nested query, one of which is exemplified by the query in the previous section. In this case, the WHERE clause of the outer query compares a single value against a list of values retrieved by the inner query. If the comparison value is IN the list retrieved by the inner query, then the condition of the outer WHERE clause is satisfied and the current row of the table in the outer query's FROM clause is added to the result set. A value from each row of the table in the outer query's FROM clause is compared to the list retrieved by the inner query. Whenever that value matches one of the items in the inner query's result set, the current row in the outer query's table is added to the outer query's result set.

The NOT IN conditional operator in a nested query

The NOT IN operator acts as you would expect in a nested query. The WHERE clause of the outer query compares a single value against the result set of the inner query. If that value is NOT IN the inner query's result set, then the current row of the table in the outer query's FROM clause is added to the outer query's result set. If you apply this to Xanthic Systems, as in the following,

```
SELECT * FROM CUSTOMERS
    WHERE CustomerID NOT IN (SELECT CustomerID FROM INVOICE
                        WHERE (TotalCharge) > 1000) ;
```

you retrieve the records of all customers who have no single invoice with a total charge exceeding $1,000.

Nested Queries That Return a Single Value

When you use a nested query with the IN or NOT IN operators, the subquery returns a list of values. Another kind of nested query uses the comparison operators:

- =
- <>
- >
- <
- >=
- <=

For this kind, the outer query's WHERE clause compares a value against a single value returned by the subquery. For the comparison operators to work, you must be able to guarantee that the result set returned by the subquery consists of no more than one value. Look again at the Xanthic Systems customers and invoices to illustrate how this kind of nested query works.

In a previous section, I showed how to retrieve the records of all customers who had bought more than some specified value, such as $1,000, on a single invoice. This can be valuable information to a sales manager. Another thing that the sales manager may like to know is the identity of the one customer who bought the most on a single invoice. You can also use the following nested query to answer this question:

```
SELECT * FROM CUSTOMERS
    WHERE CustomerID =
        (SELECT CustomerID FROM INVOICE
            WHERE TotalCharge = (SELECT MAX (TotalCharge) FROM INVOICE)) ;
```

This nested query returns the customer record for Centurion Ltd., the company who made the largest order. Incidentally, this query uses two levels of nesting to produce the desired result. There is a potential problem with this retrieval. The innermost subquery is guaranteed to return a single value because there can be only one maximum value of an invoice's TotalCharge column. The outer subselect, however, may return more than one value if more than one invoice in the INVOICE table has a total charge equal to the largest total charge. As sales manager, you are probably interested in all customers who have made a purchase equal in value to the largest purchase that any customer has made. Consequently, you may want to combine both forms of subquery that we have looked at so far.

```
SELECT * FROM CUSTOMERS
  WHERE CustomerID IN
    (SELECT CustomerID FROM INVOICE
        WHERE TotalCharge = (SELECT MAX (TotalCharge) FROM INVOICE)) ;
```

This query finds the maximum value of TotalCharge with the innermost subquery; then with the outer subquery finds the CustomerIDs of all customers having at least one invoice with that value of TotalCharge; then with the outermost query returns the customer records of all those customers.

In the above examples, I use the "equals" comparison operator (=), but the other five comparison operators can also be used. The important point is that the subselect that is the right-hand operand in a comparison must return a single value in order to be comparable to the value on the left of the comparison operator.

The ALL, SOME, and ANY Quantifiers

**20 Min.
To Go**

One way to make sure that a subquery returns a single value is to use an aggregate function within the subquery, such as the MAX function used in the previous section. The other aggregate functions (COUNT, MIN, AVG, SUM) can also be used this way, guaranteeing the return of a single value. Another way to guarantee the return of a single value is to use one of the quantified comparison operators (ALL, SOME, ANY) to quantify the subquery. The best way to explain the quantified comparison operators is through examples.

The NASTAFF and EUROSTAFF tables introduced in Session 11 provide good subjects for queries using the quantified comparison operators. Figure 13-2 shows NASTAFF; Figure 13-3 shows EUROSTAFF.

```
SELECT * FROM NASTAFF ;
```

	DeptID	DepartmentName	DepartmentManager	Headcount
1	1	Database Architecture	R. Orbison	12
2	2	Database Programming	K. Rogers	23
3	3	Application Development	W. Nelson	35
4	4	Quality Assurance	G. Frey	6
5	5	Documentation	C. Twitty	15

SPEAKERS-E SPEAKERS-E5A0M8\Adm Xanthic   0:00:00   5 rows Ln 1, Col 24

Connections: 1

Figure 13-2 *Xanthic's NASTAFF table*

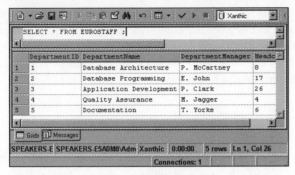

Figure 13-3   *Xanthic's EUROSTAFF table*

The various departments in North America and Europe have different headcounts, some functions requiring more people and some requiring fewer. In general, the North American departments have larger staffs than the corresponding European departments. There are some questions a human resources manager may want to ask about this data.

One question may be, "What departments in North America have a higher headcount than all the European departments?" We can ask this question in SQL as follows:

```
SELECT * FROM NASTAFF
    WHERE Headcount > ALL
        (SELECT Headcount FROM EUROSTAFF) ;
```

This returns only the row for North America's Application Development department, which has a headcount of 35. None of the other North American departments has a headcount exceeding the 26 of Europe's Application Development department.

The following query returns an empty result set:

```
SELECT * FROM EUROSTAFF
    WHERE Headcount > ALL
        (SELECT Headcount FROM NASTAFF) ;
```

None of the European departments is larger than the largest North American department.

Another question may be, "What European departments have a higher headcount than any of the North American departments?" This question can be formulated in SQL as follows:

```
SELECT * FROM EUROSTAFF
    WHERE Headcount > ANY
        (SELECT Headcount FROM NASTAFF) ;
```

This query returns Europe's Database architecture, Database Programming, and Application Development departments, which are all larger than North America's Quality Assurance department. Europe's Documentation department is equal to North America's Quality Assurance department, so it is not included in the result set.

Substituting the SOME **quantifier for the** ANY **quantifier does not change the result because** SOME **and** ANY **are synonymous. The question, "What European departments have a higher headcount than some North American departments?" is equivalent to the question, "What European departments have a higher headcount than any of the North American departments?"**

Nested Queries as Existence Tests

**10 Min.
To Go**

In our discussion of nested queries so far, I have pointed out that there are three possible results that a subquery may pass to the outer, enclosing query:

- Multiple rows may be returned
- One row may be returned
- No rows may be returned

There are times when all you want to know is whether the subquery returned anything or not. What is returned is not important. The only thing you care about is whether there was something in the result set or not. By introducing a subquery with an EXISTS or a NOT EXISTS keyword, you can reduce a potentially complex retrieval to a simple TRUE/FALSE decision. When you precede a subquery with the EXISTS keyword, if the subquery retrieves one or more rows, a TRUE value is returned to the outer statement. If the subquery returns an empty set, a FALSE value is returned to the outer statement. When you precede a subquery with the NOT EXISTS keyword, the opposite occurs.

Nested queries used as existence tests are examples of correlated subqueries. Correlated subqueries work differently from the ones covered so far. In all the nested queries looked at so far, the innermost subquery is executed first; its result is passed up to its enclosing query, which then uses it to arrive at its own result. If this enclosing query is itself a subquery, it passes its result up to the statement that encloses it.

Correlated subqueries work differently. For these nested queries, the condition of the outer query is correlated with the condition of the inner subquery. The example in the next section shows what I mean.

Using the EXISTS predicate

When I covered the IN operator earlier in this session, I showed how it can be used to retrieve the customer records of customers who had bought more than $1,000 worth of product on a single invoice. That same information can be retrieved using a correlated subquery as an existence test, as shown by the following statement:

```
SELECT * FROM CUSTOMERS
    WHERE EXISTS
        (SELECT CustomerID FROM INVOICE
            WHERE TotalCharge > 1000
            AND CUSTOMERS.CustomerID = INVOICE.CustomerID) ;
```

The "AND CUSTOMERS.CustomerID = INVOICE.CustomerID" part of the subquery's WHERE clause provides the correlation between the inner and outer queries because it refers to the CUSTOMERS table as well as the INVOICE table. This query works as follows:

- Extract CUSTOMERS.CustomerID from the first row of the CUSTOMERS table.
- Compare CUSTOMERS.CustomerID with the INVOICE.CustomerID field in every row in the INVOICE table.
- If a match is found, and if for that row TotalCharge is greater than 1000, add that row of the CUSTOMERS table to the query's result set.
- Move to the next row of the CUSTOMERS table and repeat the process until the end of the CUSTOMERS table is reached.

Using the NOT EXISTS predicate

NOT EXISTS works just like EXISTS but in the opposite direction. Suppose you want to know which customers have never bought more than $1,000 worth of product in a single invoice. You can use the same query shown in the previous section, but with the NOT EXISTS keyword rather than EXISTS. It looks like this:

```
SELECT * FROM CUSTOMERS
    WHERE NOT EXISTS
        (SELECT CustomerID FROM INVOICE
            WHERE TotalCharge > 1000
            AND CUSTOMERS.CustomerID = INVOICE.CustomerID) ;
```

This returns all the rows from the CUSTOMER table that were not returned by the query in the previous section.

Other Correlated Subqueries

In addition to EXISTS and NOT EXISTS, you can also introduce a correlated subquery with IN, NOT IN, or any of the six comparison operators. Here's an example using IN:

```
SELECT * FROM CUSTOMERS
    WHERE CustomerID IN
        (SELECT CustomerID FROM INVOICE
            WHERE TotalCharge > 1000
            AND CUSTOMERS.CustomerID = INVOICE.CustomerID) ;
```

This query retrieves the five customers who have bought over $1,000 worth of product on a single invoice. Unlike the first example query of this session, which also used the IN keyword, this one is a correlated subquery. It is yet another example of the fact that with SQL there are generally several different ways to obtain the same desired result.

To illustrate the use of a comparison operator in a correlated subquery, suppose Xanthic's human resources manager wants to know what the North American staffing levels were for departments that had staffing levels of over ten people in Europe. A correlated query using the "equals" comparison operator (=) finds out.

```
SELECT * FROM NASTAFF
   WHERE DeptID =
      (SELECT DepartmentID FROM EUROSTAFF
          WHERE Headcount > 10
          AND NASTAFF.DeptID = EUROSTAFF.DepartmentID) ;
```

This query takes DeptID from NASTAFF and compares it against DepartmentID from EUROSTAFF. When they match, it checks EUROSTAFF to see if the current department's headcount exceeds ten. If it does, the current row from NASTAFF is added to the result set. This process continues until all rows of NASTAFF have been compared to all rows of EUROSTAFF.

Done!

REVIEW

Nested queries provide a means from drawing data from multiple related tables to produce a result set that answers a question you have about the data in a database. There are several different kinds of nested queries. Some nested queries include a subquery that returns a list of values. The subqueries in another kind of nested query return only a single value. One way to assure the return of only a single value is to use one of the aggregate operators in the subquery. Another way to assure the subquery returns only a single result is to use one of the quantified comparison operators (ALL, SOME, ANY) with the subquery.

You can use a subquery to see if any of the records in a table satisfy a stated condition, using the EXISTS or NOT EXISTS keywords. Use the EXISTS and NOT EXISTS keywords only in correlated subqueries. The IN and NOT IN keywords can also be used in correlated subqueries, as can the comparison predicates.

QUIZ YOURSELF

1. What does the following nested query return when it is executed? (See "The IN conditional operator in a nested query.")

```
SELECT * FROM CUSTOMERS
   WHERE CustomerID IN (SELECT CustomerID FROM INVOICE
                          WHERE (TotalRemitted) > 500) ;
```

2. Using the Xanthic CUSTOMERS and INVOICE tables, construct a nested query that retrieves the customer records of all customers who had at least one invoice with a total charge greater than the average total charge for all invoices. (See "Nested Queries That Return a Single Value.")

3. Formulate a query that returns all the rows from EUROSTAFF where the headcount equals the headcount of any department in NASTAFF. (See "The ALL, SOME, and ANY Quantifiers.")

4. Formulate a query that returns all the customer information on customers who, on a single invoice, have bought products valued at more than 10 percent of the total value of all invoices combined. (See "Nested Queries That Return a Single Value.")

5. Formulate a query with a correlated subquery that returns all the customer information on customers who have bought products valued at more than 10 percent of the total value of all invoices combined. (See "Other Correlated Subqueries.")

Adding, Updating, and Deleting Data

Session Checklist

✔ Filling a table with data

✔ Updating table data

✔ Deleting table rows

✔ Nesting SELECT statements within INSERT, UPDATE, and DELETE statements

30 Min.
To Go

S o far this weekend, I have focused on the variety of ways you can use SQL to retrieve the information you want from a database. This, of course, presupposes that there is data in the database for you to retrieve. That data has to get in there somehow. Most database management systems provide user-friendly tools for adding data to a database, changing the data that is already in the database, or deleting that data that you no longer want in the database. These tools vary from one DBMS product to another. You can also add, change, and delete data with SQL statements. This session describes those statements and gives examples of how you may use them.

Adding Data to a Table

Most database management systems provide you with a means of entering data into a table, similar to the SQL Server 2000 screen shown in Figure 14-1.

There are currently seven records in the CUSTOMERS table, and the cursor is sitting in the eighth row, waiting for you to enter another record. A data entry operator can enter records into a database using this tool, one at a time. For just about any database, even one with thousands or millions of records, someone, somewhere, performed this tedious task at some time in the past.

CustomerID	Name	Address1	Address2	City	StateOrProvince	PostalCode	Country	ContactName	ContactP
1440	Acme Corp.	1400 Desert Drive	<NULL>	Tucson	AZ	88888	USA	Wile E. Coyote	(555) 55
2339	Booneco	25 Bryant Road	<NULL>	Springfield	KY	36515	USA	Dan'l Boone	(241) 55
3141	Centurion Ltd.	100 Main Street	Suite 100	Rome	NY	10202	USA	John Pershing	(608) 55
4772	Dome Depot	6 Buckminster Blvd.	<NULL>	Carbondale	IL	61423	USA	Sam Fuller	(312) 55
5347	Edo Enterprises	5540 River Road	Suite 324	Raleigh	NC	27606	USA	Ben Nigata	(919) 55
5771	House of Clay	12 Main Street	<NULL>	Acoma Pueblo	NM	87034	USA	Doris Sanchez	(505) 55
8333	Jam & Jelly Exporters	415 McLoughlin Road	<NULL>	Vancouver	BC	V5Y1V4	Canada	Maurice Jones	(604) 55

Figure 14-1 *Data entry table for Xanthic Systems'* CUSTOMERS *table*

Clearly, if records that are close to what you want exist in electronic form somewhere, it may be wise to import them into your database and modify them rather than having someone type them in from scratch one by one. Importing tools vary from one DBMS to another, so I don't cover that aspect of the task here.

Modifying the structure of database records is something I talk about in Session 19. Session 19 is also where I describe creating database tables from scratch.

Here I assume that database tables of the desired structure already exist. All you need to do is type data into that structure. There are three ways to do it:

- Enter data into a screen form.
- Enter data into a table, such as the one shown in Figure 14-1.
- Enter data using the SQL INSERT statement.

Entering data into a screen form

Use of a screen form presupposes that you or some other database application developer has built the screen form. Most DBMSs have a form creation tool to help you do this, which is good because SQL has no form creation capability. If you are creating a database application, you can create a screen form using the host procedural language (C, Visual Basic, Java, or whatever) that provides the basic structure of your application. Screen forms are the best data entry method for users with the lowest level of expertise.

One nice thing about the screen form method is that you can incorporate code that checks for invalid entries before adding them to the database. This helps to maintain database integrity, which I discuss at length in Session 21.

Entering data into a table

Data entry into a table such as the one shown in Figure 14-1 is fairly straightforward but not quite as easy or as reliable as the screen form method. With a screen form, you have control over the layout the data entry operator sees. You can use your knowledge of human factors and ergonomics to make it easy for the person to make valid entries and less likely to invalid entries. The table method does not give you the ability to put helpful text on the screen as the screen form method does. It also does not display the data entry fields in an ergonomic way; it just shows them in a tabular form, based on the order they appear in the table. The tabular method also does not allow you to use your host language to make data validity checks after each entry is made. The bottom line is that if you are going to provide the capability to enter data by table rather than by screen form, you need to be sure that the data entry operators are more highly trained and conscientious than would be necessary if you provided screen forms for data entry instead.

Entering data using the SQL INSERT statement

Data entry using the SQL INSERT statement is not at all convenient, but it works. Actually, behind the scenes, SQL translates data that is entered either with a screen form or a data entry table into an INSERT statement, which is what actually puts the new data into the database. INSERT's primary value to you as an application developer comes when you already have data in electronic form, stored in an array. You can write a host language procedure that references the data items in the array and then makes use of an embedded INSERT statement to add the items to a database table one at a time.

Here's the syntax of the SQL INSERT statement:

```
INSERT INTO table1 [(column1, column2, ..., columnn)]
    VALUES (value1, value2, ..., valuen) ;
```

The list of column names is optional, as indicated by the square brackets. If you do not list columns, the default is to use the table's column order. The values in the value list must be in an order that matches the order of the columns the values are to go into.

To add a new department to Xanthic's EUROSTAFF table, you can use the INSERT statement as follows:

```
INSERT INTO EUROSTAFF (DepartmentID, DepartmentName, DepartmentManager,
Headcount)
    VALUES (6, 'Sales', 'D. Bowie', 12) ;
```

This adds a new row to the EUROSTAFF table, as shown in Figure 14-2.

If you are loading data into all the columns in their original order, you may omit the optional column list, but it is not good practice to do so. The column list provides documentation of exactly what you are doing. If the structure of the table changes in the future, inserting according to the old structure will generate errors (and without a column list it will be hard to tell what is causing them).

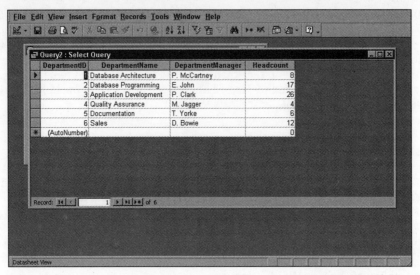

Figure 14-2 *A new row has been inserted into the EUROSTAFF table*

Changing the Data in a Table

**20 Min.
To Go**

In ancient Babylonia, scribes wrote business information onto clay tablets, which then hardened into permanent records. Now archaeologists unearth the tablets and find the same information that was written on them thousands of years ago. The pace of business has picked up somewhat over the past three or four thousand years to the point that data that cannot be easily changed to reflect new conditions is of limited value.

Things change. Customers move. Commodity prices change. Employees are promoted. Products are enhanced. Databases that can't be modified to reflect changes in the world would be about as useful as Babylonian cuneiform tablets. SQL enables you to change existing data in a database table with the UPDATE statement. You can update a single field, multiple fields, or all fields of a single record, multiple records, or all records in a table.

Updating one row selectively

To show the updating of a single row in a table, suppose Xanthic Systems has just learned that their customer, Acme Corp., has moved to a new address in Sedona, Arizona. This move affects Acme's address and telephone numbers. You can make the needed change with a single SQL UPDATE statement such as this one:

```
UPDATE CUSTOMERS
    SET Address1 = '777 Redrocks Road',
        City = 'Sedona',
        PostalCode = '87777',
        ContactPhone = '(555) 555-7777',
        ContactFax = '(555) 555-7778'
    WHERE CustomerID = 1440 ;
```

The address changes are made, while unchanged fields, such as Name and StateOrProvince, are not affected. Because CustomerID is the primary key of the Acme Corp. record, we can be sure that no records are changed except the one that holds Acme's information.

Updating multiple rows

In the above example, Xanthic wanted to change one and only one record. There are times, however, when a change in the outside world affects multiple rows in a database table. SQL's UPDATE statement can make a change to multiple rows in a single operation. To illustrate this, say that Xanthic management decides to rename the Quality Assurance departments at all divisions to Quality Control. Because department names are stored in the MANAGERS table, all the rows of that table that hold the information on the managers of the Quality Assurance departments will have to be changed. The following UPDATE statement makes the desired change:

```
UPDATE MANAGERS
    SET DepartmentName = 'Quality Control'
    WHERE DepartmentName = 'Quality Assurance' ;
```

All rows where the department name is 'Quality Assurance' are affected, and in those rows only the DepartmentName field is changed.

Updating all rows

It is even easier to update all the rows at once than it is to selectively update one or several rows. If you are updating all rows, there is no need for a WHERE clause. Use of this form of the UPDATE statement is rare because there seems to be little point in dedicating a table column to an attribute when every row in the table will have the same value for that attribute. However, a situation may arise that would make this a useful capability. Consider a scenario where Xanthic's North American business drops precipitously, and they must execute a major layoff to reduce expenses. One way is to say that no North American department may have more than six employees. Department managers have laid off all but six employees in their respective departments. You can update the NASTAFF table to reflect this unfortunate occurrence:

```
UPDATE NASTAFF
    SET Headcount = 6 ;
```

Now all departments in North America show a headcount of six. When business improves, department managers can start hiring again, at which time you can update NASTAFF to show the arrival of the new people.

 Access 2000 does not support the UPDATE statement.

Deleting Data from a Table

Just as sometimes you need to change existing data in a table, sometimes you need to remove data completely. If you never removed any data, you would fill up your hard disk and your performance would slow to a crawl. The database engine would spend most of its time wading through records that it never accessed. Removal of data that you no longer need is an important part of database maintenance. SQL makes it easy to remove one or more rows from a database table. For example, suppose that bad business conditions have forced Xanthic management to give up on the idea of setting up a Research division. Reluctantly, they decide to remove 'Research' from the DIVISION table until such time as conditions improve. Here's the code to do it:

```
DELETE FROM DIVISION
    WHERE DivisionID = 7 ;
```

The entire row where DivisionID = 7 is wiped out.

Oracle 9i includes the TRUNCATE TABLE **statement, which is not included in the SQL:1999 standard.** TRUNCATE TABLE **deletes all the records in a table. It differs from** DELETE FROM **in that you cannot selectively delete rows with a** WHERE **clause. A second difference is that a** TRUNCATE **statement cannot be rolled back. (See Session 24 for more information on rollback.) Because** TRUNCATE **does not create rollback records, it executes very fast. However, the lack of rollback capability leaves a database vulnerable to corruption if a failure should occur before the** TRUNCATE **operation is committed. (See Session 24 for information on committing transactions, too.)**

Nested INSERT, UPDATE, and DELETE Statements

**10 Min.
To Go**

Chapter 13 covers nested queries, where all the subqueries as well as the outermost query were SELECT statements. In SQL nested statements, all the subqueries must be SELECT statements, but the outermost statement may also be an INSERT, UPDATE, or DELETE. These statements work the same way as the INSERT, UPDATE, and DELETE statements described earlier in this chapter. The only difference is that the condition in the statement's WHERE clause contains a subquery. The subquery evaluates either to a list of values, a single value, or a NULL value.

Adding data to a table, taken from another table

Suppose Xanthic's North American business has deteriorated so badly that top management has decided to dissolve the North American division management structure and assign all the North American department managers to the European division management staff. To add the North American departments to the EUROSTAFF table, you can use an INSERT statement that incorporates a subselect to retrieve all the rows from the NASTAFF table.

```
INSERT INTO EUROSTAFF
    SELECT * FROM NASTAFF ;
```

Because EUROSTAFF and NASTAFF have the same structure, this code takes all the NASTAFF records and appends them to the EUROSTAFF table.

Changing the data in a table, based on the contents of another table

An UPDATE statement can also use a subselect to pull the data it needs from another table. To illustrate, consider that Xanthic has eliminated division level management in North America and given their responsibilities to Europe's division level management. This requires that the DIVISION table be updated to reflect the change. The following UPDATE statement does this:

```
UPDATE DIVISION
    SET RegionID = 2, RegionName = 'Europe'
    WHERE RegionID = (SELECT RegionID FROM REGION
                         WHERE RegionName = 'North America') ;
```

The subselect retrieves the RegionID for North America from the REGION table (just in case you don't remember North America's RegionID number, but you do remember the name 'North America'). The RegionID from the REGION table is matched with the RegionID from the DIVISION table. Wherever such a match is found, the RegionID is changed to 2 and the RegionName is changed to Europe in the DIVISION table.

Deleting data from a table, based on the contents of another table

Suppose House of Clay has gone out of business and all of their checks have bounced on you. You want to remove from the INVOICE file all sales made to House of Clay. A DELETE statement with a subquery does the job:

```
DELETE INVOICE
    WHERE CustomerID =
        (SELECT CustomerID
            FROM CUSTOMERS
                WHERE Name = 'House of Clay') ;
```

This statement removes from the INVOICE table all sales to House of Clay.

Done!

REVIEW

Although all popular database management systems provide tools for adding, changing, or deleting database data, you can also perform those operations with SQL. Generally the DBMS tools are easier to use but are largely restricted to operating on one record at a time. With SQL, you have complete flexibility to perform complex operations on multiple records. The INSERT, UPDATE, and DELETE statements give you all the power you need to manipulate the data in your database and keep it reflective of the real-world entities it is modeling.

Quiz Yourself

1. Name an advantage of using a screen form to enter data into a database table. (See "Adding Data to a Table.")

2. Write an SQL statement that will add a new row to the NASTAFF table. The new entry should have a department ID of 10, a department name of 'Nanotechnology', a manager named 'E. Drexler', and a headcount of three. (See "Adding Data to a Table.")

3. What is a good way to make sure when you are updating a table row that no other rows are accidentally updated at the same time? (See "Changing the Data in a Table.")

4. Write an SQL statement that will delete all the data from the DIVISION table. (See "Deleting Data from a Table.")

5. What four kinds of SQL statements can incorporate subselects? (See "Nested INSERT, UPDATE, and DELETE Statements.")

SESSION

15

Using SQL within an Application

Session Checklist

✔ How SQL relates to standard programming languages

✔ SQL within an application program

✔ SQL outside an application program

✔ Out-of-sight SQL

**30 Min.
To Go**

In previous chapters, I have given numerous examples of SQL statements. In each case it has been a single statement, by itself, as you would enter it from a keyboard. This is fine for learning about SQL, but it is not the way SQL is typically used.

SQL is a rich, powerful, and therefore complex language. Most computer users will never learn it. SQL's major use is as a part of application programs that operate on databases. The principal users of SQL, and coincidentally the intended readers of this book, are the application programmers who will create and maintain those application programs. In this session, you see how SQL is integrated into database application programs so that computer users can take advantage of its power without even knowing that they are using it.

Standard Programming Languages and SQL

SQL is not a complete programming language in the sense that Java, C, Visual Basic, and other familiar programming languages are complete. It was specifically designed to operate on databases and the data they contain. Consequently, it does not include many of the fundamental structures that are taken for granted in a standard programming language. As a result, database developers use a combination of SQL and a standard programming language to build their database applications.

There are a few ways that you, as a database application developer, can make SQL work together with a standard programming language:

- Embed SQL statements at appropriate spots in the code written in the standard language.
- Create SQL modules that the main program, written in a standard language, calls as sub-procedures.
- Let somebody else worry about the integration. Rapid development (RAD) tools such as Sybase's PowerBuilder, or Borland's Delphi or C++ Builder enable you to integrate SQL into the base PowerBuilder, Pascal or C++ code that the tool generates.

Why not do everything with a standard programming language?

Because SQL does not have a complete set of basic programming elements, why bother with it? Why not write your entire application in Java, C++, or the language of your choice? Here's why: Although Java and C++ are wonderful tools for building non-database applications, they were never designed to deal with relational databases. They do not have the specialized data handling capabilities that characterize SQL. The database engines that are the functional core of any database management system understand instructions fed to them in SQL. They do not understand and cannot respond appropriately to commands in any other language.

Using SQL with a procedural language

SQL differs in a fundamental way from programming languages you may be familiar with, such as Java, C, or Visual Basic. Those languages are all procedural languages. A *procedural language* processes data according to a procedure defined by the programmer. It deals with the data in a step-by-step manner, one piece at a time. In contrast, SQL is a *set-oriented language*. It operates on a whole set of data at once. The set may consist of several, several hundred, or several million records.

You can't write a full database application with SQL alone because it lacks the elements that enable you to perform complex calculations or execute a step-by-step sequence of operations. These are areas where procedural languages excel. By using SQL together with a procedural language, you take advantage of the strengths of both, while each covers the weaknesses of the other. SQL does all the data handling, and the procedural language performs calculations, controls the flow of execution, and displays results.

A major challenge to the successful cooperation of SQL with a procedural language is the incompatibility of data types. In Session 3, I describe the SQL data types. The data types recognized by C++ for example, are different. There is no standard for data types across the procedural languages. They do not agree with each other or with SQL. In order for SQL to work with a procedural language, there must be a mechanism for converting the data type of any data that is passed from one environment to the other. SQL does this with the CAST operator I describe in Session 3.

A second challenge to successful cooperation between SQL and any procedural language comes from their very different modes of operation. Procedural languages create procedures that operate step-by-step on data elements one at a time. SQL is non-procedural and operates on an entire set of data at once. You can generally overcome the mode of operation challenge by partitioning the workload. Perform the procedural operations with the procedural language and the set-at-a-time database operations with SQL.

Embedded SQL

The most common method of using SQL together with a procedural language is to embed individual SQL statements at appropriate spots within a program written in the procedural host language. At first glance this seems like a strange thing to do. The host language compiler would generate an error every time it came to one of those alien SQL statements. Similarly, the database engine that accesses the database would fail to recognize any host language commands that it received.

The compiler problem is solved by passing any program that contains SQL through a pre-processor before sending it to the compiler. The pre-processor converts the SQL statements to function calls that the compiler knows how to handle. The compiler then passes its output on to a linker, which links to the SQL functions and produces an executable program. None of the code of the executable program is ever sent to the database engine. Only the SQL, in the form of host language functions, goes to the database engine. The engine executes the SQL and sends any results back to the host language program.

The following code is a small program written in Oracle's Pro*C language, containing embedded SQL.

**20 Min.
To Go**

```
EXEC SQL BEGIN DECLARE SECTION;
     VARCHAR uid[20];
     VARCHAR pwd[20];
     VARCHAR ename[10];
     FLOAT salary, comm;
     SHORT salary_ind, comm_ind;
EXEC SQL END DECLARE SECTION;
main()
{
     int sret;              /* scanf return code */
     /* Log in */
     strcpy(uid.arr,"FRED");    /* copy the user name */
     uid.len=strlen(uid.arr);
     strcpy(pwd.arr,"TOWER");   /* copy the password */
     pwd.len=strlen(pwd.arr);
     EXEC SQL WHENEVER SQLERROR STOP;
     EXEC SQL WHENEVER NOT FOUND STOP;
EXEC SQL CONNECT :uid;
printf("Connected to user: percents \n",uid.arr);
     printf("Enter employee name to update:  ");
     scanf("percents",ename.arr);
     ename.len=strlen(ename.arr);
     EXEC SQL SELECT SALARY,COMM INTO :salary,:comm
                 FROM EMPLOY
                 WHERE ENAME=:ename;
     printf("Employee: percents salary: percent6.2f comm: percent6.2f
        \n", ename.arr, salary, comm);
```

```
      printf("Enter new salary:   ");
      sret=scanf("percentf",&salary);
      salary_ind = 0;
      if (sret == EOF !! sret == 0)     /* set indicator */
           salary_ind =-1;    /* Set indicator for NULL */
      printf("Enter new commission:   ");
      sret=scanf("percentf",&comm);
      comm_ind = 0;    /* set indicator */
      if (sret == EOF !! sret == 0)
           comm_ind=-1;           /* Set indicator for NULL */
   EXEC SQL UPDATE EMPLOY
              SET SALARY=:salary:salary_ind
              SET COMM=:comm:comm_ind
              WHERE ENAME=:ename;
printf("Employee percents updated. \n",ename.arr);
      EXEC SQL COMMIT WORK;
      exit(0);
}
```

There are several things to notice about this code, and you don't have to be a C programmer to see them.

- First, you can see that an EXEC SQL directive precedes every SQL statement embedded in the code. This directive indicates to the preprocessor that the current line is an SQL statement rather than a host language command. The preprocessor converts the SQL to functions and replaces the SQL statements in the main program to function calls.

- Second, right up at the top of the program, notice the DECLARE section, where variables that are passed between the host program and SQL are declared.

- After the declarations, the executable part of the program solicits a user name and password, validates the entries, and connects the user.

- The purpose of this code is to update salary and commission information for employees of an organization. The SQL first retrieves the current salary and commission information from the database with a SELECT; then after the host language accepts input from the user, it sends updated salary and commission information back to the database for storage using an UPDATE statement.

- When all is complete, SQL commits the transaction, and the program exits.

Here are the pros and cons of embedded SQL:

- Embedded SQL is good in that it is easy to follow the flow of execution of the program (providing you are fluent in both the host language and in SQL). SQL statements appear in the code listing at the very points in time where they are executed. It is relatively easy to get a concept of what the program is doing and how it is doing it.

- Embedded SQL is not so good if there are bugs in your code (and let's face it, there always are). Standard host language debuggers generally do not know how to handle the embedded SQL and do not operate properly when they encounter it.

Module Language

The primary alternative to embedded SQL is module language. Applications that use module language store all the SQL as procedures in a separate module. This way the main program is written 100 percent in the host language, and the SQL module is written 100 percent in SQL. There are several big advantages to using module language instead of embedded SQL.

- Because the main program contains nothing but host language code, debuggers will have no problem operating on it.

- Because the main program contains nothing but host language code and the SQL module contains nothing but SQL, you can assign an expert host language programmer to write the main program and an expert SQL programmer to write the module. There is no need for a rare superstar programmer who is an expert in both.

- Because the host language code is separated from the SQL, the application is much more portable than would be a comparable application written with embedded SQL. You can easily migrate the SQL to another system that uses a different host language. The SQL modules carry over with little or no modification.

One disadvantage of module language compared to embedded SQL is that, because the SQL is separated from the main program, it is harder to follow the logical flow of execution by looking at the source listings.

Just about any DBMS you are likely to use offers embedded SQL. Fewer offer module language, and those that do may not offer an interface to the host language you prefer to work with. Your organization may have a policy as to which method for incorporating SQL into an application they prefer. If not, choose the method that fits best with the personnel and software tools that you have.

RAD Tools and Hidden SQL

**10 Min.
To Go**

Because SQL is a data sublanguage designed specifically to operate on relational databases, it has no provision for creating user interfaces. For many simple applications, building the user interface is a major part of the total task. Development tool vendors have created a class of tools called rapid application development (RAD) tools. RAD tools take much of the tedious drudgery out of building applications with procedural languages such as C or Java. To a large extent, they automate the construction of an application's user interface. They also automate access to flat file data storage systems and simple relational database systems.

Borland Corporation has been a leader in the RAD tool area with their Delphi, C++ Builder, and JBuilder products. Delphi is a RAD tool based in Borland's Object Pascal language that runs in a Microsoft Windows environment. Kylix is Borland's new version of Delphi that runs under Linux. C++ Builder is a Windows RAD tool that is based on C++, and JBuilder is their RAD tool that is based on Java. It runs under Windows, Linux, and Solaris. All of these tools have similar capabilities, so which one you choose to use is largely a matter of personal preference. Whichever underlying language you favor will likely determine which RAD tool you select.

Figure 15-1 shows the Design view of the JBuilder 5 Integrated Development Environment (IDE) after I used it to build the JBuilder version of the famous "Hello World!" application. The IDE looks complicated, and it is. However it is also powerful enough for you to build an enterprise class database-driven application.

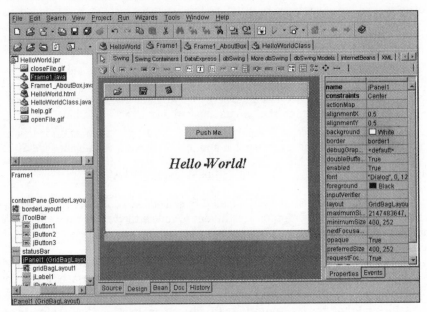

Figure 15-1   *JBuilder 5 Design view of an application*

As you may expect from the name JBuilder, this IDE generates Java code, meaning you have to know Java in order to make any modifications to the automatically generated code. Java is a good language to know because it is designed to run on any platform and has all the features necessary for building Web-enabled applications. Considering the speed with which the World Wide Web has permeated our society, it makes sense to be proficient in the language that is most commonly spoken by Web applications.

A robust extension of Borland's JBuilder is Borland® Enterprise Studio for Java™. It combines JBuilder 5, the leading Java development environment, with Borland AppServer 4.5, a platform applications server, with Rational Rose Professional J Edition, the leading visual modeling tool, with Rational Unified Process®, which ensures best practices and methodology in software development, and with Macromedia® Dreamweaver® UltraDev™ 4, in a single comprehensive package. This suite of integrated tools gives you the power to build enterprise-level e-business software that provides the front-end for a database back-end such as Oracle 9i, SQL Server 2000, PostgreSQL 7.1, or IBM's DB2.

What the RAD tools don't do is perform complex database operations. For that you need the SQL provided by database management systems such as those listed in the previous paragraph. The Borland tools have a utility called the Database Desktop, with which you can draft database queries, and then view the result sets that come back. For more complex tasks, you can embed SQL statements in programs written in the RAD tool's underlying language. This use of

SQL is very much like that described in the Embedded SQL section above, except that you can generate the non-database parts of the program much more quickly and easily with a RAD tool than you can with a language such as C++, Java, or Pascal.

Done!

REVIEW

SQL is a data sublanguage. It is the most powerful tool available today for dealing with database data. However it has no facilities for building user interfaces and minimal ability to control the flow of execution of an application program. To create commercial grade data-driven applications, you must use SQL together with a standard programming language such as Java, C++, or Visual Basic. The standard language will handle the user interface and the flow of execution, while SQL will perform the interactions with the database.

There are two primary methods of combining SQL with a procedural host language: embedded SQL and module language. In embedded SQL, single SQL statements are placed at appropriate points within a host language program. You must run such programs through a preprocessor before compiling them, to keep the host language's compiler from complaining every time it hits an SQL statement.

Module language does not try to mix SQL in with host language code. All the SQL is placed in a separate module. Whenever the main program needs to execute an SQL procedure, to goes to the SQL module to get it. The SQL then goes to the database engine, which executes it and returns any results back to the main program.

RAD tools provide a great way to automate the building of an application's user interface and provide a framework for a database application. All popular RAD tools give you the option of writing procedural code in their underlying language (C++, Java, or whatever) and of embedding SQL statements in that code.

QUIZ YOURSELF

1. How does a procedural language deal with data? (See "Using SQL with a procedural language.")
2. How does SQL deal with data? (See "Using SQL with a procedural language.")
3. How does SQL deal with data type incompatibility? (See "Using SQL with a procedural language.")
4. Why is a preprocessor needed for host language programs that contain embedded SQL? (See "Embedded SQL.")
5. What part of the application development task is most accelerated by using a RAD tool? (See "RAD Tools and Hidden SQL.")

Using SQL:1999 Flow of Control Structures within an Application

Session Checklist

✔ Taking one of two branches with IF

✔ Taking one of multiple branches with CASE

✔ Preventing data corruption with atomicity

✔ Executing code multiple times with LOOP

✔ Another way to execute code multiple times using WHILE

✔ Yet another way to execute code multiple times using REPEAT

✔ Operating on selected table rows multiple times using FOR

**30 Min.
To Go**

One of the biggest complaints about SQL from the beginning has been its inability to cause the flow of execution to branch on a condition. Another big lack has been SQL's inability to perform a sequence of operations. Such capabilities are among the most basic ones provided by even the weakest of procedural languages. In fact, some people have speculated that SQL stands for Scarcely Qualifies as a Language.

The SQL:1999 specification set about to remedy those long-standing deficiencies by the addition of new capabilities. New commands go a long way toward providing the desired functionality. At this point, however, some of these capabilities are so new that they have not yet been included in all database management systems currently available. When these new functions are phased into specific products depends on what priority the DBMS vendors give them and the timing of new releases.

SQL:1999 specifies a full set of branch on condition and looping constructs, which enable you to do more processing within SQL and less switching back and forth between SQL and its host procedural language. In principle this is great, but as yet support for these new constructs is spotty. Table 16-1 summarizes which popular DBMS products support them.

Table 16-1 *Support for SQL:1999 Branching and Looping Structures*

Structure	Oracle 9i	SQL Server 2000	Access 2000	PostgreSQL 7.1	MySQL 4.0
IF	Yes	Yes	No	No	No
CASE	Yes	No	No	Yes	No
LOOP	Yes	No	No	No	No
WHILE	Yes	Yes	No	No	No
REPEAT	No	No	No	No	No
FOR	No	No	No	No	No

Taking One of Two Branches with IF

If you are familiar with any general purpose programming language, you probably already have a pretty good idea of what the IF conditional statement does. It has the following form:

```
IF condition
THEN
    statement1
ELSE
    statement2
END IF
```

The condition must evaluate to a value of TRUE, FALSE, or UNKNOWN. If it evaluates to TRUE, then statement1 is executed. If it evaluates to either FALSE or UNKNOWN, then statement2 is executed.

> **SQL Server 2000 and Oracle 9i both support the IF statement, but Access 2000, PostgreSQL 7.1 and MySQL 4.0 do not.**

The IF statement is very handy if you want to choose between two actions based on the truth value of a condition. It is less helpful if you want to choose between more than two actions based on a more complex condition. The new CASE statement is designed to address such situations.

Taking One of Multiple Branches with CASE

Many decisions are not of the either/or variety, but may have three or more possible outcomes. If an expression has one value, you may want to do one thing; if it has a second value, you may want to do a second thing; if it has a third value, you may want to do a third thing, and so on. You can handle such situations with nested IF statements, but it is cumbersome to do so. The CASE statement is designed for just this kind of application.

There are two types of CASE statement, the simple CASE and the searched CASE. As you may infer from the names, the searched CASE is a little more powerful than the simple case. Everything that you can do with a simple CASE statement, you can also do with a searched CASE statement, but the reverse is not true.

 Do not confuse the CASE **statement with the** CASE **conditional expression described in Session 9. An expression reduces to a value, which may form part of an SQL statement. The** CASE **statement, although having the same name and a similar function, is an entirely different thing. It causes one of the SQL statements or statement blocks contained within it to be executed.**

Simple CASE

A simple case statement evaluates a single condition, and depending on the result, performs one of several actions. It takes the following form:

```
CASE selector
    WHEN expression1
        THEN statement1
    WHEN expression2
        THEN statement2
    ...
    WHEN expressionN
        THEN statementN
    ELSE statementX
END CASE
```

When the selector is equal to the expression in one of the WHEN clauses, the statement or statement block after the associated THEN keyword is executed. If the first WHEN clause does not satisfy the condition, the next one is checked. This continues until the expression in a WHEN clause equals the selector. If none of the WHEN clause expressions equal the selector, the ELSE clause is executed.

Here's an example of how you may use this:

```
CASE vcountry
    WHEN 'USA' OR 'Canada'
        THEN SELECT * FROM CUSTOMERS
        WHERE Country = 'USA' OR Country = 'Canada' ;
    WHEN 'UK'
        THEN SELECT * FROM CUSTOMERS
        WHERE Country = 'UK' ;
    WHEN 'Vietnam'
        THEN SELECT * FROM CUSTOMERS
        WHERE Country = 'Vietnam'
    ELSE SELECT * FROM CUSTOMERS
        WHERE Country NOT IN ('USA','Canada','UK','Vietnam') ;
END CASE
```

This structure checks the value of the variable *vcountry*. If vcountry contains either "USA" or "Canada," the records for the customers in those two countries are retrieved. If vcountry contains "UK," the records for the customers in that country are retrieved. Similarly, if vcountry contains "Vietnam," the records of Vietnamese customers are retrieved. If vcountry contains anything else, the records for all the customers in countries other than those named above are retrieved.

Microsoft Access 2000, Microsoft SQL Server 2000, and MySQL 3.23 do not support the CASE **statement. Oracle 9i and PostgreSQL 7.1 do.**

Searched CASE

A searched CASE statement is similar to a simple CASE, the difference being where a simple CASE tests for a single condition, a searched CASE tests for multiple conditions. Searched CASE statements take the following form:

```
CASE
    WHEN search_condition1
        THEN statement1
    WHEN search_condition2
        THEN statement2
    ...
    WHEN search_conditionN
        THEN statementN
    ELSE statementX
END CASE
```

When search_condition1 is TRUE, then statement1 is executed. If search_condition1 is not TRUE, then search_condtion2 is tried, and so on through search_conditionN. If none of the search conditions evaluates to TRUE, then statement X is executed.

Here's an example of this kind of CASE statement:

```
CASE
    WHEN vTotalCharge >= 10000
        THEN SET vCommissionRate = 0.1
            AND SET vBonusRate = 0.02 ;
    WHEN vProduct = 'Custom Database Application'
        AND vTotalCharge >= 5000
        THEN SET vCommissionRate = 0.07 ;
    WHEN vProduct = 'Order Entry Module'
        THEN SET vCommissionRate = 0.05 ;
    ELSE SET vCommissionRate = 0.03 ;
END CASE
```

This statement determines the compensation for Xanthic's salespeople, depending on the value of the sales they make. Any invoice with a total charge of at least $10,000 is worth a 10 percent commission rate and a 2 percent bonus to the person who makes the sale. Sales of custom database applications with a value between $5,000 and $10,000 are worth a 7 percent commission. Sales of the order entry module earn the salesperson a 5 percent commission, and all other sales produce a 3 percent commission for the person who makes the sale. Each one of the search conditions can be any expression that evaluates to a TRUE or FALSE value.

Preventing Data Corruption with Atomicity

20 Min. To Go

The ancient Greeks coined the word *atom* to mean the smallest piece of a given kind of matter that still retains all the characteristics of that kind of matter. So, for example, an atom of gold is the smallest piece of gold that you can have. You can break a gold atom up into protons, neutrons, and electrons, but if you do, you don't have gold anymore. The meaning of the word *atomic* has been generalized to mean anything that is indivisible.

A single SQL statement is a trivial example of an atomic block of instructions. It either executes successfully or it fails to do so. Both outcomes are acceptable. If it executes successfully, your application produces a correct result. If it fails, your database is unchanged, an error condition is generated, and you can take corrective action.

What about a compound statement made up of a series of SQL statements? There is a potential problem here because such a series is not necessarily atomic. What if some of the statements execute successfully, modifying database tables in the process, but then one of the statements in the sequence fails? You could be in big trouble. You don't have the correct final result of all your operations and you cannot get back to the condition you were in before you started either. The database is in an unknown state.

Atomicity was not a problem before SQL:1999 because SQL-92 only allowed for executing one SQL statement at a time. With SQL:1999 it became possible to execute blocks of statements. In order to maintain data integrity, it is necessary that an entire block of SQL statements be atomic. SQL:1999 provides for this with the BEGIN ATOMIC keywords to introduce a compound statement.

An atomic block of SQL statements is treated as a unit. Either all the statements in the block execute successfully, or the state of the database is rolled back to what it was before execution of the block started. In either case, your database is left in a known state. Here's an example of the use of the ATOMIC keyword:

```
BEGIN ATOMIC
    INSERT INTO CUSTOMERS (CustomerID, Name, Address1, Address2,
        City, StateOrProvince, PostalCode, Country, ContactName,
        ContactPhone, ContactFax, ContactEmail, Notes)
        VALUES (:custid, :name, :addr1, :addr2, :city, :state,
            :postcode, :country, :contname, :contphone, :contfax,
            :contemail, :notes) ;
    INSERT INTO INVOICE (InvoiceNumber, CustomerID, InvoiceDate,
        TotalCharge, TotalRemmitted, FormOfPayment, Salesperson)
        VALUES (:invnum, :custid, :invdate, :totcharge, :totremit,
            :formpmt, :empname)
    END ;
```

This code records a new customer's first purchase. The host language program captures customer and purchase information into variables, which are sent to the SQL code as parameters. Salespeople enter purchasers into the CUSTOMERS table only if they have bought something. Thus, Xanthic does not want it to be possible for the insert into the CUSTOMERS table to succeed and the insert into the INVOICE table to fail. You can prevent both problems by enclosing the INSERT statements into an ATOMIC block.

Executing Code Multiple Times with LOOP

The IF and CASE statements give you a way of altering the flow of program execution based on a condition. LOOP and the rest of the statements in this session give you the ability to execute the same statement or block of statements repeatedly. The LOOP statement is the simplest of these.

 Oracle 9i supports the LOOP statement, but Access 2000, SQL Server 2000, PostgreSQL 7.1, and MySQL 4.0 do not.

The simplest implementation of the LOOP statement produces an infinite loop, as shown in the following code:

```
LOOP
    SELECT * FROM CUSTOMERS ;
END LOOP
```

This code retrieves and displays the contents of the CUSTOMERS table and continues doing so forever. This is not a particularly useful way to use the LOOP structure.

What is needed is a way to stop looping when you have achieved your objective. SQL:1999 specifies that the LEAVE keyword be used for this purpose. Oracle 9i, however, uses the EXIT keyword instead. It works exactly the same way the LEAVE keyword is supposed to work. Here's an example using the SQL:1999 syntax:

```
vID = 0 ;
RegionPreload:
LOOP
    SET vID = vID + 1 ;
    IF vID > 8
        THEN LEAVE RegionPreload ;
    END IF
    INSERT INTO REGION (RegionID)
        VALUES (vID) ;
END LOOP RegionPreload
```

This code loads the RegionID column of the first eight rows of a newly created REGION table with eight consecutive integers, starting with 1. After the eighth time through the loop, the LEAVE keyword causes execution to break out of the loop and continue with the next instruction after the END LOOP keywords. This example also shows the SQL:1999 method of labeling a loop. Oracle 9i does it a little differently, using "<<RegionPreload>>" instead of the "RegionPreload:" label, and the EXIT keyword instead of the LEAVE keyword.

Another Way to Execute Code Multiple Times Using WHILE

**10 Min.
To Go**

Another method of looping uses the WHILE structure. To show how WHILE may be used, let's retrieve all the odd numbered invoices from the INVOICE table. In SQL Server 2000, the syntax is:

```
DECLARE @n INT ;
SET @n = 1 ;
WHILE @n < 282
BEGIN
    SELECT * FROM INVOICE
        WHERE InvoiceNumber = @n ;
    SET @n = @n + 2 ;
END ;
```

SQL Server 2000 requires that the first character of a variable name must be the "@" sign. Assuming the invoice numbers start with 1 and go up to 281, this code retrieves all the odd-numbered invoice records and none of the even-numbered records.

Oracle 9i syntax is a little different. The same retrieval is expressed:

```
DECLARE n INT ;
SET n = 1 ;
WHILE n < 282 LOOP
    SELECT * FROM INVOICE
        WHERE InvoiceNumber = n ;
    n := n + 2 ;
END LOOP ;
```

The syntaxes of both the above constructions differ from the SQL:1999 standard, which looks like:

```
DECLARE n INT ;
SET n = 1 ;
WHILE n < 282
    DO SELECT * FROM INVOICE
        WHERE InvoiceNumber = n ;
    SET n = n + 2 ;
END WHILE ;
```

Access 2000, PostgreSQL 7.1 and MySQL 4.0 do not support the WHILE structure.

Yet Another Way to Execute Code Multiple Times Using REPEAT

The REPEAT statement is very much like the WHILE statement, except the loop condition is checked at the end of the loop rather than at the beginning. Here's the SQL:1999 syntax for the same retrieval that I showed for the WHILE loop.

```
DECLARE n INT ;
SET n = 1 ;
REPEAT
    SELECT * FROM INVOICE
        WHERE InvoiceNumber = n ;
    SET n = n + 2 ;
UNTIL n = 282
END REPEAT ;
```

Access 2000, SQL Server 2000, Oracle 9i, MySQL 4.0, and PostgreSQL 7.1 do not support the REPEAT **structure.**

Operating on Selected Table Rows Multiple Times Using FOR

SQL:1999 also specifies a FOR loop, which, like the REPEAT loop, is not supported by the current versions of Access, SQL Server, Oracle, PostgreSQL, or My SQL. It declares and opens a cursor, fetches the rows of the cursor, and executes the body of the FOR statement once for each row. It then closes the cursor.

I describe cursors in detail in Session 27.

Oracle 9i has a FOR loop structure, but it is different from that specified by SQL:1999. It does not use a cursor to access specific rows in a table, but rather executes a series of SQL statements a specified number of times. The Oracle 9i syntax is given below:

```
FOR counter IN [REVERSE] lower_bound..higher_bound LOOP
        sequence_of_statements
END LOOP ;
```

The sequence of statements within the loop is executed the number of times specified by the difference between the lower bound and the higher bound. If the optional REVERSE keyword is used, the counter counts down instead of counting up.

With regard to the SQL:1999 FOR loop, it is enough to know that a cursor points to a specific row in a table and processing is restricted to that row. This is in contrast to SQL's usual mode of operation, which is a set at a time rather than a row at a time. Because none of the implementations I have been considering supports the SQL:1999 FOR loop, and because it has limited applicability to common tasks anyway, I say no more about it here.

Done!

REVIEW

Oracle 9i has the best support of the SQL:1999 conditional branching and looping features, while Access 2000 and MySQL 4.0 do not support any of them. SQL Server 2000 and PostgreSQL 7.1 provide some support for these new features.

Compound statements that consist of multiple SQL statements should be encapsulated within an ATOMIC structure to assure that either all of them or none of them are executed.

QUIZ YOURSELF

1. Suppose the variable vCustID contains the CustomerID of one of the customers in the CUSTOMERS table. If vCustID = 2339, write an IF structure that retrieves all the rows from the INVOICE table where vCustID equals 2339. If vCustID is anything else, do not make a retrieval. (See "Taking One of Two Branches with IF.")

2. If a variable may take on any of five different values, and you want to execute one of five different SQL statements depending on which of the five values the variable assumes, what kind of structure should you use to implement this logic? (See "Taking One of Multiple Branches with CASE.")

3. In a WHILE loop, where do you put the termination condition: at the beginning of the loop, in the middle, or at the end? (See "Another Way to Execute Code Multiple Times Using WHILE.")

4. What is the value of enclosing a sequence of SQL statements in an ATOMIC block? (See "Preventing Data Corruption with Atomicity.")

III

Saturday Afternoon Part Review

1. How do tables on which you can use the UNION, INTERSECT, and EXCEPT operators differ from tables where it is legal to use joins?

2. The NASTAFF table and the EUROSTAFF table both have the same structure. Write an SQL query that produces a result set that consists of the names of all the department managers in both tables.

3. Assuming two UNION-compatible tables AUTHORS and EDITORS, what would be returned by the following query?

```
SELECT * FROM AUTHORS
INTERSECT
SELECT * FROM EDITORS ;
```

4. In what clause of a query are table aliases declared?

5. What is the difference between the syntax of a cross join and that of an equi-join of the same columns of the same two tables?

6. What is the difference between an equi-join and a condition join of the same columns of the same two tables?

7. How many levels of nesting may you have in a nested query?

8. What kinds of statements are allowed in subqueries of a nested query?

9. Some retrievals can be made by either an ordinary nested query or by a correlated nested query, returning the same result in either case. What consideration might cause you to choose one type of query over the other?

10. What is the best facility for a database application programmer to provide users for the entry of new rows into a database table?

11. When a user enters a new row of table data into a screen form, what must your application do to store that data into the database?

12. When you issue an INSERT statement that fills less than all of the fields with data, what happens to the unnamed fields?

13. Why are programs that include embedded SQL harder to debug than programs that use module language?

14. Why are programs that include embedded SQL easier to understand than programs that use module language?

15. Why aren't major business applications developed entirely with easy-to-use RAD tools?

16. Why should you always use the ATOMIC keyword when executing a block of SQL statements?

17. What is the main functional difference between a WHILE loop and a REPEAT loop?

18. Of all the SQL:1999 branching and looping structures, which one is the most widely supported by DBMS vendors?

PART

IV

Saturday Evening

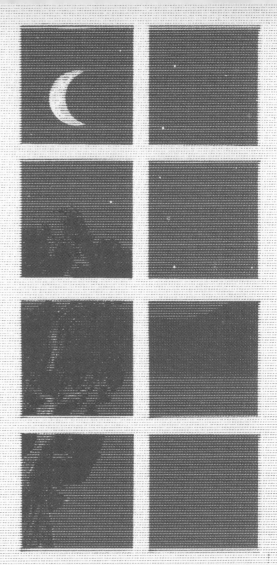

Connecting to a Remote Database

Session Checklist

✔ Going native with native drivers

✔ Discussing ODBC

✔ Reviewing what occurs when the application makes a request

**30 Min.
To Go**

With a standalone desktop database system, communication is never an issue. The data-driven application you write has only one place to go for data — the database on your hard disk. Your desktop database management system provides the interface between your application code and the database. This simple situation, once very common, has largely been replaced by client/server database systems that reside on a local area network (LAN) or wide area network (WAN), or Web-based systems that operate over the Internet. In these more complicated configurations, you must communicate with different database back ends different ways.

I discuss Web-based systems in Session 26.

Consider client/server systems: A simple client/server system has one server machine that hosts the database. Multiple client computers are connected to the server over a LAN. Users sit at the client machines, which execute your database application program. Larger systems can have multiple servers, each holding different databases. The part of your program written in host language is executed on the client machine, but the SQL is sent over the network to a server. Before it is sent to the server, the SQL must be translated into something the database understands. There are several different methods of doing this.

Native Drivers

The simplest form of communication between an application and a database is through a native driver. Figure 17-1 shows how a native driver specific to Oracle 9i connects your application to an Oracle 9i database.

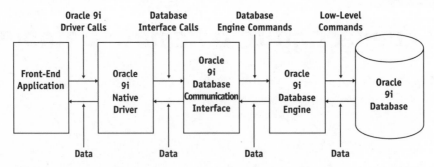

Figure 17-1   *Database system using an Oracle 9i native driver*

This arrangement is not much different from that of a standalone desktop database system. The Oracle 9i native driver is specifically designed to take SQL from the application and translate it into Oracle 9i database commands. When the database returns a result set, the native driver translates it into a standard SQL result set and passes it back to the application.

Because native drivers are specifically designed to work with a particular database, they can be highly optimized for that specific situation and thus have very good performance. That specificity, which makes possible the native driver's greatest strength, is also its biggest weakness. When you build a database system that uses a native driver to connect to one type of database, say Oracle 9i, the connection does not work with any other type of database, such as SQL Server.

When you write a database application, the part of the application that communicates with the database is called the *application programming interface* (API). When you are communicating to databases through native drivers, every native driver is different from all the others, so the API is different for each one, too. This complicates the design and development of applications that must deal with multiple data sources.

Native drivers are great if you know that the application you are writing will have to interface with only one specific data source, both now and in the future. You can't beat the performance of a well-designed native driver. However, if there is a possibility that your application may need to pull data from more than one source, you may want to consider one of the interface options that are not product specific.

ODBC

An application may need to access data in multiple databases of incompatible types. Incorporating multiple APIs into your code is not a desirable solution. Happily, there is a better way. ODBC, which stands for *Object DataBase Connectivity,* is a widely accepted standard method of communicating with most popular database formats. It accomplishes this by adding an extra layer between the application and the database. Figure 17-2 shows this arrangement. It is unlikely that you would want to connect any realistic application to five different data sources, as shown in Figure 17-2, but with ODBC, you could.

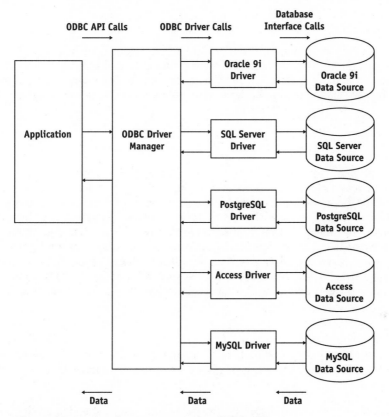

Figure 17-2   *Database system using ODBC API*

The application communicates directly with the driver manager. The front end of the driver manager always presents the same API to the application. The back end of the driver manager connects to a driver that is specific to the database on the back end. The driver, in turn, connects to the database. This arrangement means that the application programmer never has to worry about the details of how to connect to the database on the back end. All you have to do is make your program compatible with the ODBC API, and you will be successful. The driver manager makes sure that the correct driver is in place to communicate with the database.

ODBC is a direct response to the needs of developers who are designing applications to run on client/server systems. People designing for standalone PCs running integrated DBMS systems don't need ODBC. Neither do people designing for proprietary mainframes. The whole point of ODBC is to present a common interface to database applications, so that the application developer does not have to write code specific to whatever platform the data is located on. ODBC translates standard syntax coming from the application into custom syntax specific to the back-end database being accessed. It even allows an application to access multiple different back-end databases at the same time, without getting confused. To provide its function, ODBC can be conceptually (and physically) divided into four major components.

ODBC major components

The four major components are the application, the driver manager, the driver, and the data source. The application is the component closest to the user, and the data source is the component that holds the data. Each different type of data source has its own driver. The driver manager manages communication between the application and the data source, through the driver.

20 Min. To Go

Application

The *application* is a piece of software that interacts directly with the user and requires access to data. If you are an application programmer, the application is the one ODBC component that you create. It can be a custom program written in a procedural language such as C++ or Visual Basic. It can be a spreadsheet or a word processing package. It can be an interactive query tool. Just about any piece of software that works with data and interacts with a user can be the application portion of an ODBC system. The data accessed by the application can be from a relational database, from an ISAM (Indexed Sequential Access Method) file or from a straight ASCII text file. ODBC provides a lot of flexibility in what kinds of applications can use it and in what kinds of data those applications can access.

Driver manager

The driver manager is a library (under Windows it is a dynamic link library) that provides a common interface to applications, regardless of what data source is being accessed. It performs such functions as:

- Determining which driver to load, based on the data source name supplied by the application
- Loading and unloading drivers
- Calling driver functions
- Implementing some functions itself
- Performing error checking

A dynamic link library (DLL) is a library of routines that is linked to an application at runtime. In the case of a driver manager, their routines perform the various functions listed above.

The value of the driver manager is that the application can make function calls to it without regard for which driver or data source is currently in use. After the application identifies the needed driver and data source by sending the driver manager a connection handle, the driver manager loads the driver and builds a table of pointers to the functions in that driver. The application programmer does not need to worry about maintaining a table of pointers to functions in the driver. The driver manager does it "under the covers."

Driver managers are written and distributed by the companies that write drivers. Microsoft, Merant, Borland, and OpenLink Software are examples of companies that provide the driver manager component of ODBC systems.

Drivers

Drivers are libraries that implement the functions of the ODBC API. Each driver has a common interface to the driver manager, but its interface to its data source is customized to that particular data source.

Companies that specialize in driver development, such as those listed in the previous section, have developed and made available drivers for most of the popular data sources in use today. As a result, there is no need for most people to write their own drivers. Only those working with unusual data sources, or those requiring functions not supported by standard drivers, will need to write their own drivers. Tools for writing drivers are available.

There are two different kinds of drivers: file-based drivers and DBMS-based drivers. File-based drivers are used in one-tier configurations, and DBMS-based drivers are used in two-tier configurations.

File-based drivers File-based drivers are so named because the driver processes the data source directly. A file-based driver must be capable of processing SQL statements and performing the appropriate operations on the database. There is no DBMS involved. File-based drivers apply to desktop databases such as dBASE, Paradox, and FoxPro as well as spreadsheet files and other flat files. You can use a file-based driver on a standalone PC or on a network. Figure 17-3 shows a typical one-tier configuration.

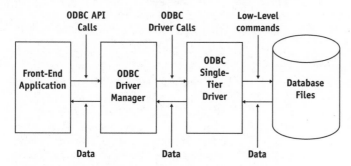

Figure 17-3 *Architecture of one-tier driver systems*

In the standalone system, the application, driver manager, driver, and data storage are all on the same system. In the network case, the application, driver manager and the driver are on the client, and only the data source is on the server machine. All the intelligence is on the client.

DBMS-based drivers DBMS-based drivers operate on multi-user systems operating in true client/server mode. This mode of operation features a balance between the client and server machines. Both do significant processing. The application, driver manager, and driver all reside on the client machine. Together they comprise the "client" part of the client/server system. The data source is composed of the DBMS, such as SQL Server, Oracle, or DB2, and the database itself. These components are located on the server machine. DBMS-based drivers are generally easier to write than file-based drivers because they only need to translate ODBC-compatible SQL statements to commands the database engine understands and handle any results that come back. Figure 17-4 shows the two-tier configuration.

Data sources

The data source, as the name implies, is the source of the data that is accessed by the application. It can be a spreadsheet file, an ASCII file, or a database under the control of a DBMS. The user need not know the technical details of the data source, such as file type, DBMS, operating system, or hardware. The name of the data source is all the user needs to know.

Can ODBC Drivers Perform as Well as Native Drivers?

You may have heard that ODBC was good because it frees the application developer from having to customize applications to each potential target data source. You may also have heard that ODBC was bad because database access through an ODBC interface was slower than access using a database's native drivers. This criticism makes sense, because it seems that going through an extra layer of processing cannot help but slow things down. In fact, database access using ODBC 1.0 *was* significantly slower than the same access through a native driver. Going through an extra layer of processing does slow things down. However, using ODBC does not require you to go through that extra layer.

One big reason ODBC 1.0 access was slow was because the early drivers that implemented it merely accepted SQL from the application and converted it to the DBMS's native API calls. This has to be slower than a system that generates the native API calls in the first place. Performance of ODBC 2.0 and later drivers has been much better. This is largely due to the fact that these more recent drivers have been written to use the DBMS's underlying data stream protocol rather than the native API. Instead of making an ODBC call that makes a native API call that uses the data stream protocol, current ODBC drivers use the data stream protocol directly. With this architectural change, ODBC driver performance has become competitive with native driver performance, even exceeding it on some benchmarks.

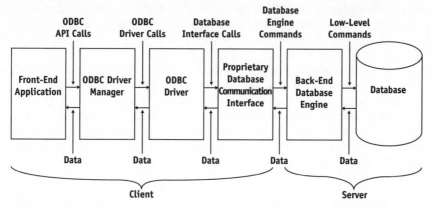

Figure 17-4   *Architecture of a two-tier driver system*

What Happens When the Application Makes a Request

**10 Min.
To Go**

Application development consists of writing, compiling, linking, executing, and debugging. Once an application is functioning the way you want it to, you can release it to users. Applications that use ODBC are linked to the Driver Manager's import library at link time. The import library contains those parts of ODBC that deal with importing instructions from the application. Under Windows, the import library is named ODBC32.LIB. In addition to ODBC32.LIB, a running application also makes use of ODBC32.DLL and a driver compatible with the data source. ODBC32.DLL remains loaded in memory as long as any running application requires it. When the last ODBC-enabled application terminates, ODBC32.DLL is unloaded from memory.

Handles

ODBC makes extensive use of the concept of *handles*. A handle is an integer value that identifies an object used by an application. ODBC uses three types of handles that are related to each other in a hierarchical fashion: the environment handle, the connection handle, and the statement handle.

The *environment handle* is ODBC's global context handle. Every application that uses ODBC must first allocate an environment handle, and when it finishes, it must free that handle. Every executing application has one and only one environment handle.

An application connects to one or more data sources. Each such connection is managed by a *connection handle*. The connection handle identifies the driver used in the connection and for the routing of the ODBC function calls. The driver manager keeps a list of all connection handles associated with an environment handle. The application uses the connection handle to establish and also to break the connection to a data source. The connection handle also passes error codes for connection errors back to the application and sets connection options.

A third kind of handle used by ODBC is the *statement handle*. Statement handles process SQL statements and catalog functions. When the application sends a function call that contains a statement handle to the driver manager, the driver manager extracts a connection handle from it to route the function call to the correct driver.

An application can have one and only one environment handle. Conversely, each environment handle can be assigned to one and only one application. A single environment handle can "own" multiple connections, each represented by a single connection handle. Each connection can "own" multiple statements, each represented by a single statement handle. Figure 17-5 shows how to use environment handles, connection handles, and statement handles to establish a connection to a data source, execute some SQL statements, and then to break the connection.

Allocate Environment Handle
↓
Set Environment Attribute
↓
Allocate Connection Handle to Oracle 9i
↓
Connect to date source
↓
Get information about data source
↓
Allocate Statement Handle
↓
Set statement attributes (optional)
↓
Execute SQL statements
↓
Free Statement Handle
↓
Disconnect from data source
↓
Free Connection Handle
↓
Free Environment Handle

Figure 17-5 *Handles establish the connection between an application and a data source.*

Stages

An ODBC operation takes place in distinct stages. Each stage builds on the one that preceded it. Handles provide the mechanism for the exchange of commands and information. First an environment is established. Next a connection between application and data source is built; then an SQL statement is sent to the data source for processing. Results are returned from the data source to the application, and finally the connection is terminated.

Stage 1: The application allocates environment and connection handles in the driver manager

ODBC-enabled applications communicate with the rest of the ODBC system by making function calls. The first step in the process is to allocate an environment handle and a connection handle. The function calls SQLAllocEnv and SQLAllocConnect do the job. The driver manager allocates space in memory for the requested handles and returns the handles to the application. SQLAllocEnv initializes the ODBC interface, in addition to allocating memory for global information. If the SQLAllocEnv function executes successfully, execution can proceed to the SQLAllocConnect function. SQLAllocConnect allocates memory for a connection handle and its associated connection information. SQKAllocConnect takes the active environment handle as input and returns a pointer to the newly allocated connection handle as an output. Depending on which development tool they are using, application programmers may or may not have to explicitly allocate environment and connection handles.

Stage 2: The driver manager finds the appropriate driver

After environment and connection handles have established a link between the application and the driver manager, the next step in the process is to link the driver manager to the appropriate driver. There are two functions for accomplishing this task, SQLConnect and SQLDriverConnect. SQLConnect is the simpler of the two, requiring only the connection handle, data source name, user identifier, and user password as input parameters. When the establishment of a connection requires more information than SQLConnect provides, SQLDriverConnect is used. It passes a connection string to the driver attached to the data source.

Stage 3: The driver manager loads the driver

In a Windows system, after the connection between the driver manager and the driver has been established, the driver manager obtains a library handle for the driver. It then calls the Windows function GetProcAddress for each function in the driver. The function addresses are stored in an array associated with the connection handle.

Stage 4: The driver manager allocates environment and connection handles in the driver

Now that the driver has been loaded, environment and connection handles can be called in it. The functions SQLAllocEnv and SQLAllocConnect can be used for this purpose, as they were used to call the environment and connection handles in the driver manager. If the application uses the function SQLSetConnectOption to set options for the connection, the driver manager calls the driver's SQLSetConnectOption function at this time to enable those options to be set.

Stage 5: The driver manager connects to the data source through the driver

Now at last, the driver manager completes the connection to the data source by calling SQLConnect or SQLDriverConnect. If the driver is a one-tier driver, there is no network connection to make, so this stage is trivial. If it is a multi-tier driver, the driver now calls the network interface software in the client machine, which connects to the server machine that holds the data source. To make this connection, the driver uses information that was stored in the ODBC.INI file when the data source name was created.

After the connection is established in a client/server system, the driver usually sends the user name and password to the server for validation. If the user name and password are valid, the driver returns a standard SQL_SUCCESS code to the driver manager. If they are not valid, the server returns an error code to the driver. The driver then translates this error code to the standard ODBC error code and returns it to the driver manager as SQLSTATE. The driver manager then returns SQLSTATE to the application.

Session 29 describes SQLSTATE and error handling in general.

Stage 6: The data source (finally) executes an SQL statement

With the connection at last established, an SQL statement can be executed. Even this, however, is a multi-stage process. First a statement handle must be allocated. The application does this by issuing an SQLAllocStmt call. When the driver manager receives this call, it allocates a statement handle and then sends an SQLAllocStmt call to the driver. The driver then allocates its own statement handle before returning control to the driver manager, which then returns control to the application.

After the statement handle has been allocated, an SQL statement can be executed. There is more than one way to do this, but the simplest is with the SQLExecDirect function. SQLExecDirect takes a character string as input and sends it to the server. The character string should be a valid SQL statement. If necessary, the driver translates the statement from ODBC-standard SQL to commands understood by the data source on the server. When the data source receives the request for action, it processes the command and then returns any results to the application via the driver and driver manager. The exact details of this processing and how the results are returned to the client application may differ from one data source (DBMS) to another. These differences are masked by the driver, so that the application always sees standard ODBC responses, regardless of what data source it is communicating with.

Done!

REVIEW

SQL is the language everyone uses to connect to relational databases. However, just having a language is not enough. The details of establishing and maintaining a connection to a database vary from one implementation to another. There are a variety of methods for making such connections. Depending on your needs, one of these methods will probably be best.

Native drivers have high performance, but are good to use only if you will never want your application to function with more than one data source. An ODBC interface is good where multiple data sources are possible, either now or in the future, although it is not particularly optimized for use with the Java language. JDBC is specifically designed to work with applications written in Java. ASP and ADO are Microsoft technologies designed for applications that are served on the World Wide Web. They are optimized to work with Access and SQL Server database back ends.

Quiz Yourself

1. What is an API? (See "Native Drivers.")
2. When may it be good to use a native driver to interface an application to a data source? (See "Native Drivers.")
3. What is the main value of an ODBC driver manager in connecting an application to a data source? (See "ODBC.")
4. What is an ODBC handle? (See "Handles.")

Stored Procedures and Triggers

Session Checklist

✔ Using stored procedures to enhance performance and data integrity

✔ Responding to user actions with event-driven programming and triggers

✔ Creating a trigger

✔ Firing a trigger

**30 Min.
To Go**

System performance is a critical concern in any installation, whether on a standalone computer, a local or wide area network, or a Web-based system. For data-driven applications, database integrity is also of primary importance. In this session, I look at both areas.

In any system where the database is hosted on a different machine from the user's machine, the speed with which data can be transmitted between the two can be a major bottleneck to performance. One way of addressing this problem is to reduce the amount of traffic between the server and the client. Because the database is on the server, the more processing that can be done locally on the server, the better. Stored procedures are parts of applications that reside on the server rather than on the client with the rest of the application.

Database integrity can be compromised whenever an INSERT, UPDATE, or DELETE is performed. This is particularly important on Web-based systems, where anyone, even hackers and other hostile visitors, may access the system. Stored procedures (which you control because they're on the server rather than the client) can help to protect your database. *Triggers* are a specific kind of stored procedure that is often used to ensure database integrity.

Client/Server Architecture and the Web

In a classic client/server environment, the database resides on the server, and the database application resides on the client machine. The application sends SQL queries over the network to the DBMS on the server, which accesses the data in the database and sends a response, possibly including a result set, back to the client. This arrangement can easily involve considerable network traffic

Figure 18-1 is a schematic diagram of a simple client/server local area network.

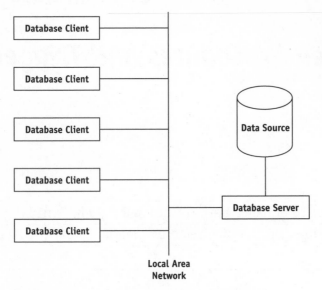

Figure 18-1   *A two-tier client/server system*

In Figure 18-1, the database application clients form one tier, and the database server is the other tier. The database application clients provide the user interface to the database application, and the database server performs operations on the database. A typical operation is for the user to request that a query be run on the database. The portion of the application running on the database client passes the request to the database server, which, in turn, translates the request into a form the data source can understand and respond to. The data source then sends a result set to the database server, which passes it on to the database application client, which displays it to the user.

The simple two-tier architecture has been largely replaced on all but the smallest LANs with a three-tier architecture. The three-tier architecture, schematically represented in Figure 18-2, includes a new tier on the server side. This new tier, called *middleware,* takes over some of the computational burden that on a two-tier system would be done by the database application client, as well as some of the computational burden that would be done by the database server.

Three-tier architecture has several advantages.

- Because there are potentially many more client machines than servers, it makes sense to minimize overall system cost by minimizing what the client machines are called upon to do. Client machines with less functionality are less expensive. That cost saving is multiplied by the number of client machines on the network.

- Removing computational chores from the database server frees up its resources to concentrate on its most important task, transferring data in and out of the data source.

- A more modular system is easier to maintain and easier to troubleshoot if problems arise. The more components there are, the easier it is to isolate a problem to whatever is failing.

- The new middleware tier is an ideal place to put stored procedures, described in the next section.

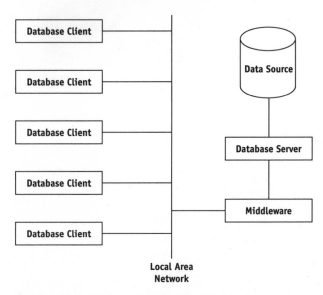

Figure 18-2 *A three-tier client/server system*

The Internet has been called a network of networks. It is essentially thousands of client/server networks that have all been hooked together. As is the case with client/server networks, we can talk about two-tier and three-tier Web architecture. However, in the Web case, the tiers are somewhat different.

A two-tier Web system consists of a Web server and multiple Web clients, connected to each other by the Internet. Figure 18-3 gives some idea of the relationship of the elements of the system.

As you can see, there is no data source in this system. The Web user visits a Web site; the Web server downloads HTML pages to the user's Web browser on the client machine. The server may also download Java applets, small programs that provide some dynamic functionality to the Web site. However, the two-tier Web architecture does not support database access. Database access requires a three-tier Web system.

A three-tier Web system retains the user's Web browser and the Web server, but adds the server extension program, database server, and data source shown schematically in Figure 18-4. The Web browser constitutes one tier; the combination of the Web server and the server extension program constitutes the second tier, and the combination of the database server and the data source constitutes the third tier.

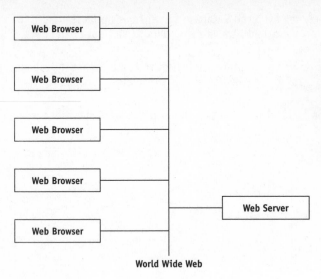

Figure 18-3   *A two-tier Web system*

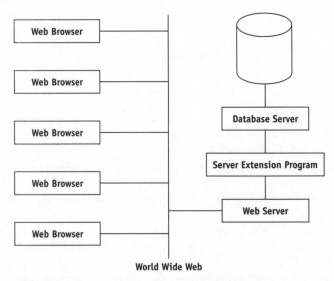

Figure 18-4   *A three-tier Web database system*

The communication between the client's Web browser and the Web server is done according to the HyperText Transfer Protocol (HTTP). This is fine for serving and displaying Web pages, but is not something that a database understands. The server extension program translates the communications coming from the Web server into something the database server understands. Then as a result set comes back from the database server, the server extension program translates it into something the Web server can handle. In this way true database applications, such as e-commerce programs that sell you things over the Web, can be written.

Enhancing Performance and Data Integrity with Stored Procedures

In a classic Web-based system, everything except the Web browser initially resides on the server. When the client connects to the server, an applet is downloaded to the client, where it executes, sending SQL queries to the server. This arrangement involves considerable network traffic, especially while the applet is being downloaded to the client. When there are multiple clients — and there almost always are — the problem multiplies.

There are several benefits to having at least some of the application code reside on the server.

- Everything that stays on the server does not have to be sent over the network to the clients. Fewer network round trips means less network traffic and better performance.
- Code that runs on the server can be protected from corruption by accidental or malicious user actions. You have much more control over your own server than you do over thousands of Web-client machines.
- Compiled code on the server runs faster than interpreted code running on the client. Client side application code is typically interpreted by a virtual machine that translates it into a form the DBMS can understand.
- Code written to be run on the server can be optimized for that environment. There is no need to be concerned with what the client machine hardware, operating system, or browser happens to be.
- Code residing in modules on the server, being isolated from the rest of the application, are easier to debug if they contain errors and easier to optimize if they are slow.

The application modules that reside and execute on the server are called stored procedures. Stored procedures first appeared in the ANSI/ISO specification in SQL:1999, but major DBMS vendors have supported their own proprietary versions of stored procedures for some time. Oracle 9i, SQL Server 2000, Access 2000 and PostgreSQL 7.1 all support some version of stored procedures. MySQL 4.0 does not support stored procedures.

Stored procedures in SQL Server 2000

SQL Server 2000 operates with its own version of SQL, called Transact-SQL, or T-SQL for short. T-SQL complies with the SQL-92 Entry Level standard, and also includes proprietary extensions that support stored procedures. The extensions include flow of control structures, local and global variables, exception-handling code, as well as math and string functions. With the release of the SQL:1999 standard, much of this functionality is now a part of ANSI/ISO standard SQL, but it will probably be a while before T-SQL syntax matches ANSI/ISO syntax completely.

When an application invokes a stored procedure, it can send the procedure parameters that affect how it executes. The procedure in turn can send output parameters to the application, as well as status codes and result sets.

Suppose Xanthic's sales manager wants to run a list of all the customers in a particular state or province on a frequent basis. She can create a T-SQL stored procedure to do it as shown in the following code:

```
CREATE PROCEDURE ListStateCust
   @StateOrProvince CHAR (2)
 AS
   SELECT *
      FROM CUSTOMERS
      WHERE StateOrProvince = @StateOrProvince ;
```

@StateOrProvince is an input parameter that the user employs to specify which state or province contains the customers of current interest. To execute the procedure for British Columbia, use the following code:

```
EXECUTE ListStateCust 'BC'
```

This returns a result set listing all customers located in British Columbia.

You can call a stored procedure from another stored procedure. In SQL Server 2000 this nesting of stored procedures can extend to 32 levels.

A stored procedure, such as the one created above, depends on the stability of any tables it references. If the structure of a referenced table changes in such a way that the action of the stored procedure is no longer appropriate, problems can arise at run time. SQL Server 2000 addresses this concern by automatically compiling and optimizing a stored procedure whenever the structure of a table it uses changes or when the procedure is first run after SQL Server is started. You can also force a recompile using the system stored procedure sp_recompile as follows:

```
sp_recompile 'ListStateCust' ;
```

You can change a stored procedure with an ALTER PROCEDURE statement. The ALTER PROCEDURE statement completely replaces the existing procedure of the same name, without changing the permissions that have been granted to the procedure. To change the example procedure shown above so that it returns only the customer's name rather than the entire record, use the following code:

```
ALTER PROCEDURE ListStateCust
   @StateOrProvince CHAR (2)
 AS
   SELECT Name
      FROM CUSTOMERS
      WHERE StateOrProvince = @StateOrProvince ;
```

The action of SQL Server 2000 here differs from the way SQL:1999 defines the ALTER PROCEDURE statement. SQL:1999 states that you can use ALTER PROCEDURE to change the language, parameter style, SQL-data access indication, null-call clause, DYNAMIC RESULTS SETS, or NAME of an external routine, but not to change what the procedure actually does. SQL Server 2000, as in the example above, allows you to change what the procedure does.

You can remove a stored procedure with the DROP PROCEDURE statement. DROP PROCEDURE RESTRICT drops only the named procedure. If any other objects depend on the named procedure, such as other stored procedures or triggers, the DROP PROCEDURE RESTRICT statement fails. To drop the named procedure and all objects that depend on it, use the DROP PROCEDURE CASCADE syntax. DROP PROCEDURE CASCADE is not part of core SQL and may not be available on all implementations. To drop the ListStateCust stored procedure, use:

```
DROP PROCEDURE RESTRICT ListStateCust ;
```

Stored procedures in Oracle 9i

The creation and operation of stored procedures in Oracle 9i is much like the corresponding operations in SQL Server 2000, but the syntax is a little different. Here is the listing of customers by state procedure as it would be written for Oracle 9i:

```
CREATE OR REPLACE PROCEDURE ListStateCust
    (StateOrProv IN CHAR (2))
AS
BEGIN
    SELECT *
        FROM CUSTOMERS
        WHERE StateOrProvince = StateOrProv ;
END ;
```

This syntax does double duty. You can use it either to create a new stored procedure or to modify an existing one. The CREATE OR REPLACE syntax is proprietary to Oracle and does not comply with the SQL:1999 standard. Also note that an Oracle stored procedure encloses the action part of the procedure within a BEGIN...END block, which is not needed by SQL Server 2000 when the action part of the procedure consists of a single SQL statement.

Oracle 9i's ALTER PROCEDURE statement complies with SQL:1999 in a way that SQL Server's ALTER PROCEDURE statement does not. You cannot use Oracle 9i's ALTER PROCEDURE statement to change what a stored procedure does. To change what a procedure does, use CREATE OR REPLACE PROCEDURE. To get rid of a stored procedure that you no longer want, use the DROP PROCEDURE syntax shown below:

```
DROP PROCEDURE ListStateCust ;
```

Oracle 9i does not support the RESTRICT and CASCADE keywords. If you drop a procedure that other objects depend upon, Oracle invalidates those other objects. When they are referenced later, Oracle attempts to recompile them. If the dropped procedure has not been recreated, an error will be generated.

Stored procedures can be written in SQL as shown in the above examples, but they can also be written in a host language such as C++ or Java, with or without embedded SQL.

Responding to User Actions with Event-Driven Programming and Triggers

You are probably familiar with at least some aspects of event-driven programming. Simply put, an *event-driven program* is one in which the occurrence of one event can cause another event to happen. An everyday example would be to place your mouse pointer over an icon on the screen and then press your left mouse button. Placing the pointer over the icon is one event (a hover event), which may cause a small text box to appear, describing what the icon does. The mouse click is an event (a left click event), which causes something else to happen. Relational database management systems support a special kind of event-driven programming using a stored procedure called a trigger. Whenever you affect a database table with either an INSERT, UPDATE, or DELETE statement, you can accompany that event with the firing of a trigger.

 As noted earlier, MySQL 4.0 does not support stored procedures. Because triggers are a kind of stored procedure, MySQL 4.0 does not support them, either.

Whenever a specified event occurs, namely the execution of an INSERT, DELETE, or UPDATE statement, a trigger may fire, meaning that the SQL statements contained in the trigger stored procedure execute. Triggers are often used to enforce business rules, to maintain activity logs, or to apply constraints. Enforcing business rules and applying constraints are ways that you can use triggers to maintain database integrity.

Creating a Trigger

10 Min. To Go

You create a trigger with a CREATE TRIGGER statement, specifying the table affected by the triggering event, the operation on that table that causes the trigger to fire, and whether you want to trigger to fire before or after the event. Say for instance you want to make an entry in a log file every time an insert is made into the CUSTOMERS table. You can create a trigger to do that as follows:

```
CREATE TRIGGER CustInsert
    AFTER INSERT ON CUSTOMERS
        REFERENCING OLD ROW AS Old
    FOR EACH ROW
        INSERT INTO CUSTLOG
            VALUES (Old.Name) ;
```

This statement assumes that a log file named CUSTLOG exists and has a single column that is compatible with the Name column of the CUSTOMERS table. Every time an insert into the CUSTOMERS table is made, the CustInsert trigger fires and adds the name of the customer being inserted to the CUSTLOG file.

 The syntax used in the above example works with Oracle 9i, but SQL Server 2000 does not support the REFERENCING clause and does not allow a table column name in the VALUES clause. So with SQL Server 2000 you can add a record to a log file recording that an insert, update, or delete event has taken place, but you cannot record what was inserted, updated, or deleted.

Firing a Trigger

You fire a trigger by executing the event it is looking for. You can fire the CustInsert trigger created in the previous section by executing a statement such as:

```
INSERT INTO CUSTOMERS (CustomerID, Name, Address1, City,
    StateOrProvince, PostalCode)
VALUES (2001, 'Sam & Tori Memphis Style Bar-B-Que',
    '2341 Bells Road', 'Brownsville', 'TN', '38543') ;
```

This event fires the trigger that adds a record to the CUSTLOG file, indicating the addition of 'Sam & Tori Memphis Style Bar-B-Que' to the CUSTOMERS file.

Done!

REVIEW

Stored procedures take some of the work that has traditionally been performed by the client in a client/server system and put it on the server. This configuration can deliver improvements in both performance and data integrity. Although stored procedures were recently introduced to standard SQL by the SQL:1999 specification, major SQL implementations, such as SQL Server, Oracle, and PostgreSQL, have had proprietary versions of stored procedures for years. They are now in the process of migrating their proprietary versions into compliance with the standard.

Triggers are a specific kind of stored procedure that execute when an INSERT, UPDATE, or DELETE statement changes a database table. You can set the trigger to fire either before, after, or instead of the INSERT, UPDATE, or DELETE statement that activates it. Options available for triggers as well as detailed syntax differ from one implementation to another. Consult the documentation for your specific implementation to make sure your triggers will work.

QUIZ YOURSELF

1. Why does code in a stored procedure on the server run faster than the same code would run as part of an application program on the client? (See "Enhancing Performance and Data Integrity with Stored Procedures.")
2. If you want to change the action of a SQL Server 2000 stored procedure, what statement should you use? (See "Stored procedures in SQL Server 2000.")
3. If you want to change the action of an Oracle 9i stored procedure, what statement should you use? (See "Stored procedures in Oracle 9i.")
4. What value is there to logging the changes that have been made to a table? (See "Creating a Trigger.")

Database Structure

Session Checklist

✔ Creating tables so data has a place to live

✔ Matching real-world changes by altering table structure

✔ Dropping obsolete tables

✔ Opening and closing windows on the data by creating and dropping views

**30 Min.
To Go**

S o far I have talked almost exclusively about how to deal with data in databases — how to put data into database tables, how to change table data, how to delete data from tables, and how to retrieve data from tables. This is all very valuable information, but somewhere, somehow, those tables must have been created.

In this session, I describe how to create tables so that they can hold the data that is the main object of our interest. In addition, I cover how to change the structure of those tables, so that as the organization's data needs change, the database can change, too. Sometimes needs change so drastically that tables that were important before are no longer needed at all. I also describe how to get rid of such obsolete tables, freeing up valuable storage and likely improving overall performance at the same time.

Creating Tables

Today's database management systems, such as SQL Server 2000 or Access 2000, ease the task of creating database tables by giving you screen forms where all you have to do is fill in the blanks with column names, data types, and any applicable constraints. I for one don't believe in making extra work for myself, so I use these facilities without apology. However, you can also create tables using nothing more than SQL statements. The statements of SQL's Data Definition Language (DDL) do the job. The DDL statements CREATE, ALTER, and DROP, respectively, enable you to create new tables, change the structure of existing tables, and remove tables that you no longer need.

Specifying table columns

We have already had a look at several example tables, such as the CUSTOMERS table. Each table has one or more columns. Each column represents an attribute of the entity that the table models. So, just as real world customers have attributes such as an identifying number, a name, an address, and so on, the CUSTOMERS table has corresponding columns named CustomerID, Name, Address1, and so on.

If you created the CUSTOMERS table using SQL Server 2000's Enterprise Manager, it likely has a structure like that shown in Figure 19-1.

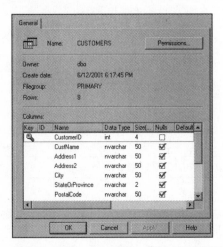

Figure 19-1 *Structure of the CUSTOMERS table, as maintained by SQL Server 2000's Enterprise Manager*

There are four primary pieces of information that SQL Server maintains about a table:

- The names of the columns
- The data type of each column
- The maximum length of each column
- Whether or not NULL values are allowed in each column

I say quite a bit about NULL values in Session 21, so I do not go into depth on that aspect of the table definition here.

One of the nice things about creating a table using a screen tool such as the one shown in Figure 19-1 is that the DBMS does a lot of the work for you. You fill in the column name and specify a data type; then the DBMS enters default values in the Length and Allow Nulls columns. On the other hand, one of the not so nice things about creating a table using a screen tool such as the one shown in Figure 19-1 is that the DBMS does a lot of the work for you. How's that for a paradox?

The DBMS uses default values for Length and Allow Nulls that are adequate for most cases — adequate, but not necessarily optimal. Consider Figure 19-1. SQL Server has assigned all the character fields a length of 50 ASCII characters (except the StateOrProvince column, which I overrode). This is probably a big waste of space for most, if not all, of the columns. Another default is to allow NULL values for all columns defined. You have to manually override this behavior if you want to force certain columns to have a definite value.

If you create your tables with SQL rather than a screen form, you have very fine-grained control over their structure. You can not only explicitly specify column names, data types, field lengths, and nullability, but also foreign keys and constraints.

I discuss constraints in Session 21 and foreign keys in Session 22.

Here, I cover basic table creation using SQL.

Let's create the CUSTOMERS table. We already know what columns we want. They are:

- CustomerID
- CustName
- Address1
- Address2
- City
- StateOrProvince
- PostalCode
- Country
- ContactName
- ContactPhone
- ContactFax
- ContactEmail
- Notes

I have used CustName for the customer's name rather than Name as I did in earlier sessions, because although Name is not a reserved word in SQL:1999, in some implementations Name *is* a reserved word. To avoid confusing the DBMS' SQL parser, it is better to use CustName.

After you know what your columns should be, think about what is the best data type for each and what is the maximum length entry that is likely for each column. When you have these things in mind, you are ready to create the table. Use the CREATE TABLE statement as follows:

```
CREATE TABLE CUSTOMERS (
    CustomerID                      INTEGER,
    CustName               CHAR (25),
    Address1               CHAR (25),
    Address2               CHAR (25),
    City                            CHAR (20),
       StateOrProvince              CHAR (2),
       PostalCode                   CHAR (10),
    Country                CHAR (20),
       ContactName         CHAR (30),
       ContactPhone        CHAR (20),
    ContactFax                      CHAR (20),
    ContactEmail           CHAR (30),
    Notes                           CLOB ) ;
```

This statement creates an empty CUSTOMERS table, ready to accept data that you can enter using an INSERT statement. As I state in Session 3, the CLOB data type is for character strings that are too long for the normal character types. For some customers, you may want to accumulate a lot of facts in the Notes column.

 You can use SQL to create tables in Access 2000, but it isn't at all obvious how to do it. You must use the Access query tool and enter the CREATE statements as if they were queries.

Designating a primary key

20 Min. To Go

One of the major threats to a table's data integrity is the possibility that two different records may become confused. For example, what if Xanthic had two customers in two different cities, both named "Main Street Photo"? When Main Street Photo orders product, where do you send it? Database developers resolve this problem by guaranteeing that the value in a row for a column or the values in that row for a combination of columns is different from the corresponding values of all other rows in the table. That column or combination of columns that is guaranteed to contain a unique value is called the *primary key* of the table.

There are a variety of ways of guaranteeing uniqueness of a primary key. One way to guarantee uniqueness is to use an ID number that automatically increments every time you add a record to the table. There are other ways as well. A product may have a unique serial number or model number. A person may have a unique government-issued identifier, such as the United States' Social Security Number. By making such a number the primary key of your table, you avoid a host of data integrity problems. You can specify the primary key of a table when you create it. We could have done so when we created the CUSTOMERS table in the previous section by adding a PRIMARY KEY constraint to the CustomerID column. The table definition looks like this:

```
CREATE TABLE CUSTOMERS (
    CustomerID                      INTEGER         PRIMARY KEY,
    CustName               CHAR (25),
    Address1               CHAR (25),
    Address2               CHAR (25),
```

```
     City                        CHAR (20),
        StateOrProvince          CHAR (2),
        PostalCode               CHAR (10),
     Country               CHAR (20),
        ContactName        CHAR (30),
        ContactPhone       CHAR (20),
     ContactFax                  CHAR (20),
     ContactEmail          CHAR (30),
     Notes                       CLOB ) ;
```

One of the features of the PRIMARY KEY constraint is that it does not allow the insertion of a new record whose primary key duplicates the value of the primary key of a record that is already in the table. It also does not allow the insertion of a new record whose primary key field has a NULL value. Because a NULL value means that the value is unknown, that unknown value may duplicate the primary key value of an existing record. To eliminate that possibility, the DBMS does not allow a record with a NULL primary key to be inserted.

Altering Table Structure

Even if you have done an absolutely perfect job of determining your users' needs and have created tables accordingly, you will probably have to change the structure of some of those tables sooner or later. The world changes; the market changes; the company changes; management changes; everything changes. When the things that the database is modeling change, the database must change, too. SQL gives you the ability to change the structure of tables that you (or other people) have previously created.

Changes that are most likely to be needed are the addition of new columns or the deletion of old ones. You will want to add new columns when your application is called upon to track new attributes of the entity your table models. For example, you may now find that your CUSTOMERS table should have a column for the contact person's cell phone. You can add that column as follows:

```
ALTER TABLE CUSTOMERS
   ADD COLUMN ContactCellPhone CHAR (20) ;
```

You can also use the ALTER TABLE statement to get rid of columns that you no longer want. There are two possible situations. First, the column you want to drop has no views, constraints, or other objects that depend on it. Second, the column you want to drop does have objects that depend on it. You want to handle these two situations differently.

Let us say that you want it drop the ContactFax column if no other objects depend on it, but you do not want to drop it if even one object depends on it. Use the following syntax:

```
ALTER TABLE CUSTOMERS
   DROP COLUMN ContactFax RESTRICT ;
```

If nothing depends on the ContactFax column, it is dropped from the CUSTOMERS table. However, if something does depend on the ContactFax column, the RESTRICT keyword causes the ALTER TABLE statement to fail and no change to the CUSTOMERS table is made.

On the other hand, if you are sure you want to drop the ContactFax column, and further-more, you want to also drop any objects that depend upon it, you can do that with the fol-lowing syntax:

```
ALTER TABLE CUSTOMERS
   DROP COLUMN ContactFax CASCADE ;
```

This statement drops the ContactFax column regardless of whether anything depends on it. If any objects do depend on the ContactFax column, the CASCADE keyword assures that they are dropped from the database, too.

Dropping Tables

**10 Min.
To Go**

If you can create tables with SQL, you had better be able to delete them with SQL as well. Otherwise, your hard disk gradually fills up with obsolete tables, and your performance slows to a crawl. Happily, SQL has a facility for dropping tables that is analogous to the action of DROP COLUMN in the ALTER TABLE statement. Consider:

```
DROP TABLE CUSTOMERS RESTRICT ;
```

This statement drops the CUSTOMERS table if no objects depend on it. If any objects *do* depend on the existence of the CUSTOMERS table, this DROP TABLE statement fails. Alternatively:

```
DROP TABLE CUSTOMERS CASCADE ;
```

This statement drops the CUSTOMERS table regardless of whether any objects depend on its existence. Any objects that do depend on CUSTOMERS are dropped also.

> DROP, **particularly with the** CASCADE **option, is a dangerous statement. When you drop a table, it is gone for good. Be absolutely sure you know what you are doing when you use the** DROP **statement.**

Creating and Dropping Views

One of the major advantages of databases over flat file systems is flexibility. Different people in an organization can use the data in a database for different purposes. In the case of Xanthic Systems, the sales manager may want information on how much sales volume is coming from each customer. The production manager may want to know the current inven-tory level of each product and the number sold since the last time the INVOICE table and its associated INVOICELINE table were archived and reinitialized. Database tables that you have created according to a logical schema do not fall neatly into either of these needs.

The sales manager needs to pull data from the CUSTOMERS table and the INVOICE table. The production manager needs data from the INVOICELINE table and the INVENTORY table. INVOICELINE is a table related to the INVOICE table that holds the details of what products appear on each line of an invoice.

To give both of these people visibility of the data they need, without confusing them with irrelevant data they don't need, you can create views that display what is wanted and hide what is not wanted. A view selects columns from one or more tables, creating a virtual table. The result sets that I have talked about throughout this book are another kind of virtual table. A view is a more substantial virtual table than a result set, however, because it is named and defined in the database's metadata. It has a logical existence, but the data that it seems to contain actually resides in the base tables that it draws from.

For example, the sales manager's CUSTSALES view draws CustomerID and CustName from the CUSTOMERS table and TotalCharge from the INVOICE table. The SQL to create the required view is something like the following:

```
CREATE VIEW CUSTSALES
    (CustomerID, CustName, TotalCharge)
    AS SELECT CUSTOMERS.CustomerID, CustName, TotalCharge
    FROM CUSTOMERS, INVOICE
    WHERE CUSTOMERS.CustomerID = INVOICE.CustomerID ;
```

 Because both the CUSTOMERS **and** INVOICE **tables contain a column named CustomerID, you must specify which one you are taking the view's CustomerID column from. CustName occurs only in** CUSTOMERS **and TotalCharge occurs only in** INVOICE**, so you don't need to tell SQL where the corresponding columns in the new view come from.**

If the sales manager wanted a view that showed only the purchases of customers in Arizona, adding a condition to the above CREATE statement does the job:

```
CREATE VIEW CUSTSALES
    (CustomerID, CustName, TotalCharge)
    AS SELECT CUSTOMERS.CustomerID, CustName, TotalCharge
    FROM CUSTOMERS, INVOICE
    WHERE CUSTOMERS.CustomerID = INVOICE.CustomerID
    AND CUSTOMERS.StateOrProvince = 'AZ' ;
```

The production manager's STOCKING view draws ProductID, ProdName, and InStock from the INVENTORY table as well as QuantitySold from the INVOICELINE table. Create the STOCKING view similarly to the way you created the CUSTSALES view.

```
CREATE VIEW STOCKING
    (ProductID, Prodname, InStock, QuantitySold)
    AS SELECT INVENTORY.ProductID, INVENTORY.ProdName,
        InStock, QuantitySold
    FROM INVENTORY, INVOICELINE
    WHERE INVENTORY.ProductID = INVOICELINE.ProductID ;
```

From these examples, we can surmise that you can create a view by selecting columns from one, two, or more existing tables where one or more conditions are satisfied.

Dropping a view is very similar to dropping a table. Once again, objects may or may not depend on the view that you want to drop. You can use the RESTRICT or CASCADE keywords, depending on how you want to handle those dependent objects. To drop the CUSTSALES view you can use:

```
DROP VIEW CUSTSALES RESTRICT ;
```

This drops the view if no objects depend on it, but fails to drop the view if one or more objects do depend on it. Alternatively, you can use:

```
DROP VIEW CUSTSALES CASCADE ;
```

This drops the view regardless of whether any objects depend on it. Any objects that do depend on the dropped view are also dropped.

Done!

REVIEW

SQL's Data Definition Language, consisting of the CREATE, ALTER, and DROP statements, enable you to build the structure or skeleton of a database:

- Use the CREATE statement to create tables and views.
- Use the ALTER statement to change the structure of existing tables.
- Use the DROP statement to eliminate unwanted tables and views from your database.

QUIZ YOURSELF

1. Why may you want to use SQL to create tables rather than your DBMS's table creation tool, even though using SQL would be more work? (See "Specifying table columns.")
2. What is the purpose of a primary key in a table? (See "Designating a primary key.")
3. Why must a primary key never have a NULL value? (See "Designating a primary key.")
4. What SQL statement should you use to add a new column to an existing table? (See "Altering Table Structure.")
5. If you want to drop a table regardless of whether other objects depend on it, what keyword should you add to your DROP TABLE statement? (See "Dropping Tables.")

Database Design

Session Checklist

✔ Deciding on relevance

✔ Acting early to avert disaster

✔ Turning entities and attributes into tables and columns

✔ Linking tables by identifying relationships

✔ Relating tables to each other

✔ Supercharging performance by creating indexes

**30 Min.
To Go**

In Session 19, I describe how to create database tables using SQL. You can certainly create tables that way, but in a real development project, it is not wise to just sit down and start creating tables. You should do some serious thinking first, as well as interviewing everyone who has an interest in the project. Different people probably have different ideas about what the system should be and do. You need to get a clear consensus that everyone can accept before entering the design phase of the project.

Ask a lot of questions, such as:

- What are the important entities to track?
- Who will be using the system?
- Who will be using the information generated by the system?
- What reports will you want to generate on a regular basis?
- Will anyone want to make ad hoc queries? If so, what kind?

When you have a clear idea of what the software system will be called upon to do, you can start conceptualizing the schema that will produce what is needed. The *schema* of a database, which is held in the database's metadata, is its structure.

Deciding What Is Relevant and What Is Not

As you talk to domain experts, system users, managers, stockholders, and other people related to the system, you will start to get an idea of what entities and other items are relevant to the system you have been called upon to design. Domain experts can tell you what the system is all about. Users can tell you what they need to get out of the system to do their jobs. Managers can give you a "big picture" idea of what is important. If you are developing for a public company, stockholders may need to be considered, too. The important point here is that most database applications must serve the needs of multiple constituencies. To meet those needs, you need to discover those constituencies, talk to them, and find out what is important to them.

After you have talked to everyone, you will probably find that there are conflicting ideas about what is important to include in your application. One group may place high importance on one kind of information and no importance on another. A second group may reverse those priorities. You want to make sure you are aware of everyone's needs and desires before going any further.

Averting Disaster

After you have compiled the wish lists of all the stakeholders in the development, it is likely that developing everything that everybody wants will cost more than the organization is able or willing to pay. At this point, you need to go back to the decision makers who control the budget and get a decision on which features should be implemented right away, which should be deferred until later, and which should not be done at all.

After you have a written agreement on what will be delivered (and the deadline for delivery), get your responsible client (the person who will pay you) to sign and date it. This can help to protect you from *scope creep*. Scope creep is an insidious disease that causes the scope of a project to slowly but relentlessly expand far beyond what you originally agreed to do. Scope creep can turn a reasonable project into an impossible monstrosity. It is best to lay ground rules at the beginning so that it never has a chance to start.

**20 Min.
To Go**

Defining Tables and Columns

After you have gathered all the input from stakeholders and reached agreement with them on what is important, you can decide which entities they have mentioned deserve to become tables in your database. Some of the things mentioned deserve to be modeled as tables. Some are better modeled as columns of tables. And some are business rules that can be applied to tables as constraints.

Entities that are important to the conduct of an enterprise should be modeled as database tables. Attributes of those entities become columns of the tables. Let's illustrate this process, using the sales efforts of Xanthic Systems as an example. A number of things are important to Xanthic. Among them are the following:

- Prospects
- Customers
- Employees

- Products
- Invoices

It makes sense for each of these entities to be modeled with a table. After we look into things a little deeper, we may find that other tables are needed, too. Each of the above listed entities has attributes that become columns in the tables we create. We can use SQL to create the tables as follows:

```
CREATE TABLE PROSPECTS (
    CustomerID              INTEGER         PRIMARY KEY,
    CustName                CHAR (25),
    Address1                CHAR (25),
    Address2                CHAR (25),
    City                    CHAR (20),
    StateOrProvince         CHAR (2),
    PostalCode              CHAR (10),
    Country                 CHAR (20),
    ContactName             CHAR (30),
    ContactPhone            CHAR (20),
    ContactFax              CHAR (20),
    ContactEmail            CHAR (30),
    Notes                   CLOB ) ;

CREATE TABLE CUSTOMERS (
    CustomerID              INTEGER         PRIMARY KEY,
    CustName                CHAR (25),
    Address1                CHAR (25),
    Address2                CHAR (25),
    City                    CHAR (20),
    StateOrProvince         CHAR (2),
    PostalCode              CHAR (10),
    Country                 CHAR (20),
    ContactName             CHAR (30),
    ContactPhone            CHAR (20),
    ContactFax              CHAR (20),
    ContactEmail            CHAR (30),
    Notes                   CLOB ) ;

CREATE TABLE EMPLOYEES (
    EmployeeID              INTEGER         PRIMARY KEY,
    EmployeeName            CHAR (30),
    Address1                CHAR (25),
    Address2                CHAR (25),
    City                    CHAR (25),
    StateOrProvince         CHAR (2),
    Postal Code             CHAR (10),
    HomePhone               CHAR (13),
    OfficeExtension         CHAR (4),
    HireDate                DATE,
    JobClassification       CHAR (10),
    HourlySalaryCommission  CHAR (1) ) ;
```

```
CREATE TABLE PRODUCTS (
     ProductID                INTEGER         PRIMARY KEY,
     ProductName              CHAR (30),
     ProductDescription       CHAR (50),
     Cost                     NUMERIC (12,2),
     RetailPrice              NUMERIC (12,2),
     DiscountPriceA           NUMERIC (12,2),
     DiscountPriceB           NUMERIC (12,2),
     DiscountPriceC           NUMERIC (12,2) ) ;

CREATE TABLE INVOICE (
     InvoiceNumber            INTEGER         PRIMARY KEY,
     CustomerID               INTEGER,
     InvoiceDate              DATE,
     TotalCharge              NUMERIC (12,2),
     TotalRemitted            NUMERIC (12,2),
     FormOfPayment            CHAR (20),
     Salesperson              CHAR (30) ) ;
```

You now have a table for each of the objects in the model that you have determined is important enough to be an entity. You have defined columns for each table that correspond to the attributes of the entities. Now you must address the question, "How do these tables that I have just defined relate to each other?"

Identifying Relationships

Xanthic Systems has its database logically divided into tables, each of which stores the attributes of an important entity. In most cases, people making retrievals from the database want to pull information from more than one table at a time. A marketing manager may want to find out where sales are coming from by pulling location information from the CUSTOMERS table and sales total information from the INVOICE table. A payroll clerk may want to compute commissions and print checks by pulling sales data from the INVOICE table and personnel information from the EMPLOYEES table.

Many different people may want to combine table data in many different ways. In order for this to work, the relationships between the tables must be well defined and clearly understood. You as the developer must lay down some rules for these relationships. Here are some considerations that apply to Xanthic Systems.

- Customers make purchases. When they do, an invoice is generated. Each invoice-generating purchase is made by one and only one customer. A customer can and hopefully will make multiple purchases. Thus a customer can be related to multiple invoices, but each invoice must be related to one and only one customer.

- Salespeople make sales. When they do, an invoice is generated. Each sale is made by one and only one salesperson. A salesperson can and hopefully will make multiple sales. Thus a salesperson can be related to multiple invoices, but each invoice must be related to one and only one salesperson.

- Products get sold. When they do, an invoice is generated. A product may be sold to multiple customers in multiple sales transactions that generate multiple invoices. An invoice may contain multiple line items, each one of which records the sale of a different product. Thus a product can be related to multiple invoices, and an invoice can record the sale of multiple products.

- Prospects have not yet made any purchases, so they are not related to invoices, products, or salespeople.

Figure 20-1 graphically shows the ways these entities are related, in the form of an entity-relationship diagram.

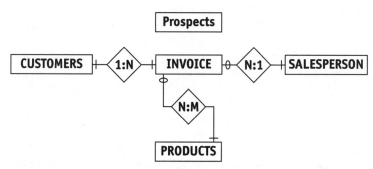

Figure 20-1 *Relationships of Xanthic Systems' main entities*

The diagram in Figure 20-1 requires some explanation. Each rectangle represents the entity named within it. The diamonds represent the maximum cardinalities of the relationships between tables. 1:N represents a one-to-many relationship. The 1 side can at most have a value of one. The N side can have a value that is not specified precisely but may be greater than one. N:1 represents a many-to-one relationship. N:M represents a many-to-many relationship, where both N and M represent numbers that may be greater than one and not necessarily equal to each other.

The slash marks and ovals next to the entity rectangles represent minimum cardinality. A slash next to an entity means that at least one instance of that entity must exist in the relationship. An oval next to an entity means that there may be no instances of that entity.

As an example, consider the INVOICE/SALESPERSON relationship. If an invoice exists, then it must hold the name of the salesperson that made the sale. The salesperson must exist, so there is a slash next to the SALESPERSON rectangle. However, a newly hired salesperson may not have made any sales yet. A salesperson can exist, even if no invoices bear that salesperson's name, so there is an oval next to the INVOICE rectangle.

There are no relationships connecting the PROSPECTS entity to any of the other entities. This mirrors the real life situation. If no one is assigned to do anything about the prospects, they probably will not become customers. If management decides to assign prospects to salespeople for follow-up, then a relationship can be added to the diagram.

The minimum cardinalities I have specified in Figure 20-1 are just examples, based as they are on Xanthic Systems' common practice. Other organizations may define things differently. Whatever the common practice of an organization may be, make sure you have modeled it accurately in your entity-relationship diagram. The diagram is the basis for refining the structure of your database.

**10 Min.
To Go**

Transforming Entity Relationships to Table Relationships

After establishing the major entities and the relationships between them, the next step in building a database is to create tables that correspond to the entities and do so in such a way that the relationships between the entities are realized as relationships between the corresponding tables.

There are three basic kinds of relationships:

- **One-to-one:** These relationships are the simplest. One row of the first table corresponds to one and only one row of the second table, and one row of the second table corresponds to one and only one row of the first table.

- **One-to-many (or many-to-one):** One-to-many relationships, illustrated in Figure 20-1 as linking the CUSTOMER entity to the INVOICE entity and linking the SALES-PERSON entity to the INVOICE entity, are more complex but still directly translatable to relationships between tables. One row of the first table corresponds to multiple rows of the second table, but each row of the second table corresponds to one and only one row of the first table.

- **Many-to-many:** Many-to-many relationships, exemplified in Figure 20-1 by the relationship between the INVOICE entity and the PRODUCTS entity, are the most complex. They are not directly translatable to relationships between tables. You can solve this problem by adding a linking table between the two tables involved in the many-to-many relationship.

You can add an INVOICELINE table between the INVOICE table and the PRODUCTS table. This decomposes the many-to-many relationship into two one-to-many relationships. One invoice can contain multiple invoice lines, but each invoice line is contained in one and only one invoice. One product can appear on multiple invoice lines, but each invoice line records the sale of one and only one product. Figure 20-2 shows the entity-relationship diagram for this modified model.

In Session 19, I discuss the importance of primary keys, which guarantee that every row in a database table is distinguishable from every other row in that table. Keys serve an additional, very important purpose. They serve as the bridge that links one table to another. In order to actualize the relationships shown in Figure 20-2, two linked tables must share one or more columns. In a one-to-many relationship, the shared column or columns must be the primary key of the table on the one side of the relationship. On the many side of the relationship, the shared column or columns constitute a *foreign key*.

In the preceding section I show how to create the PRODUCTS and INVOICE tables with SQL. You can now create the INVOICELINE table similarly.

```
CREATE TABLE INVOICELINE (
     InvoiceLineNo         INTEGER              PRIMARY KEY,
     InvoiceNumber         INTEGER,
     ProductID             INTEGER,
     ProductName           CHAR (30),
     UnitPrice             NUMERIC (12,2),
     Quantity              INTEGER,
     ExtendedPrice         NUMERIC (12,2) ) ;
```

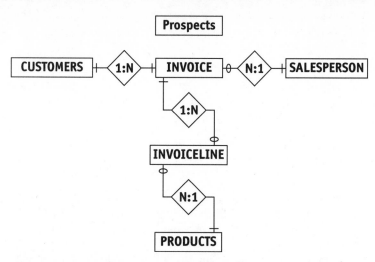

Figure 20-2 *Modified model of Xanthic Systems' main entities*

InvoiceLineNo is the primary key of the INVOICELINE table. InvoiceNumber is a foreign key that links INVOICELINE to the INVOICE table, and ProductID is a foreign key that links INVOICELINE to the PRODUCTS table. Similarly, the CustomerID column in the INVOICE table is the foreign key that links it to the CUSTOMERS table. The Salesperson column links the INVOICE table to the EMPLOYEES table. It corresponds to the EmployeeName column in the EMPLOYEES table.

To establish these relationships, you must state them explicitly in the table definitions. It is best to do this at the beginning with the CREATE TABLE statements, although you can do it later with ALTER TABLE statements. Because none of these tables contain any data yet, I can drop them and then recreate them without losing any information. I demonstrate the process here with CREATE TABLE statements:

```
DROP TABLE INVOICE ;
CREATE TABLE INVOICE (
    InvoiceNumber          INTEGER          PRIMARY KEY,
    CustomerID             INTEGER,
    InvoiceDate            DATE,
    TotalCharge            NUMERIC (12,2),
    TotalRemitted          NUMERIC (12,2),
    FormOfPayment          CHAR (20),
    SalespersonID          INTEGER,
    CONSTRAINT CustFK FOREIGN KEY (CustomerID)
        REFERENCES CUSTOMERS (CustomerID),
    CONSTRAINT SalesFK FOREIGN KEY (SalespersonID)
        REFERENCES EMPLOYEES (EmployeeID)
) ;
```

```
DROP TABLE INVOICELINE ;
CREATE TABLE INVOICELINE (
    InvoiceLineNo           INTEGER                PRIMARY KEY,
    InvoiceNumber           INTEGER,
    ProductID               INTEGER,
    ProductName             CHAR (30),
    UnitPrice               NUMERIC (12,2),
    Quantity                INTEGER,
    ExtendedPrice           NUMERIC (12,2),
    CONSTRAINT InvNum FOREIGN KEY (InvoiceNumber)
        REFERENCES INVOICE (InvoiceNumber)
) ;
```

Now the tables for Xanthic Systems' new database are structured properly, but there is one more thing to consider before starting to fill the tables with data. The speed with which you can retrieve data from a database depends on how quickly the database engine can find the records you ask for in your SQL query statements. For tables with a large number of records, retrieval times can be agonizingly slow. One thing you can do to speed things up dramatically is to use indexes.

Creating Indexes

What if a table contains thousands or millions of records, and you only want to retrieve one of them? This is analogous to finding a needle in a haystack. It may take a long time. One remedy to this is to maintain the table in order, sorted by whatever retrieval key you are going to use. There are a couple of problems with this approach. One is that you may want to do a retrieval based on the value in one column one time and do another retrieval based on the value in another column at another time. If you sort the table to optimize one retrieval, you will deoptimize the second. A second problem has to do with the fact that it takes a long time to sort a large table. If you have to re-sort the table every time you add or delete records, you will spend so much time sorting there will be no time left to do useful work. Maintaining large tables in sorted order is not practical.

You can design rapid retrieval into your database without sorting tables by using indexes. An *index* is a table of pointers. Each pointer points to a row in a data table. It is much easier to maintain the index in sorted order than it is to maintain a data table in sorted order. You make a retrieval by rapidly finding in the index table the pointer to the record in the data table that you want and then following the pointer to wherever in the data table your target record is. The result is almost as fast as if the data table had been in sorted order.

You can create an index for every field in the data table that you may want to use as a retrieval key. Thus each index is always optimized for the specific retrieval it was designed to facilitate. Whenever you add or delete records in the data table, you do not have to re-sort the indexes. All you have to do is change the affected pointers to the new values. This can be done almost instantaneously, unlike sorting, which may force you to move most of the rows in the table.

The SQL:1999 standard does not specify how to create indexes, but all popular implementations provide a method for doing so. Here's an example of how SQL Server 2000 creates two indexes:

```
CREATE INDEX CustNameIdx
   ON CUSTOMERS
      (CustName) ;
CREATE INDEX CustPostalCodeIdx
   ON CUSTOMERS
      (PostalCode) ;
```

The same syntax works with Oracle 9i databases, Access 2000 databases, MySQL databases and PostgreSQL databases.

Destroying Indexes

If you can create something, you'd better be able to destroy it, too. It is particularly important to be able to destroy indexes. Every time a table is changed, all of its indexes are updated. That updating takes time and system resources. If you have indexes on a table that you no longer use, deleting them improves performance. All the DBMS products we are considering here perform this operation with the DROP INDEX statement, as shown in the following example:

```
DROP INDEX CustNameIdx ;
```

Appropriate indexing can make a database application a performance champion. Inappropriate or no indexing can make a database application totally unusable. Make sure you give sufficient attention to creating and maintaining the right indexes for the way your database is used by the applications running against it.

Done!

REVIEW

Before you can create a useful database application, you must design and build the database that will hold the data. Proper structure of that database is critical to both performance and data integrity. At the outset, you must determine what elements of the real world system being modeled need to be included in the database, and whether they should be tables or columns of tables. At the outset, it is also important to make sure that the scope of the project is well-defined and agreed to.

When you know the size and nature of the task, you can then define entities, establish relationships, and create tables. Establish the relationships between tables with foreign key constraints; then create indexes that enable users to retrieve the information they need efficiently.

QUIZ YOURSELF

1. Who should you talk to before starting to design a database application that you have been assigned to develop? (See "Deciding What Is Relevant and What Is Not.")
2. What is the biggest danger of scope creep? (See "Averting Disaster.")

3. If two tables are linked by a one-to-many relationship, what field of what table provides that link? (See "Identifying Relationships.")

4. What is the maximum cardinality of the one side of a one-to-many relationship? (See "Identifying Relationships.")

5. If your entity-relationship model has a many-to-many relationship in it, what should you do before converting it to a relational model? (See "Transforming Entity Relationships to Table Relationships.")

PART

IV

Saturday Evening Part Review

1. Why is it not a good idea to use native drivers when your application must communicate with multiple data sources?

2. What are the four major parts of ODBC?

3. Which part of ODBC determines which driver to load to service a request for data from the application?

4. How does the use of stored procedures improve overall system performance on a network?

5. If the structure of a table used by a stored procedure changes, what should be done to the stored procedure to assure that it is compatible with the new table structure?

6. What type of stored procedure is often used to enforce business rules?

7. What SQL statement would you use to add a column to an existing table?

8. Why does SQL not allow a primary key with a NULL value?

9. Why might you want to create a view of a single table?

10. When is scope creep more harmful to your financial position: when you are working on a fixed price contract, or when you are being paid by the hour?

11. When transforming an entity-relationship (E-R) model to a relational model, what do the E-R model's entities and attributes become in the relational model?

12. Under what circumstance would it not make sense to build an index for a database table?

☑ Friday

☑ Saturday

☑ Sunday

PART

V

Sunday Morning

Integrity and Constraints

Session Checklist

✔ Identifying problems with database data

✔ Database integrity and how to maintain it

✔ Protecting your database by applying constraints

**30 Min.
To Go**

A database doesn't have much value if you can't count on its contents to be correct. Unfortunately, there are a number of different ways that bad data can get into a database. There are several things that you can do to protect your database from bad data, but none of them are completely foolproof. In this session, I call your attention to several possible sources of data corruption, and then describe some things you can do to prevent it.

Problems with Database Data

There are a variety of different threats to the integrity of your data. These threats strike at different times, in different ways, and call for a variety of countermeasures. Next I explore some of the things that can happen and what you can do about them.

Your source data is wrong

You can have a problem before you start. You need to fill the tables in your database with data. This data has to come from somewhere, perhaps written records, odd slips of paper, people's vague recollection, Web sites, scientific journals, or supermarket tabloids. Some of the information contained in these sources may be incorrect. If a data item is incorrect but still reasonable, it may be difficult to determine that there may be a problem with it.

On the other hand, if the value of the data item is not reasonable, you can infer that there must be a problem somewhere and deal with the problem appropriately. For example, if you're dealing with genealogy and the source you have says a person's marriage date preceded his or her birth date, you can be pretty sure that at least one of those dates is wrong. In a corporate database, if an employee's termination date precedes his or her hire date, you can draw the same conclusion. So when your source data is faulty, sometimes you can easily tell that there is a problem and sometimes you cannot. Later in this session, I show how applying constraints to a database can discover some of these problems and prevent bad data from entering the database.

The source data gets entered incorrectly

Most data of interest does not start out in digital form. Somewhere, at some time, a human being has to enter the data into a computer, usually via a keyboard. At this stage in the process, data entry errors are a real possibility. Even if your source data is 100 percent correct, if the data entry operator makes errors while typing, bad data gets into your database. As in the previous case, if an entry falls outside of the expected range, a constraint that checks for range errors pinpoints the problem. Erroneous entries that happen to fall within the expected range, however, are not caught by such a constraint.

Update errors

After the data is in a database table, it is still vulnerable to corruption. A person making updates, insertions, or deletions may make errors. He may make the right update to the wrong row or the wrong update to the right row. He may insert a row that shouldn't be inserted or delete a row that shouldn't be deleted. One strategy here is to not allow anyone who is prone to errors to make updates. This helps some, but even the best data entry operator is not perfect all the time. Constraints on the database do flag range errors, but are of no help when erroneous entries that are nonetheless within the acceptable range are made.

Hardware failure

The hardware on which your database is running can fail. This can be something as subtle as a cosmic ray flipping a bit in memory or as dramatic as a tornado destroying your building. Perhaps more likely is a power failure or brownout that happens at just the precise instant that your database is vulnerable during a write operation. No amount of software integrity features or database constraints can protect you from this class of problems. The best defenses against hardware failures are procedural. Error correcting hardware, frequent backups, and off-site storage of backup media can be lifesavers should disaster strike. A good backup policy, rigidly enforced, is cheap insurance against an event that can destroy months of work and priceless data.

Software bugs

Database applications tend to be large and complex. If they don't start out that way, eventually they grow to be large and complex as more functionality is added over time.

Furthermore, database applications rely on database management systems, which also tend to be large and complex. All of this rides on top of a computer operating system, which is even larger and more complex. All of these large, complex pieces of software almost certainly harbor hidden bugs. Hidden software bugs tend to surface at the most inopportune times, destroying the maximum possible amount of work.

The best defense against software bugs is the same as it is for hardware failure. Back up frequently and religiously. A software bug may not do as much damage as a tornado, but it can totally wipe out the copy of your program on disk. If may even corrupt several generations of your backups if you don't notice it right away. Make sure the effort you put into your backup procedure matches the importance of the material you are backing up.

Intentional damage

Not everybody likes you. Even the Dalai Lama and the Pope have their detractors. Consider the possibility that someone may want to hurt you or your organization by trashing your database or your application. Someone may even harm you without having you specifically in mind. There are people out there who unleash computer viruses and worms just for the sheer thrill of having affected thousands of people. If one of these hits the computer that holds your database, you can lose it all.

Physical isolation is a good preventative for this type of threat. Don't put your database on a machine that is accessible over the Internet. Don't let unauthorized people use any of the computers that can access the database. Restrict the access rights of authorized users to include only what they need in order to do their jobs.

In the case of Internet access, you have a greater problem if your database is serving data over the Web. In this case, a robust firewall can be invaluable, along with constant vigilance. There is no sure preventative here. Hackers have penetrated some of the most technologically sophisticated Web sites in the world, including the US Department of Defense and the White House. Make sure any database accessible over the Web is as well protected as you can make it.

Data redundancy

Problems can arise if you store the same data item more than once in a database. Consider the case where you have a CUSTOMERS table that stores customer addresses and an INVOICE table that also stores customer addresses. After a customer has made a number of purchases, she informs you that she has a new address. Because of the redundant address data in your database, you must update not only one row in the CUSTOMERS table, but also many rows in the INVOICE table. If you fail to update even one of those rows, you now have inconsistent data. Inconsistencies can proliferate over time, gradually degrading the value of your database.

The best solution to the problem of data redundancy is to structure your database so as to minimize it. You cannot eliminate data redundancy completely because related tables must share a common column that serves as a primary key in one and a foreign key in the other. However, you can minimize any redundancy that goes beyond that.

20 Min.
To Go

Maintaining Database Integrity

With all the problems enumerated in the previous section that can potentially corrupt the data in your database, the importance of maintaining database integrity is evident. Three distinct types of integrity have been identified (entity, domain, and referential), and each requires different actions from the database developer.

Entity integrity

The real world entities that you model with database tables may be physical things such as customers or products, or they may be conceptual things such as invoices or library catalogs. A table has entity integrity if it is entirely consistent with the entity that it models. Of course, this does not mean that it is identical to the entity it models. It only means that as far as it goes, there are no contradictions between the structure and content of the table and its corresponding real world entity.

You can ensure that the tables you build have entity integrity by cataloging all significant entity attributes and assigning appropriately defined table columns to them. Furthermore, any business rules that apply to the entity should be modeled with constraints. I discuss constraints in detail later in this session.

Domain integrity

Bad source data or data entry errors can often be discovered and dealt with if your system has domain integrity. The domain of a data item is the set of all possible values that the data item may have. Any piece of data that falls outside of the domain for the field it is being put into must be in error. By adding domain constraints to your database, you can at least be assured that any data entered falls within the acceptable range. The DBMS does not detect any erroneous data entered into a field that nonetheless falls within the domain for that field. Thus domain constraints give you partial, but not complete, protection against bad source data and data entry errors.

As an example, say you wanted your CUSTOMERS table to accept only entries where the customer's country was either USA or Canada. You can apply the following domain constraint:

```
CREATE DOMAIN CountryDom CHAR (50)
    CHECK (COUNTRY IN ('USA', 'Canada'));
```

After creating the domain, create any tables that contain the column specified in the domain constraint. Thus you should issue the above CREATE DOMAIN statement before issuing the CREATE TABLE CUSTOMERS statement.

Referential integrity

Well-designed tables have entity integrity and domain integrity. This is excellent, but tables in relational databases are related to each other, and those relationships must have integrity also. Referential integrity is the name give to the concept that all the tables in a database are consistent with each other.

Inconsistencies can easily corrupt a database if you don't take steps to prevent them. Consider the CUSTOMERS table and the INVOICE table. There is a one-to-many relationship between CUSTOMERS and INVOICE, creating a parent-child relationship. Suppose your customer Acme Corp. has gone out of business. They are never going to buy from you again, so you want to delete them from the CUSTOMERS table to free up some valuable disk space and improve processing speed. If you delete Acme from the CUSTOMERS table (the parent side of the relationship), what should you do with Acme's orders recorded in the INVOICE table (the child side of the relationship)? If you leave them alone, they are "orphan records." They refer to a customer number that no longer exists in the CUSTOMERS table, which is an inconsistency. On the other hand, if you delete all of Acme's orders from the INVOICE table, your calculations of total sales are wrong. You must make a decision on how you want to handle this situation, as it will probably occur fairly often.

You can deal with such cases by adding a clause to the foreign key constraint you place on the INVOICE table. In Session 20, I created the INVOICE table with the following SQL statement:

```
CREATE TABLE INVOICE (
    InvoiceNumber          INTEGER        PRIMARY KEY,
    CustomerID             INTEGER,
    InvoiceDate            DATE,
    TotalCharge            NUMERIC (12,2),
    TotalRemitted          NUMERIC (12,2),
    FormOfPayment          CHAR (20),
    SalespersonID          INTEGER,
    CONSTRAINT CustFK FOREIGN KEY (CustomerID)
        REFERENCES CUSTOMERS (CustomerID),
    CONSTRAINT SalesFK FOREIGN KEY (SalespersonID)
        REFERENCES EMPLOYEES (EmployeeID)
) ;
```

Now we see that this table definition has a problem when either a customer is dropped or an employee leaves. We can remedy those problems in one of several ways as follows:

```
CREATE TABLE INVOICE (
    InvoiceNumber          INTEGER        PRIMARY KEY,
    CustomerID             INTEGER,
    InvoiceDate            DATE,
    TotalCharge            NUMERIC (12,2),
    TotalRemitted          NUMERIC (12,2),
    FormOfPayment          CHAR (20),
    SalespersonID          INTEGER,
    CONSTRAINT CustFK FOREIGN KEY (CustomerID)
        REFERENCES CUSTOMERS (CustomerID)
            ON DELETE RESTRICT,
    CONSTRAINT SalesFK FOREIGN KEY (SalespersonID)
        REFERENCES EMPLOYEES (EmployeeID)
            ON DELETE CASCADE
) ;
```

By adding ON DELETE RESTRICT to the REFERENCES CUSTOMERS clause, we preserve referential integrity. If you try to delete a customer from the CUSTOMERS table that has purchases recorded in the INVOICE table, the DBMS returns an error code rather than performing the deletion. If you try to delete an employee from the employee table and that employee happens to be a salesperson who has sales recorded in the INVOICE table, the employee is deleted from the EMPLOYEES table and all the sales made by that employee are deleted from the INVOICE table.

You may or may not want to delete the sales of an ex-employee from the INVOICE table. If you want to retain those records because eventually that account will be assigned to another salesperson, you can modify the REFERENCES clause in another way:

```
CONSTRAINT SalesFK FOREIGN KEY (SalespersonID)
    REFERENCES EMPLOYEES (EmployeeID)
        ON DELETE SET NULL
```

This replaces the departed salesperson's EmployeeID with a NULL that you can later replace with the EmployeeID of the new salesperson.

Some of the same problems that can occur when you delete a record from the parent in a parent-child relationship can also occur when you update the primary key of a parent record. A primary key update disconnects any child tables that are linked via that primary key. Usually updating a primary key is a bad idea, but sometimes it is justifiable. When you do make such an update, you need to consider how to handle any records in child tables that will be affected. You may want to cascade the update with ON UPDATE CASCADE, or you may want to prevent the update with ON UPDATE RESTRICT.

Applying Constraints

10 Min.
To Go

In addition to the obvious components of a system, the entities, attributes, and relationships, there are the less obvious business rules. Business rules pose a particular challenge to the database developer because they are often not documented. System users know what the rules are and pass them on verbally to new coworkers. As a developer you need to tease this domain knowledge out of the domain experts who hold it.

When you design your database, you can translate your entities into tables, your entity attributes into table columns, your entity relationships into table relationships, and your business rules into constraints. Even if you are building a scientific database or some other non-business database, there are still going to be rules that apply to the entities in your system. You need to translate these into constraints in the database.

Sometimes you want to constrain what can be entered into a single table column. Other times you want to make a constraint that applies to an entire table. You may also want to place a constraint that deals with more than one table, on the database. These three types of constraints are called column constraints, table constraints, and assertions respectively.

Column constraints

When creating or altering a table, you specify three things about each column: the column name, its data type, and any constraints on that column. In Session 20, I state that a table's primary key should be unique and should not have a NULL value. You can enforce these rules with column constraints, and apply constraints to any other columns at the same time. Let's look at an example where I create a CUSTOMERS table using column constraints on CustomerID and also on CustName. I want to force the user to enter a customer's name or I will not accept a new customer record.

```
CREATE TABLE CUSTOMERS (
    CustomerID              INTEGER        NOT NULL,
    CustName                CHAR (25)      NOT NULL,
    Address1                CHAR (25),
    Address2                CHAR (25),
    City                    CHAR (20),
    StateOrProvince         CHAR (2),
    PostalCode              CHAR (10),
    Country                 CHAR (20),
    ContactName             CHAR (30),
    ContactPhone            CHAR (20),
    ContactFax              CHAR (20),
    ContactEmail            CHAR (30),
    Notes                   CLOB,
    UNIQUE (CustomerID)
) ;
```

The three column constraints applied in the above definition ensure that no record is added to the CUSTOMERS table that has a NULL CustomerID or a NULL CustName, or whose CustomerID duplicates an existing CustomerID (the UNIQUE constraint).

Table constraints

Table constraints apply to an entire table. They include the column constraints, such as the NOT NULL and UNIQUE constraints shown above. In addition, PRIMARY KEY, FOREIGN KEY, and CHECK constraints, which can apply to one or more columns, round out the set of possible table constraints. In the section on referential integrity in this session I show an example of the PRIMARY KEY and FOREIGN KEY constraints, repeated here:

```
CREATE TABLE INVOICE (
    InvoiceNumber           INTEGER        PRIMARY KEY,
    CustomerID              INTEGER,
    InvoiceDate             DATE,
    TotalCharge             NUMERIC (12,2),
    TotalRemitted           NUMERIC (12,2),
    FormOfPayment           CHAR (20),
    SalespersonID           INTEGER,
    CONSTRAINT CustFK FOREIGN KEY (CustomerID)
        REFERENCES CUSTOMERS (CustomerID)
            ON DELETE RESTRICT,
    CONSTRAINT SalesFK FOREIGN KEY (SalespersonID)
        REFERENCES EMPLOYEES (EmployeeID)
            ON DELETE CASCADE
) ;
```

I can add a CHECK constraint to prevent the user from entering a negative TotalCharge. That produces the following statement:

```
CREATE TABLE INVOICE (
    InvoiceNumber          INTEGER         PRIMARY KEY,
    CustomerID             INTEGER,
    InvoiceDate            DATE,
    TotalCharge            NUMERIC (12,2),
    TotalRemitted          NUMERIC (12,2),
    FormOfPayment          CHAR (20),
    SalespersonID          INTEGER,
    CONSTRAINT CustFK FOREIGN KEY (CustomerID)
        REFERENCES CUSTOMERS (CustomerID)
            ON DELETE RESTRICT,
    CONSTRAINT SalesFK FOREIGN KEY (SalespersonID)
        REFERENCES EMPLOYEES (EmployeeID)
            ON DELETE CASCADE,
    CHECK (TotalCharge >= 0.0)
) ;
```

In this case the PRIMARY KEY constraint, each of the FOREIGN KEY constraints, and the CHECK constraint all apply to only one column. However, they can apply to multiple columns if the tables involved had multi-column primary keys and if I were setting a range limit to more than one column with a CHECK constraint.

Assertions

Assertions are constraints that apply to more than one table. They are not a part of core SQL and are not currently supported by SQL Server 2000, Access 2000, Oracle 9i, PostgreSQL 7.1, or MySQL 4.0. However, when assertions are finally supported, and adhere to SQL:1999 syntax, an example would look like this:

```
CREATE ASSERTION
    CHECK (NOT EXISTS (SELECT * FROM CUSTOMERS, PROSPECTS
        WHERE CustName = ProspectName)) ;
```

This statement checks whether any of the customer names in the CUSTOMERS table match any of the prospect names in the PROSPECTS table. If an assertion returns a FALSE value, then the statement that makes the assertion go false (such as an attempted INSERT into the CUSTOMERS table of a company in the PROSPECTS table) is not committed. The INSERT fails.

Done!

REVIEW

Ensuring that the data that goes into your database is accurate and stays that way is vital. There are many things that can go wrong, and there are things you can do to prevent them from going wrong. When accepting data into a table, decide what the set of permissible values should be; then set a constraint to allow only those values. Recognize that hardware failures can happen or software bugs can surface at the most inopportune time, and protect yourself as best you can from such unhappy possibilities. At a minimum, this entails a strict multi-stage backup regimen. Make sure that you have actualized all of a system's business rules with constraints. If there are business rules that you do not translate into constraints, your database is likely to accept bad data and become progressively more corrupt.

QUIZ YOURSELF

1. What is the best way to prevent bad source data from getting into your database? (See "Problems with Database Data.")

2. What is the best way to protect your database from hardware failures and software bugs? (See "Problems with Database Data.")

3. Why is data redundancy a problem for data integrity? (See "Problems with Database Data.")

4. What are the three main types of integrity? (See "Maintaining Database Integrity.")

5. What constraint would you apply to a column to assure that no two rows contain the same value in that column? (See "Applying Constraints.")

Designing High-Integrity Databases

**30 Min.
To Go**

You want the databases you build to contain good information. Unfortunately, if your database tables are not structured properly, it will be difficult to keep your data from becoming progressively more corrupt. In this session, I discuss some of the most common structural problems that threaten data integrity in a database and how to modify database structure to avoid them.

Problems with Table Structure

In Session 1, I talk about the advantages of storing data in a structured database as compared to an unstructured flat file system. In the sessions that follow, I describe database structure in terms of two-dimensional tables with rows and columns. However, I did not formally describe exactly what a table is. In relational database practice, the notion of a table is somewhat more restricted than it is in common everyday use. In this book, when I speak of a table, I am talking about a structure with the following properties:

- Each cell in the table must contain a single value, if it contains any value at all. Repeating groups and arrays are not allowed as values.

- All the entries in any column must be of the same kind. A column that contains a customer name in one row must contain customer names in all rows that contain values.

- Each column has a unique name.
- The order of the columns doesn't matter.
- The order of the rows doesn't matter.
- No two rows may be identical.

Any table that has the properties listed above is said to be in First Normal Form (1NF). The idea of normal forms as applied to databases was introduced in a paper by E. F. Codd in 1970. That paper provided the theoretical foundation for relational database design. By insisting that all tables in a database must be in 1NF, you can avoid many problems. However, tables in 1NF are still susceptible to defects called modification anomalies.

Modification anomalies are problems that corrupt the data in a table when you modify it with either an insertion or a deletion. Consider the following example.

Suppose Xanthic Systems is expanding and has just moved into a new facility. The new facility has separate labs for different development teams. A new database table lists employees, the teams they are on, and the locations of the labs for each team. Table 22-1 shows what this table looks like.

Table 22-1 *Xanthic Systems Technical Employee Locator*

Employee Name	Team	Room
Descartes, R.	Applied Mathematics	201
Babbage, C.	Computation Hardware	102
Lovelace, A.	System Software	101
Von Neumann, J.	Architecture	202
Hopper, G.	Language Development	103

This table looks fine. It satisfies all the criteria of 1NF and it tells us what we want to know. It tells us which lab each employee works in and where that lab is located. Is there a problem here?

Yes, there is a problem. What if Ms. Lovelace decides to move to England to marry a poet? If we remove her record from the table, we not only lose the fact that she works on the Systems Software team; we also lose the fact that the System Software team is located in room 101. This type of problem is called a *deletion anomaly*.

There is another problem. Suppose management decides to create a quantum computing team and hires E. Schrödinger as team leader. This fact cannot be recorded in the table until a building and room is assigned to the lab for the new team. This is called an *insertion anomaly*.

Yet another problem arises if Dr. Von Neumann is assigned to assist Mr. Babbage on the Computation Hardware team. To see how this may be a problem, look at Table 22-2.

Table 22-2   *Xanthic Systems Technical Employee Locator*

Employee Name	Team	Room
Descartes, R.	Applied Mathematics	201
Babbage, C.	Computation Hardware	102
Lovelace, A.	System Software	101
Von Neumann, J.	Architecture	202
Von Neumann, J.	Computation Hardware	102
Hopper, G.	Language Development	103

If I want to go see Dr. Von Neumann, should I look for him on the first floor or the second? The problem arises because we are asking one table to do too many things. On the one hand, we want it to tell us which teams various employees are on. On the other hand, we want it to tell us where the labs are for the various teams. It may not do a good job of telling us where to look for a particular employee.

Fixing Structural Problems with Normalization

The problem in the previous section stems from keys and dependencies. For a table to be in 1NF, every row must be distinguishable from every other row — every row must be unique. One way to guarantee that every row in a table is unique is to force it to have a primary key, which, by definition, is unique. All of the non-key attributes must depend on the key. Another way of saying the same thing is to say that if we find the primary key, we have also found all the non-key attributes for the row that has that primary key.

In the table illustrated in Table 22-1, it looked like Employee Name would be a good primary key. However, as soon as it became possible for an employee to be a member of more than one team, as shown in Table 22-2, Employee Name was not unique any more. At this point, the combination of Employee Name and Team could serve as a primary key. A key that is made up of more than one column is called a *composite key*.

The problem exposed by Table 22-2 comes about because Room, a non-key attribute, depends on Team but does not depend on Employee Name. When we have found Employee Name, we have not necessarily found Room. This problem motivated the creation of second normal form (2NF). A table is in 2NF if it is in 1NF and all non-key attributes are dependent on all of the primary keys. From this we see that any table that is in 1NF and has a single-column primary key is automatically in 2NF also.

Dependencies, Keys, and Ideas

**20 Min.
To Go**

In the 1970s, a race developed between anomalies and normal forms. As every new class of anomaly was recognized, a new, more restrictive normal form was invented to eliminate it. The conditions that can lead to anomalies became increasingly arcane and less likely to happen in actual practice. The remedy that all these normal forms use to eliminate the chance of anomalies is to break a table up into two or more tables such that all the non-key attributes depend on the key, the whole key, and nothing but the key. We can apply this to the database table illustrated in Table 22-2, breaking it up into two tables, each of which represents only one idea. Table 22-3 and Table 22-4 are the two resulting tables.

Table 22-3 *Xanthic Systems Technical Employee Team Assignments*

Employee Name	Team
Descartes, R.	Applied Mathematics
Babbage, C.	Computation Hardware
Lovelace, A.	System Software
Von Neumann, J.	Architecture
Von Neumann, J.	Computation Hardware
Hopper, G.	Language Development

Table 22-4 *Xanthic Systems Lab Locator*

Team	Room
Applied Mathematics	201
Computation Hardware	102
System Software	101
Architecture	202
Computation Hardware	102
Language Development	103

The Team Assignment table (Table 22-3) deals with the single idea of staff team assignments. The primary key is composed of both the Employee Name and Team columns. Now, if Ms. Lovelace leaves the firm to go to England, she can be removed from the team assignment table without our losing the fact that the System Software lab is located in room 101, which is preserved in the Lab Locator table (Table 22-4).

We can add Dr. Schrodinger to the Team Assignment table, as a member of the Quantum Computing team, even though no lab for that team has yet been assigned. The Lab Locator table deals with the single idea of where the labs for the various teams are located. The comings and goings of individual employees do not affect those room assignments.

The above example illustrates an important principle for designing databases with high integrity. A database table should deal with one and only one main idea. If you have a table that deals with more than one idea, break it up into smaller tables, each of which deals with only one idea. Couple this principle with the one stated above that all the non-key attributes of a table should depend on the key, the whole key, and nothing but the key. If you follow those two principles, you can be almost certain that your database is free of modification anomalies. I say "almost" certain because the normal forms developed in the 1970s (1NF, 2NF, 3NF, BCNF, 4NF, 5NF) have not been proven to eliminate all possible modification anomalies. That achievement had to wait until the 1980s.

The Simplicity of Domain Key Normal Form

In 1981, R. Fagin published a paper in the scholarly literature that introduced a new normal form that he called Domain/Key Normal Form (DKNF). In the paper he proved mathematically that a database whose tables are all in DKNF is anomaly-free. Surprisingly, DKNF is also much easier to understand than the other normal forms. The only problem with DKNF is that no method is known for automating the process of putting a database table into domain/key normal form. Human understanding is needed. This is not true of the other normal forms. If you start with a table in 1NF, algorithms exist for putting it into higher normal forms.

A database table is in DKNF if every constraint on the table is a logical consequence of the definition of keys and domains. The only things you need to understand to have a good grasp of DKNF are constraints, keys, and domains.

- A constraint is a rule that governs the static values of columns. Static values are those that do not vary with time.
- A key is a unique identifier of a table row.
- A domain is a description of the values that a column may hold.

If you enforce all key and domain restrictions on a table, then the table is in DKNF and guaranteed to be free of modification anomalies. To show how to put a table into DKNF, let's look at Xanthic's Technical Employee Locator table (Table 22-2), which we know contains anomalies, so cannot be in DKNF.

Table:	EMPLOYEELOCATOR(EmployeeName, Team, Room)
Key:	EmployeeName, Team
Constraints:	Team → Room* 100 <= Room <= 299

* Team → Room means Team determines Room. Room is functionally dependant on Team.

We know that the room numbers must fall between 100 and 299 because Xanthic's building has only two floors and the room numbering starts at 100 and 200 respectively.

The question we need to ask ourselves is, "Is every constraint on the table a logical consequence of the definition of keys and domains." There are two constraints. All we have to do is define the domain for Room as 100 <= Room <= 299 in order to satisfy the second constraint. The first constraint is a problem however. It has nothing to do with domains and Room does not depend on the whole key. The constraint (Team → Room) is not a logical consequence of the definition of the key because it does not depend on EmployeeName.

I can bring our database into compliance with DKNF by breaking EMPLOYEELOCATOR into two tables, each of which satisfies the requirements of DKNF.

Domain Definitions:

EmployeeName IN CHAR (30)

Team IN (Applied Mathematics, Computation Hardware, System Software, Architecture, Language Development, Quantum Computation)

100 <= Room <= 299

 EmployeeName's domain is a character string of 30 characters or less. The domain of Team is the complete list of teams. The domain of Room is an integer between 100 and 299.

Table and Key Definitions:

Table: TeamAssignment (EmployeeName, Team)

Key: EmployeeName, Team

Table: LabLocator (Team, Room)

Key: Team

Constraints: Team → Room   (Logical consequence of key)

        100 <= Room <= 299   (Logical consequence of domain)

The requirements of DKNF are satisfied. Every constraint on each table is a logical consequence of the definitions of keys and domains.

Better Designs through Denormalization?

Now that I have convinced you of the wisdom of normalizing your tables all the way to DKNF, let me reverse myself and discuss why in some cases it may not be best to normalize your tables that far. When you start with a database design that is already normalized and move in the other direction, combining separate tables into a single table, it is called *denormalization*.

The benefit of normalization is that it clusters attributes that all have to do with a single idea into a single table, separating them from attributes that primarily have to do with another idea. This reduces or eliminates the chance that modification anomalies can occur within the database's tables. Think about what effect this separation of attributes may have on performance.

Generally, when a person wants to retrieve information from a database system, that information involves several different ideas. This means that data must be pulled from multiple tables in a normalized database. Often the data in those tables must be combined in some way before the part you want can be retrieved. This combination operation, usually some kind of join, but possibly involving one of the other relational operators, takes time, perhaps an unacceptably long period of time.

With normalization, there is a tradeoff between data integrity and performance. You must find the balance between those two opposing system features that is appropriate for your particular application. You can normalize your tables to the point where performance becomes totally unacceptable. The solution to this dilemma is to normalize your tables as much as you can, fill them with data, then see how well your queries perform. If performance is acceptable, great! Leave everything the way it is.

If performance is not acceptable, investigate which particular operations are slowing you down and determine whether selectively denormalizing the tables involved brings performance into the acceptable range. If it does, go ahead with the denormalization, but pay close attention to what anomalies this will potentially allow. It may allow inconsistencies to creep into your data that you know you will never care about anyway. Or it may make you vulnerable to truly disastrous anomalies. You get to decide how best to deal with the performance/integrity tradeoff.

Done!

REVIEW

For a database to have value, it must contain correct data and must not contain incorrect data. It must hold all the data you expect it to contain and none of the extraneous data that you do not expect it to contain. A key technique (no pun intended) for assuring relational database integrity is normalization. Normalization separates collections of data into tables, each of which expresses a single idea. In a fully normalized database table all non-key attributes of a table should depend on the entire key and nothing else.

Valuable as the process of normalization is for preserving database integrity, sometimes it makes sense to denormalize a database in order to enhance performance. As a developer, you must exercise your judgment in finding the best balance between performance and integrity. A database with less than 100 percent assured integrity can still be valuable. In many cases the places where integrity may be compromised have no effect on the information you actually use from the database.

QUIZ YOURSELF

1. What are the defining characteristics of a table in first normal form? (See "Problems with Table Structure.")
2. What is one way to guarantee that every row in a table is unique? (See "Fixing Structural Problems with Normalization.")
3. How many ideas should a database table deal with? (See "Dependencies, Keys, and Ideas.")
4. What differentiates Domain/Key Normal Form from all the other normal forms? (See "The Simplicity of Domain/Key Normal Form.")
5. Why would you ever want to denormalize a database? (See "Better Designs Through Denormalization.")

Controlling Access to a Database

Session Checklist

✔ Who has access to my database and what can they do?

✔ Granting privileges

✔ Revoking privileges

✔ Granting the GRANT OPTION

**30 Min.
To Go**

Databases contain information that is important to the people or organizations that create them. In Session 21, I detail a number of things, such as hardware failures, software bugs, data entry errors, and intentional damage that can corrupt or destroy that important information. Backing up the database is your best defense against hardware failures and software bugs. Protecting the privacy and integrity of your database from unauthorized human access is a function that SQL performs.

Many databases contain a variety of data items, some more sensitive than others. You may want some things to be accessible only to a select group of people, such as executive management. You may want other things to be accessible only to a different select group, such as human resources department staff. Some less sensitive information may be available to customers, and even less sensitive information, such as product data sheets, may be available to anyone.

Who Has Access to My Database and What Can They Do?

SQL has a robust facility for controlling access to database data. There are four primary data access statements: SELECT, INSERT, UPDATE, and DELETE.

- Use SELECT to retrieve and view data in a database.
- Use INSERT to put new data into a database.

- Use UPDATE to change existing data in a database.
- Use DELETE to remove data from a database.

Clearly, some people need to be empowered to do *all* the above listed database operations. These people should be among the most highly trusted people in the organization. Other people may need to be able to add data to or change data in certain specific tables, but not others. These should also be highly trusted people.

Some people, in order to do their jobs, must be able to view data in certain specific tables that other people should not view. In addition, there may be some tables that everyone in the world can view. In the following sections, I discuss the different classes of users and the access privileges that each of them may have.

The database administrator

Someone must assume primary responsibility for the maintenance and health of any database. This person is called the *database administrator* (DBA). In a very small, understaffed organization where people customarily wear many hats, one of the application developers may also serve as DBA. In larger installations, not only can the database manager position be a full time job, but there may be several assistant DBAs as well.

The database administrator has all rights to every aspect of the database. This highly trusted person can execute SELECT, INSERT, UPDATE, and DELETE statements on any and all tables in the database, as well as perform a number of other maintenance tasks. Even the smallest organization should have more than one person with DBA privileges and the knowledge needed to exercise those privileges.

There are a number of ways in which any single individual may become unavailable to the organization. They may go on vacation in New Zealand. They may be in an automobile accident. They may be hired away by a competitor. They may just be out to lunch. Even a short period of unavailability can be disastrous if it comes at the wrong time. The organization's primary DBA should have at least one backup person, preferably two.

 Because DBAs have such awesome power, they should be very careful how they exercise it. A mistake while inserting, updating, or deleting can destroy the usefulness of important tables, perhaps even endangering the economic viability of the organization. For this reason, a person with DBA privileges should log in as DBA only when there is a specific task to perform that requires DBA privileges. When the task is complete, log out as DBA, and then log back in with your own personal login, which normally would have no rights to other peoples database objects and thus much less opportunity to cause havoc with other people's data. You can still cause havoc with your own data, however.

The database object owner

After the people who hold DBA privileges, the next most privileged class of user is the database object owner. Tables, views, and a few other things are considered database objects. The person who creates a database object is its owner, unless that person specifically designates someone else as the object owner. Database object owners have full rights to the objects they own. They can SELECT, INSERT, UPDATE, or DELETE at will. However, they have no special rights to anybody else's objects.

There are some complexities involved with object ownership. For example, one person can create and own a view into a table owned by another person. However, the person owning the view is not able to see or do anything through it that they do not have the right to see or do with the table itself. In other words, creating a view into another person's table doesn't allow the view creator to do anything to the table that they can't do directly to the table. The view merely serves to filter out data that is not of interest.

Privileged users

The DBA and database owners have the right to grant access to database objects to other users. Such grantees are considered privileged users. As a database owner, you can grant SELECT, INSERT, UPDATE, or DELETE rights to whomever you choose. You can grant a different package of rights to each different privileged user if you wish, or you may grant a defined set of rights to an entire class of users, such as all executives, all salespeople, or all human resources staffers.

The public

The last group of people that can access a database includes the people who have no special access privileges. When a DBA or object owner grants rights to PUBLIC, they are granting those rights to anyone who has physical access to the database and can call it up on a client computer. Objects that are accessible to the public should not contain anything that you would want to conceal from anyone who has such access.

**20 Min.
To Go**

Granting Privileges

The DBA not only has the power to perform any legal operation on a database, but also has the power to grant to others the right to perform any legal operation on that database. In addition, database object owners can grant access to the objects they own to other people. This granting of privileges is done with the GRANT statement, which has the following syntax:

```
GRANT privilege-list
    ON object
    TO user-list
    [WITH GRANT OPTION] ;
```

The privilege list can include any combination of the SELECT, INSERT, UPDATE, DELETE, REFERENCES, and USAGE privileges. In this session I briefly describe each of these. Objects can be tables, domains, character sets, collations, or translations. I talk about these, too. The user list is a list of login IDs that receive the privileges in the privilege list. The user list can include PUBLIC, in which case everyone is a grantee of the listed privileges. The optional WITH GRANT OPTION clause gives the grantee not only the right to exercise the listed privileges, but to grant them to others.

Roles

When a DBA or object owner grants individual privileges to individual users, it is easy to make sure that exactly the right privileges are being granted to exactly the right people. However, this can also be awfully tedious. What if there are 20 people who all have the same duties and all need the same privileges? It sure would be nice to handle the whole matter in one operation rather than having to do the same thing 20 times. SQL provides for this need with the concept of roles.

A *role* is a function in the organization rather than a person. You can assign all the people who perform the same function the same role. Then, by granting a package of privileges to the role, all the people who are members of that role automatically acquire those privileges. This saves DBAs and object owners a lot of typing, especially in large organizations.

 Roles are not a part of core SQL and so may not be supported by your DBMS. Oracle 9i and SQL Server 2000 support roles, and so does PostgreSQL 7.1, but in PostgreSQL roles are called *groups*. MySQL 4.0 and Access 2000 do not support roles.

To create a role with SQL, enter code similar to the following:

```
CREATE ROLE SecurityGuard ;
```

After you have created a role, you can assign users to it and grant privileges to it in the same manner that you grant privileges to an individual user.

Looking at data

You are going to want to give some people the right to look at the data in certain database tables, in order for them to do their jobs. You can do so by granting the SELECT privilege as shown here:

```
GRANT SELECT
    ON EMPLOYEES
    TO SecurityGuard ;
```

This allows any security guard to check the status of a person trying to enter the facility after hours, claiming to be an employee.

 If a table, such as the EMPLOYEES table, contains sensitive information (for example, salary data) that should not be viewed by a security guard, you can create a view that holds only the non-sensitive data and then grant the SecurityGuard role the SELECT privilege to the view rather than to the underlying table.

For information that you want to be available to anyone and everyone, you can grant SELECT access to PUBLIC.

```
GRANT SELECT
    ON PRICELIST
    TO PUBLIC ;
```

Inserting new data

The GRANT statement works pretty much the same way for all privileges. Here's an example of how you can use it to grant the INSERT privilege:

```
GRANT INSERT
    ON PRICELIST
    TO SalesManager ;
```

This statement allows anyone that has the sales manager role to add new product records to the PRICELIST table.

Changing existing data

Things change all the time. Some types of data are more volatile than others, but it would be hard to think of a database table that didn't need to be updated at least occasionally. Somebody needs to be empowered to make those changes. You can give them the power like this:

```
GRANT UPDATE (Price)
    ON PRICELIST
    TO SalesClerk ;
```

This statement allows any sales clerk to modify entries in the Price column of the PRICELIST table. The other columns in the PRICELIST table are not affected by this grant.

Deleting obsolete data

Just as records in a database table need to be modified from time to time, sometimes you need to completely delete records. You want to be pretty careful about who you grant the DELETE privilege to because that person can completely obliterate the contents of your table. Here's an example of how you grant the DELETE privilege:

```
GRANT DELETE
    ON CUSTOMERS
    TO SalesManager ;
```

The sales manager is likely the one to personally decide which customers should be deleted from the database and which should remain.

Referencing related tables

We have seen that in a relational database, tables are related to one another. Tables that are directly related generally have the primary key of one table serving as a foreign key in the other. The intimacy of this relationship, which is beneficial in many ways, also creates the potential for a security breach. If a table that contains sensitive information is directly related to another table that does not, the second table can serve as a dangerous "back door" that allows unauthorized access to the sensitive information in the first table.

Suppose you are the chief financial officer of a company and you have a table named TARGETS. It contains information on companies your company is considering as takeover targets. Knowledge of this information can give a stock speculator an unfair advantage in trading the stock of the target companies because acquiring companies often pay a substantial premium over the current price at which the stock of a takeover target is trading. This is why you, as an insider, are not allowed to take unfair advantage of your knowledge. What if some unscrupulous employees decide to supplement their income? What can such people do?

They would only have to know a couple of key facts in order to exploit the opportunity. They would have to know that the name of your table is TARGETS, and they would have to know the name of a column in that table, for example, StockSymbol.

How can they do this? By creating a new table that references your TARGETS table.

```
CREATE TABLE CRACKER
   (StockSymbol CHAR (5)
   REFERENCES TARGETS) ;
```

Now all they have to do is attempt to INSERT into CRACKER the stock symbols of all likely candidates on the New York Stock Exchange, the American Stock Exchange, or the NASDAQ stock exchange. Any inserts that succeed are the symbols of companies in the TARGETS table. All other attempted inserts fail. Now they can buy stock in the target companies and wait for you to make your move.

You can prevent this type of harmful and illegal activity by restricting the list of people you grant references rights to. Grant them only to highly trusted people.

```
GRANT REFERENCES (StockSymbol)
   ON TARGETS
   TO Directors ;
```

With this precaution, only members of your company's board of directors, who are also considered to be insiders, are able to create tables that reference the StockSymbol column of the TARGETS table.

Using domains and other types of objects

In Session 21, in the discussion of domain integrity, I give an example of how to create a domain. Domains are valuable for maintaining integrity because they don't allow users to insert values into a column that are not members of the domain defined for that column. Domains also can save you considerable labor when creating tables.

Consider the likely scenario in business where you have multiple tables that all have a Price column. In all tables Price is of the same type and has the same constraints on it. For example, Price is always of the DECIMAL type, is never negative, and is never greater than $10,000. You can create a domain for all these Price columns in all the tables in your database that have Price columns, with a single CREATE DOMAIN statement, such as:

```
CREATE DOMAIN PRICEDOMAIN DECIMAL (10,2)
   CHECK (Price >= 0 AND Price <= 10000) ;
```

Now, after creating tables that have a Price column in them, none of these tables accept an entry with a type that does not conform to DECIMAL (10,2), nor do they accept any entry that falls outside the range 0 <= Price <= 10000.

When you create a table that has a Price column, specify the domain instead of the type for that column, similar to the following:

```
CREATE TABLE PRICELIST
   ProductID            INTEGER        PRIMARY KEY,
   ProductName     CHAR (30),
   Price           PRICEDOMAIN ;
```

The domain's type definition and constraint definition are automatically applied to the new table.

As was the case with REFERENCES, there is a security concern involved with the use of domains. In the case of a price list, you probably don't care who knows what the upper limit on your pricing is. However, there are other cases where you may want to specify a range of values with a domain, where the upper or lower limit may be confidential. Any unauthorized persons who wanted to find out those limits can easily do it by creating a table containing a column that used your domain in its definition. Then all they would have to do would be to continually insert numbers into that field until an insert failed because of a constraint violation. That failure would reveal the limit.

You can protect yourself from this type of hack by restricting who can use any domain that contains sensitive information. Apply such a restriction by explicitly granting domain usage to people authorized to have the sensitive information, and not granting such usage to anybody else. You can do that with statements similar to this:

```
GRANT USAGE ON DOMAIN PRICEDOMAIN TO SalesManager ;
```

Aside from domains, you can also grant usage to character sets, collations, and translations. Only those users granted usage of specific character sets, collations, and translations will be able to access them. There is no mystery about what a character set is. An organization's primary work may be conducted with the ASCII character set, but for some work other character sets may be needed, such as Spanish, German, Russian, or Greek. You can control the use of these character sets with a GRANT USAGE ON CHARACTER SET statement.

A *collation* is a set of rules that determine how strings in a character set compare with one another. Every character set has a default collation. In the default collation of the ASCII character set, A comes before B, B comes before C, and so on. A is considered to be less than B and B is considered to be less than C. With a GRANT USAGE ON COLLATION statement, you can enable a user to use a different collation from the default.

SQL's translation facility enables users to translate data that is stored in one character set into another character set. This is useful for instance, if your printer does not support the character set your data is stored in. You can translate it into a supported character set before printing. Give other people this ability with a GRANT USAGE ON TRANSLATION statement.

**10 Min.
To Go**

Granting the GRANT OPTION

In a large organization with a dynamic database that changes frequently, it may be too much of a burden on the DBA or database object owner to constantly be monitoring and adjusting the privileges granted to each user. SQL gives DBAs and object owners the ability to delegate the right to grant privileges. You can do this by granting privileges WITH GRANT

OPTION. This gives the grantee the right to use the privilege and also the right to pass that privilege on to other users. Here's an example:

```
GRANT INSERT
   ON CUSTOMERS
   TO SalesManager
   WITH GRANT OPTION ;
```

After this statement takes effect, the sales manager can add new customers to the CUS-TOMERS table and can also grant assistant sales managers, or anyone else, the right to add new customers also.

Revoking Privileges

If you are going to grant privileges to people, you'd better be able to revoke them, too. People's jobs change, which changes their need to access specific data. Sometimes people even leave the organization and join a competitor. In cases such as that, you definitely want to revoke any and all privileges that they have. You can revoke a grant and you can also revoke the GRANT OPTION privilege with a REVOKE statement. Syntax is:

```
REVOKE [GRANT OPTION FOR] privilege-list
   ON object
   FROM user-list [RESTRICT|CASCADE] ;
```

This syntax requires some explanation. With the optional GRANT OPTION FOR clause, you can revoke a person's right to grant the listed privileges to others, without revoking their right to use the privilege themselves. If you do not use the optional GRANT OPTION FOR clause, then the revocation will revoke the grantees privileges along with the privilege of granting those privileges to others. The user list specifies which particular users or roles are having their privileges revoked.

The most complex part of this operation involves the RESTRICT and CASCADE keywords. These come into play if the grantee whose privileges you are revoking has granted privileges to someone else, using the WITH GRANT OPTION clause.

If you revoke the listed privileges of a user or role, using the CASCADE keyword, then the listed privileges of the named grantee are revoked and so are the listed privileges of anyone the named grantee has granted privileges to, or anyone the sub-grantee has granted privileges to, all the way down the chain of privilege granting. So, like falling dominoes, a whole string of grants can potentially be revoked. Privileges that are not named in the privilege list are unaffected.

If you revoke the privileges of a user or role, using the RESTRICT keyword, then what happens depends on whether the named grantee has granted the listed privileges to someone else. If not, then the named grantee's listed privileges are revoked. However, if the named grantee has granted any of the listed privileges to someone else, the REVOKE statement fails and returns an error code.

When you revoke someone's privileges with the REVOKE statement, they may still be able to exercise those privileges. Suppose the object owner grants the DELETE privilege to person A WITH GRANT OPTION and also to person B. Now suppose person A also grants person B the DELETE privilege. If at a later time *you* revoke person B's DELETE privilege, the privilege he obtained from person A is still in effect. Chains of dependency in privilege granting can become maddeningly complex. It is the responsibility of the object owner to keep tight control of this, being very careful about to whom the grant option is given.

Done!

REVIEW

Databases can contain important information. For many organizations, the information in their databases is critical to survival. Great harm can be done if this information should be destroyed, corrupted, or if it should fall into the wrong hands. Strong measures must be available to control who has access to the contents of a database, and further to control what kind of access they have. SQL provides this control with its GRANT and REVOKE statements.

There is a hierarchy of control of database access with the database administrator at the top of the hierarchy. The DBA is omnipotent when it comes to the database; he or she can do anything. Next in the hierarchy are the various database object owners, who have absolute power within their own domains, namely the objects they have created. Database object owners can grant access privileges to people or roles that they choose. These grantees, if they have received the GRANT OPTION, can then grant the privileges they have to other people or roles. At the bottom of the access hierarchy is the PUBLIC. Any member of the PUBLIC who is not otherwise a privileged user, may only exercise those privileges that have been granted to the PUBLIC.

Defining domains can make the process of creating tables easier, but can also add complexities to a database's security system. The ability to use domains can be granted and revoked the same way that access to tables can be granted and revoked. The use of character sets, collations, and translations are also subject to grants from the object owner who created them.

QUIZ YOURSELF

1. What privilege must a person have in order to change the data in a column of a database table? (See "Who Has Access to My Database and What Can They Do?")

2. People who act as database administrators usually have two login IDs, one as DBA and one as their personal account. Which should they use when they want to work exclusively within a database they have created as part of an application development project? (See "Who Has Access to My Database and What Can They Do?")

3. If a database owner grants a privilege to a user `WITH GRANT OPTION`, will the database owner always be able to `REVOKE` that privilege at a later time? (See "Revoking Privileges.")

4. Write an SQL statement that revokes the `UPDATE` privilege on the `CUSTOMERS` table from a user named Smith. (See "Revoking Privileges.")

Protecting the Contents of a Database

Session Checklist

✔ Identifying the major threats to database integrity

✔ Avoiding resource conflicts with locking

✔ Averting data corruption with transactions

✔ Assuring database integrity with ACID

30 Min. To Go

I n Session 23, I enumerate various bad things that can happen to a database as a result of hardware failure, software bugs, or accidental or malicious human activity. Those are not the only threats that a database faces. There are also serious threats that arise from perfectly normal and legitimate human activity. In this session, I cover the tools that SQL provides to address both classes of threats.

Threats to Database Integrity

Some threats to database integrity can be parried by restricting access to the database, as covered in Session 23. Other threats, not due to accidental or intentional interference, require other solutions. One class of problems comes from the *platform,* which is the hardware and software that you are running on. Another class is a result of multi-user operation. Today, with practically all computers connected to either wired or wireless networks, multi-user operation is the norm and standalone operation the exception.

Platform problems

From the point of view of the database, the platform is everything the database relies on in order to be able to run. Thus the platform includes the database management system, the operating system, the drivers, the BIOS (Basic Input/Output System), and the system hardware, including processor, RAM, disk, and input-output devices. A problem in any one of these areas can cause your database to deliver incorrect results or, more likely, no results at all.

Generally, the highest incidence of problems occurs when a system is new. Perhaps all the components are new and thus untried. Even if the components are not new, perhaps they are being used in a new way when you install your database system. This can expose problems that have been there all along, but that never surfaced before. After all the initial problems have been solved, things usually settle down to a relatively trouble-free mode of operation. Things run pretty smoothly until one of the components of your system changes.

Problems that occur when something has changed

Every aspect of technology is changing, and changing at an ever-increasing rate. People are upgrading their hardware more often than ever before. They are moving to new releases of their operating system more often than ever before. They are even migrating to the latest release of their DBMS more often than ever before. All the upgrades, moves, and migrations add a host of new unknowns to any installation. Incompatibilities surface. Bugs that have been latent in your system all along are exposed by a new component that exercises the code the bugs are hiding in for the first time.

Problems due to incompatibilities and newly revealed latent bugs are often the hardest things to track down and fix. If your organization depends on your database being available and reliable, these kinds of problems can be very costly.

Never run important production work on a system that has just been upgraded in any way. The risks are just too great. Instead, install the upgrade on a parallel system, running a clone of your database. Work out the bugs on expendable data. Keep your live data on a system running on known, reliable hardware. Switch your live data over to the upgraded system only after it has proven itself and you are confident that it is at least as reliable as your existing system is.

Problems that occur even though nothing has changed

Although systems with a new component are at higher risk of failure, any system, even one that has been working reliably for years, can fail on you at any time. Nothing lasts forever. Hardware components wear out or deteriorate. Software may slow down or even come to a grinding halt when your database grows beyond some threshold size. Hardware problems and software problems must be addressed in fundamentally different ways.

Dealing with hardware problems

Because any piece of hardware can fail at any time without warning, your best defense is redundancy. If that sounds paradoxical, it is. Throughout this book I have warned you about the danger of redundancy in the data in your database. Redundant data is an open invitation to data inconsistency, which leads to progressive data corruption. Redundant data is a bad thing.

However, redundant hardware is a good thing. If you have two printers and one breaks, you can still print on the other one. If you have multiple hard disks in a RAID (Redundant

Array of Inexpensive Disks) and one breaks, you have not totally lost all your data — your processing is just slowed down a little until you can install a hot spare. (A *hot spare* is one you plug in while the system is still running. The operating system automatically configures it and loads it with data.)

The ultimate in hardware redundancy is to completely duplicate your main system and run the duplicate in parallel. In this case, if either system breaks, there is no downtime whatsoever. Fix the faulty machine and bring it up again; then synchronize it to the one that has been working all along. You are back at full strength again. Critical real-time systems such as airline reservation systems have this kind of redundancy. Operators of less critical systems get by with lesser levels of redundancy and are willing to suffer the consequences in downtime when failures occur.

Dealing with software problems

When your database and the applications that use it start to outgrow the DBMS or operating system that they are running on, performance can suffer, or the system may just die outright. If you can't downsize your database or application, the only solution is for the DBA to upgrade the platform they are running on. This, as noted above, leads to another set of problems. It is important to see that your software platform is being overstressed before it reaches a critical stage. Deal with it before it fails catastrophically on you. Follow these steps:

- Set up a parallel system.
- Put a clone of your production system on it.
- Work out the bugs.
- Migrate you production system to the upgraded system.

Collisions due to concurrent access

Even if your hardware and software are both rock-solid stable and working exactly the way they are supposed to work, you can still have problems if two people both try to access the same data at the same time. This type of problem is best illustrated with an example, so let's consider one.

Suppose Xanthic Systems has an order entry system that accesses four tables: ORDER, ORDERLINE, CUSTOMERS, and INVENTORY.

- The ORDER table holds all the data about each specific order, such as OrderNumber, CustomerID, Salesperson, Terms, Date, TotalSale, Tax, and Shipping.
- The ORDERLINE table holds details about each individual line on the order, such as ProductID, ProductName, Description, Quantity, Price, and ExtendedPrice.
- The CUSTOMERS table holds the CustomerID, CustomerName, Address, and so on.
- The INVENTORY table records the quantity of each of Xanthic's products that is currently in stock.

Now suppose that Xanthic has an "all or nothing" policy on shipping orders. They do not make partial shipments. If all the items on an invoice are in inventory, the order is shipped; otherwise, shipment is delayed until all items are available.

You write code for the order processing application that checks the INVENTORY table to see if everything on the order is available. If it is, you generate a packing slip and update the QuantityOnHand field of the INVENTORY table to indicate that the ordered items have now been sold and are no longer available. There are two different ways you can handle this situation.

- **Method 1:** Process each row in the INVENTORY table that corresponds to a row in the ORDERLINE table. If QuantityOnHand is large enough, mark the quantity ordered as committed, thus removing them from available stock. If QuantityOnHand is not large enough, roll back the entire order to restore the inventory levels for all items to what they were before you started processing the current order.
- **Method 2:** Check the inventory levels for all items on the order. Process the order only if the inventory levels for all items are sufficient.

If you almost always have enough inventory on hand to fill orders, then Method 1 is more efficient. Each row is accessed only once. In Method 2 each row must be accessed twice. Conversely, if you frequently get orders that cannot be filled, then Method 2 is more efficient. You don't waste a lot of time rolling back aborted orders.

Let's examine these two methods, and how they may respond to multiple users trying to access the INVENTORY table at the same time.

- **Scenario 1:** The system is written to handle orders using Method 1. User 1 starts processing Order 1, which asks for ten pieces of Item 1. Your program checks and finds that exactly ten pieces of Item 1 are available, so marks all ten pieces in QuantityOnHand as committed, them moves on to process Item 2. Meanwhile, User 2 starts processing Order 2, which asks for one piece of Item 1. Your program checks and finds that now no Item 1 is available, so User 2's order is aborted. By this time, User 1 has started checking for Item 2. Finding that none are in stock, User 1's order is aborted also. The result is that neither order gets shipped, even though User 2's order could have been. Revenue is lost and a customer is unnecessarily disappointed.
- **Scenario 2:** The system is written to handle orders using Method 2. User 1, in processing Order 1 scans the INVENTORY table to see if there is adequate stock of all 257 items on the order, and finds that there is. Meanwhile, User 2, processing Order 2, scans for the one item on his order, finds it and commits it. Now when User 1's process gets to that item again, it is no longer available and User 1's big order fails, rolling back and taking up a lot of time and system resources in the process. Revenue is lost and a high volume customer is disappointed.

Both methods of processing are susceptible to problems due to unwanted interaction between users. Preventing these types of conflicts is clearly important for any multi-user database system. The primary method for preventing such conflicts is locking.

Locking

An easy way to prevent data access conflicts is to restrict access to a resource such as a table to one user at a time. This act of restriction is called *locking* the resource. There are several varieties of locks:

- A *read lock* prevents a second user from reading the contents of a resource while it is locked by the first user.

- A *write lock* prevents a second user from changing the contents of a resource while it is locked by the first user.

- A *full lock* prevents a second user from both reading and changing the contents of a resource while it is locked by the first user.

Locks are great for preserving system integrity but can kill performance when multiple people want to access the same resource at the same time. In the example above, when Xanthic is receiving a lot of orders, many people are going to want to access the INVENTORY table at the same time. Allowing only one person to access it at a time has a drastic effect on the speed with which orders get processed.

The performance problem brought on by locking brings up the subject of *granularity*. The granularity of a lock can be coarse-grained, medium-grained, or fine-grained. An example of a coarse-grained lock would be one that locks the entire database. This is something that the DBA would use while making a structural change to the database. Coarse-grained locks should be done only when activity is at a minimum. To lock an entire table is an example of a medium-grained lock. Access to other tables is not restricted, but if many people all want to access the locked table, locking it creates a bottleneck. Locking a single row in a table is an example of a fine-grained lock. Other users can access all the other rows of the table without problem, each applying their own row lock to the row they are working on. The probability of conflict is much reduced (although not eliminated entirely).

What kind of locking should you use in Scenario 1 above? A row lock would not prevent the problem described in Scenario 1. During User 1's scan, a row lock would be placed and then released on the Item that User 2 wants to order. Later User 2 would lock that row, but find that all stock of the item is already committed. User 2 would then release the lock and abort Order 2. User 1 would then check for Item 2, find none available, and abort Order 1. A table lock would prevent the conflict, but would tie up the INVENTORY table for the entire time that Order 1 was being processed.

What kind of locking should you use in Scenario 2 above? In this case also, row locking would not help. User 1 would lock each row sequentially during the scan, releasing each one as it moves to the next. User 2 would come in behind User 1, lock a row that User 1 had already locked and released, commit the available inventory, then release the lock. Now when User 1 attempts to order the product in that row, the order fails because no uncommitted stock is left. Once again a table lock would prevent this problem. User 1, arriving first, would lock the table and perform her entire large order before releasing the lock. User 2, coming in later, would not be able to fill his small order, but that is probably the best we can do, considering the amount of product available.

Transactions

SQL controls the application and release of locks with transactions. An SQL transaction encapsulates all the SQL statements that look at or change the contents of a database. Based on what you, the programmer, specify for transaction characteristics, the SQL database engine will determine how aggressive to be in locking resources while your transaction is active. A transaction ends in one of two ways, either with a COMMIT or a ROLLBACK. If everything went as planned and there were not problems, it ends with a COMMIT. This makes permanent all the changes you have made to the database during the course of the transaction. If anything went wrong, the transaction ends with a ROLLBACK, which undoes any changes that were made during the transaction.

Before SQL:1999, ANSI Standard SQL (SQL-92) protected you by automatically considering each individual SQL statement to be a transaction. Thus as each statement in your program was executed, it was either committed or rolled back, as appropriate. Now, with SQL:1999 statements not necessarily being atomic, by surrounding your code with BEGIN ATOMIC and END keywords, you can guarantee that a series of SQL statements is considered as a single transaction and that locks remain in place until you are through with them.

Choosing the appropriate isolation level

Ideally, you would like complete and total isolation between what one user is doing with a database and what all the other users are doing. That would mean that there is no possibility of conflicts due to concurrent access of the same resource. However, total isolation comes at what can be a high cost: reduced performance. It is similar to the situation where everyone who comes to the bank is forced to wait in one long line to be served by a single bank teller. Having multiple lines going to multiple tellers is much more efficient. Everyone receives faster service and goes away happier.

SQL allows several levels of isolation that are less than complete. The less the isolation level, the greater the performance. You can choose the tradeoff between isolation and performance that is most appropriate for the task you are performing. The least protective and highest performing isolation level is READ UNCOMMITTED.

READ UNCOMMITTED

Transactions running at the READ UNCOMMITTED isolation level are susceptible to the _dirty read_ problem. A dirty read occurs when one user makes a change; then a second user reads the new value before the first user commits the transaction. If the first user rolls back the transaction rather than committing it, the second user will have retrieved an incorrect value. This can cause the second user to make a bad decision, based on bad data.

READ COMMITTED

Somewhat better than the READ UNCOMMITTED isolation level is the READ COMMITTED isolation level. It is not subject to the dirty read. However, it does have a different problem, the _non-repeatable read_. The non-repeatable read is the problem illustrated in Scenario 2 above. User 1 reads a location but does not commit her transaction yet. User 2 changes the same location and commits. Now User 1 wants to change the location, but it no longer contains the same value it did when User 1 first read it. This is a classic case of a non-repeatable read.

REPEATABLE READ

The REPEATABLE READ isolation level protects you from the non-repeatable read, as its name implies. However, it is still subject to the elusive phantom read. A _phantom read_ occurs when the data in a database changes while you are looking at it. Consider the case where User1 issues a SELECT statement that returns a result set consisting of multiple rows.

Meanwhile, User 2 updates some of the rows that User 1 had retrieved and commits the transaction. Now some of the rows that originally met User 1's search condition no longer do, and some of the rows that did not meet User 1's search condition meet it now. If User 1 now issues a statement based on what was retrieved with the original read, it operates on different data than User 1 thinks it does. The results are not correct, but there may be no way for User 1 to tell that there is a problem. User 1 can make a bad decision based on this incorrect data.

SERIALIZABLE

SERIALIZABLE is the highest isolation level provided by SQL. A transaction is serializable if the result of the transaction is the same as it would be if the transaction were run by itself, with no competing transactions running at the same time. Depending on the DBMS, serializable transactions may not actually be run serially. There can be some overlap, but not in such a way that would affect the outcome of any of the transactions involved. Serializable transactions are not subject to the phantom read, the non-repeatable read, or the dirty read. Serializable transactions are the safest, but they also have the largest impact on system performance.

**10 Min.
To Go**

The default transaction

If you don't explicitly set the characteristics of a transaction, SQL executes the transaction with default characteristics. A transaction has three characteristics: mode, isolation level, and diagnostic area size. The default values for mode and isolation level are based on two assumptions:

- People are going to want to make changes to the database.
- When in doubt, pick the safest alternative.

There are two possible modes, READ ONLY and READ-WRITE. As the names of the modes indicate, a person with READ ONLY access to the resources accessed in a transaction can SELECT but cannot INSERT, UPDATE, or DELETE anything. A person with READ-WRITE access can do all those things.

The safest isolation level is SERIALIZABLE, so the default transaction sets mode to READ-WRITE and isolation level to SERIALIZABLE. The default value for the third characteristic, DIAGNOSTICS SIZE may vary from one DBMS to another, so you have to consult your DBMS's documentation to find out what it is for your particular platform.

Setting your own transaction characteristics

If you want to build a transaction that has characteristics other than the default characteristics, you can do so with a SET TRANSACTION statement. For example, if you want a quick answer to a question and approximate results will do, you may start your transaction with the following statement:

```
SET TRANSACTION
    READ ONLY,
    ISOLATION LEVEL READ UNCOMMITTED,
    DIAGNOSTICS SIZE 4 ;
```

This statement allows the following statements in the transaction to read but not change anything. It sets the lowest isolation level to favor speed over accuracy, and sets the diagnostics size to capture error information on up to four errors that the transaction may cause.

If you wanted to make changes to the database, and data integrity is important, then you may start your transaction with a somewhat different statement:

```
SET TRANSACTION
   READ-WRITE,
   ISOLATION LEVEL SERIALIZABLE,
   DIAGNOSTICS SIZE 8 ;
```

This statement allows you to make changes to the database, sets the highest and safest isolation level and sets the diagnostic area to capture information on up to eight errors.

Making changes permanent

When you have done everything you want to do in a transaction and no error codes have been returned, to make any changes permanent and close the transaction, issue a COMMIT statement. At this point you can begin another transaction, execute SQL code that does not require the protection of a transaction, or execute host language code to alter the flow of execution of your application.

Returning the database to its original state

Everything doesn't go right all the time. Sometimes bad things happen to good people. When this happens to you in the form of a transaction that encounters errors, issue a ROLLBACK statement to return the database to the state it was in before you started. You can do this by checking for a returned error code after executing a statement that may cause an error. If no error code is returned, you can proceed with your transaction. However, if you do get an error, branch to an error handling routine that includes a ROLLBACK statement. That way, you can be sure the database is in no worse shape than it was in before you started the faulty transaction.

ACID

ACID is the acronym for the four hallmarks of a well-designed, reliable transaction. The letters stand for Atomicity, Consistency, Isolation, and Durability. When you design a transaction, make sure it has these four characteristics.

- **Atomicity:** A transaction is treated as an indivisible unit. Either it is executed in its entirety and committed or it is rolled back and leaves the database unaltered.

- **Consistency:** The state of the database after the transaction is committed is consistent with the state of the database and the input data before the transaction started. Thus if you had a starting bank balance and a deposit amount, after the transaction completes, the bank balance should equal the starting balance plus the deposit.

- **Isolation:** The full isolation characteristic of serializable transactions is ideal. In some circumstances lesser levels of isolation may be acceptable.
- **Durability:** After a transaction is either committed or rolled back, you should be able to count on the fact that the database contains the data you expect it to. Even if a catastrophic hardware failure happens after you commit but before the transaction is copied from RAM to hard disk, a durable system recovers the correct data.

Done!

REVIEW

Protecting databases from harm must be a major concern of database application programmers as well as database administrators. A variety of things can threaten database integrity and it is important to have countermeasures in place for all of them. Hardware and software problems can often be handled by judiciously adding redundancy to the hardware and by being conservative about upgrading to both new hardware and new software.

Integrity problems caused by concurrent access by multiple users require a different set of countermeasures. SQL-based database management systems provide automatic locking within the scope of transactions to prevent the corruption that can be caused by access conflicts. As is true in many areas, there is a tradeoff between system performance and data integrity. You need to find a balance of those two characteristics that is appropriate to what you are trying to achieve with your application. A well-designed DBMS ensures that your transactions are always atomic, consistent, and durable. You get to decide how high an isolation level your system will have.

QUIZ YOURSELF

1. After a database system has been running correctly for a period of time, what event is most likely to suddenly cause problems? (See "Threats to Database Integrity.")
2. How can you protect your system's productivity when you experience a hardware failure? (See "Threats to Database Integrity.")
3. What is the best time for a DBA to make structural changes to a database? (See "Locking.")
4. What is the safest isolation level for a transaction? (See "Transactions.")
5. What is the database characteristic that says a database will be recoverable even if the worst imaginable failure happens at the worst possible time? (See "ACID.")

Performance Tuning

Session Checklist

✔ Deciding on an appropriate system size

✔ Tuning applications for best performance

✔ Tuning the DBMS for best performance

✔ Addressing performance problems

**30 Min.
To Go**

A database system is a big, complex combination of many big and complex components. To achieve satisfactory performance, each of the components must be operating optimally, as well as interacting with the other components in an optimal manner. Because the demands on most systems change continually, performance optimization is a never-ending job.

A performance level that was more than adequate last week may have degraded by today to a point where users are firing off angry e-mails to the DBA. If you happen to be the person on the receiving end of those e-mails, there are a number of things you can do to restore performance to an acceptable level. Poor performance can be due to problems in any one of several areas. In this session, I discuss them all in turn and then give a step-by-step procedure for returning your system to a performance level that will brighten the day of your most dissatisfied user.

System Sizing and Capacity Planning

Clearly, the best time to address the question of how to achieve acceptable database performance is before you design the system to deliver that performance. Estimating the probable load on the server, both currently and in the foreseeable future, gives you an idea of what you need in terms of processing power, memory, and disk storage.

The main thing that a database server does is I/O (input/output). It receives requests from the client machines in the form of SQL statements, accesses data on disk, and then returns results to the clients. Thus the number of transactions the server is called upon to handle per unit time, and the time it takes to complete an average transaction, gives you a rough idea of the performance level your system must be able to provide. Actually, it must be able to provide more than that, because occasionally (or even regularly), peak load situations occur that significantly exceed the average load.

If you are able to size your system accurately and project what capacity you will need over, say, the next six months, and then put in place a system that matches your projections, you can save your organization a tremendous amount of money. Putting in an inadequate system can be tremendously expensive in terms of lost productivity and user frustration. Putting in a system with too much capacity means you have unnecessarily spent money on more capacity than you can use.

When your system is up and running, capacity planning is an ongoing activity. Needs change, usually in the direction of growth, and the configuration of your system must change to match those changing needs. When you are planning capacity for an existing system you have an advantage over the person trying to size a system that hasn't been installed yet. You can take data that records actual usage of system resources. By maintaining records over a period of months, you can see trends and proactively upgrade capacity before your system becomes overloaded.

Application Tuning

In the chain that runs from the database application to the DBMS to the database to the system hardware, the first place to look for a performance bottleneck is the application. There are two reasons for this. First, there are many things about the application that are often not considered that can have a major impact on performance. Second, problems in the application are often easier to fix than problems anywhere else in the system.

Using and tuning indexes

When you access records scattered throughout a database table with either a SELECT, UPDATE, or DELETE statement, the DBMS does a sequential scan of the table, examining each record in turn until it finds the ones you specified with your WHERE clause. Suppose, in a million-record table, there are ten records that match the search condition in your WHERE clause. The DBMS has to look at all million records to make sure it didn't miss one that satisfied the search condition. Because users typically execute many such statements, overall system performance suffers.

Indexes in a database are somewhat like indexes in a book. Imagine a one-thousand page book where the information you wanted was on ten pages scattered throughout the book. One way to find the information would be to leaf through all thousand pages one at a time, scanning each page for the desired information. This would take a long time, and you would probably give up before finishing. A better way would be to look up your target information in the book's index, and then go directly to the ten pages listed.

Database indexes use a B-Tree structure to quickly zero in on the information you want. A sequential scan of a million-record table requires a million I/O operations to find ten desired records. A good index can give you the same result in an average of 1,000 I/O operations, 1,000 times faster. On smaller tables the speedup would not be so great, but even a table with only 10,000 records can exhibit a factor of 100 speedup with indexes. Very small tables, with only a few hundred records, do not benefit from indexes. It is quicker to do a sequential scan on them.

Index keys

Index keys are the columns in a table that you use as indexes. To access a row of data in a table using an index, you must include the index key as a condition in your WHERE clause. An index based on a single column is called a *simple index* and an index based on multiple columns is called a *composite index*. Considering Xanthic's EMPLOYEES table, an index based on EmployeeID would be a simple index, while an index based on the combination of FirstName and LastName would be a composite index.

Unique indexes

Columns or combinations of columns where every value is unique make the best indexes. When you retrieve a table row with a unique index, it is guaranteed to be the exact row you want. A table's primary key is guaranteed to be unique, so primary keys make good indexes for that reason. You can also guarantee uniqueness in an index column by applying a UNIQUE constraint to it.

An index doesn't have to have unique values in every row, but the less duplication of values there is in an index, the more effective it is at reducing access time.

Tuning indexes

There are a number of things you can do to make sure your indexes are working for you and not against you. Here are some key rules to follow:

- Don't use an index if you expect to access more than 20 percent of the rows in the table. A sequential scan will probably be faster.
- What will users do most often? If they will use SELECT a lot more than INSERT, UPDATE, or DELETE, then indexes can cause dramatic speed improvements. On the other hand, if INSERT is the predominant operation on the table, adding an index can actually hurt overall performance. Updating the index after every INSERT, UPDATE, or DELETE adds to the processing burden, and because inserts always take place at the end of a table, they do not benefit from an index.
- Build your indexes to optimize performance for the actual queries that will be run most often on your system. If, over time, your query profile changes, you should change your indexes, too.
- Don't index small tables.

- Don't create any more indexes than you need. Every index you maintain on a table must be updated every time you insert, update, or delete a record.

- Use columns with small data types, such as INTEGER, for index keys, rather than columns with large data types such as VARCHAR. The longer the index key, the more time it takes to deal with it.

Minimizing network traffic

A key idea in optimizing SQL queries is to minimize the amount of network traffic that must pass between the server and the clients. Every round trip that consists of an SQL statement from the client followed by a response from the server consumes network bandwidth. Using stored procedures is one way to reduce network traffic.

I discuss stored procedures in Session 18.

Another way is to retrieve only the data you need. Instead of using the SELECT * syntax, specify explicitly the columns you want. There is no point in clogging up the network with result sets containing columns you don't need. Also, make your WHERE clauses as selective as possible so that you return no more rows than you need.

Setting isolation levels

In Session 24, I mention the four possible isolation levels for transactions in a multi-user system: READ UNCOMMITTED, READ COMMITTED, REPEATABLE READ, and SERIALIZABLE. The SERIALIZABLE isolation level gives you the best protection from possible data corruption due to an access conflict with another user. However, it also has the greatest impact on system performance. You may be able to improve performance significantly by dropping down to a lower isolation level. For example, the phantom read and non-repeatable read problems matter only if you follow a read operation with another operation that accesses the same rows. For transactions that hit the database only once, using the SERIALIZABLE isolation level is overkill. You don't need that much isolation. If you and the other database developers in your organization pay careful attention to what you are doing in your transactions and set your isolation levels no higher than they need to be, everyone benefits from higher throughput.

**20 Min.
To Go**

DBMS Tuning

If you are the application programmer, you can do quite a bit, as discussed above, to improve the performance of your application and the system in general by doing things within your application such as creating indexes, coding to minimize network traffic, and setting isolation levels. You don't, however, have any control over the DBMS. On the other hand, if you are the DBA, there are things *you* can do to improve performance for everyone. The areas that are under your control include memory management, disk configuration, and lock management.

Managing memory

Memory on a database server comes in two forms: semiconductor memory, often called *RAM* (Random-Access Memory), and hard disk memory. RAM is typically over a hundred thousand times faster than disk memory. For that reason, you want to keep your DBMS and the parts of the database that are being actively accessed in RAM. For systems that are small enough, you can keep everything in RAM, but for most practical systems, RAM is not enough.

Modern database management systems store data in virtual memory. A system's RAM is referred to as *physical memory*. The combination of RAM and a portion of the system's disk memory that has been allocated to the DBMS is called *virtual memory*. From the point of view of the database application, the virtual memory is all the same, with no distinction between the part that is in RAM and the part that is on disk. The DBMS is managing memory allocation so as to keep the executable code and the parts of the database that are being accessed most frequently in RAM and the parts that are being accessed less frequently on disk. The goal is to provide the best overall performance.

If, despite the best efforts to keep the most active data in RAM, performance is still unsatisfactory, the best solution may be at add more RAM to the system. This should have a dramatic effect. The more data that resides in RAM, the more likely that a data access request will be for RAM-resident rather than disk-resident data.

Configuring disk storage

Because, for applications that access large amounts of data, some of the data resides on hard disk storage, it is important to optimize disk performance. One way to do that is to spread the data across multiple disks. Any one disk is limited by how fast the read/write head can move from one spot on the disk to another and by the speed with which it can read and write data. Because these speeds depend on how fast disk platters can rotate and read/write heads can seek, disks operate orders of magnitude slower than processors and RAM.

One way to alleviate the disk speed bottleneck is to access multiple disks in parallel. While one disk is busy accessing one data item, another disk can be accessing another. The ideal situation would be for all the disks you have to be carrying an equal part of the load. The DBA has some control over this by deciding which disks should hold which tables. Tables that are often used at the same time should be on separate disks, so that they all can be simultaneously accessed. Reasonably enough, this process is called *load balancing*.

One thing that can seriously degrade your system performance is to have one of your hard disks fail, or *crash*, on you. After all, hard disks are mechanical devices with moving parts — and such things wear out. Modern hard disks are very reliable, but nevertheless, they do fail sometimes. When they do, if they are holding all or even some of your database, your productivity drops to zero until repairs are made and your database is restored.

A common solution to the disk failure problem is to use RAID technology. I mention *RAID* (Redundant Array of Inexpensive Disks) in Session 24 as a means of continuing processing even if a hard disk fails. I now explain how this is done.

RAID uses a process called *striping* and fault tolerance techniques. Instead of putting different tables on different disks, in a RAID the data is spread (or *striped*) across the disks in such a way that none of them holds a single table. There are several RAID levels, providing varying degrees of protection against failure. Typical is RAID Level 5, which adds extra *ECC* (Error Correcting Code) bits to the data. These extra bits carry enough information so that if any one disk in the RAID array were to fail, the remaining disks, plus their associated ECC bits, carry all the information that was on the failed disk. Processing can continue, but at a reduced rate. The most sophisticated installations also feature *hot swapping,* in which the bad disk is physically disconnected and a new blank disk is plugged in. The DBMS then recovers the lost information from the remaining disks, writes it to the new disk, and then resumes full speed operation.

RAID Level 1, also called *disk mirroring,* is a less sophisticated but more expensive technology than RAID Level 5. It merely duplicates everything on your main hard disks on a second set of disks. Thus is requires twice as much hard disk storage as a non-RAID system. RAID Level 5 will also cost more than a non-RAID system, but not twice as much. The more disks there are in a RAID Level 5 array, the less redundancy there is, and the fewer disks are needed to reliably store a given amount of data.

Managing locks

As Session 24 discusses, the locks that are placed on table rows, whole tables, or even whole databases, can have a big effect on performance. There are some things that the application programmer can do about this, such as adjusting isolation levels. At a more primitive level, the DBMS can alter locking behavior.

There are a number of types of locks, each appropriate to a different task that an application performs. For example, if you are merely reading a location with a SELECT statement, there is no harm in letting someone else read the same location at the same time. In this case the DBMS would place a *shared lock*, which allows multiple simultaneous reads but no writes to the locked location. If you are writing, however, with an INSERT, UPDATE, or DELETE statement, the DBMS will place an *exclusive lock* on the location you are writing to, which prevents anyone else from either reading or writing to the locked location. If you are the DBA and are changing the structure of a table, the DBMS places a *schema lock* to prevent all access to the table until the lock is released. Various database management systems may feature other locks.

Much of the work of managing locks is done by the DBMS without any human intervention. The DBA can control a few things, such as the maximum number of locks that the DBMS may allocate.

Responding to a Performance Problem

10 Min.
To Go
Sooner or later, every database installation starts suffering from degraded performance. To return performance to acceptable levels, it helps to follow a step-by-step procedure. The procedure should be a logical progression that takes you from a suspicion that there is a problem all the way to a complete solution of the problem and understanding of what caused it. In the following sections, I give one possible set of steps to remedy degraded performance.

Determining the root problem

First of all, you need to determine whether you have a problem at all. If your system is running satisfactorily, changing things can actually make matters worse. If users complain about performance, perhaps their expectation levels — based on prior experience with smaller, simpler applications or with more expensive, more powerful systems — are too high. It is important to verify that performance is indeed degrading. One good way to do this is to periodically run test queries that exercise a wide variety of system capabilities on a test database that does not change. Record performance each time you run the test suite, and graph results to make it easier to spot trends. If you see a trend of ever-decreasing performance, you probably have an issue that you need to address.

Generally, somewhere in the chain of components in the system (the application, the DBMS, the database, the operating system, the processor, the I/O, the RAM, the disks), one link in the chain is causing the slowdown. You must identify this weak link, which causes a bottleneck, before you can take effective corrective action. Modern database management systems provide performance monitoring tools that help you narrow down the source of the problem.

After you have a hypothesis about the source of the problem, you may want to write a test program that isolates and exposes the problem, confirming or refuting your hypothesis. Continue with this approach until you are sure you have identified the problem adequately.

Deciding on a solution

Once you know what the problem is, you are more than halfway toward solving it. There are probably a limited number of things that you can do that may restore your system to an acceptable performance level. Choose the most cost-effective solution, which is the action that solves your problem and does so at the lowest cost. You can always solve your problem with a high cost solution, such as buying a much more expensive computer, buying a much more expensive DBMS, or totally rewriting your application, but that is probably not the best course of action. Depending on where your bottleneck is, you may be able to get data flowing again by coding your transactions more efficiently, changing settings in the DBMS, allocating more resources to the database, or balancing the load on your hard disk array. If the problem lies in hardware, you may be able to solve it by adding disks, RAM, or processors.

Implementing the solution

After you have decided on a solution, and after you have carefully monitored and documented system performance, apply your proposed solution and document how performance is affected. It may get better, worse, or it may stay the same. If performance worsens, back out the change, revise your hypothesis, and try something else. It is best to change only one thing at a time, carefully recording the effect of each change. This way, when you finally do solve the problem, you will know exactly what the problem was and how it was fixed. If you change multiple things at once and the problem goes away, you can't be sure which of the things you did caused the improvement. This may be important to know for the future.

Analyzing the result

You documented the state of the system before making any changes. You made a change. You documented how performance was affected by the change. You backed out the change, then changed something else, documenting its effect also.

Now you can decide on what permanent changes to make. Perhaps two of the changes you tried yielded moderate improvement. You can implement them both at the same time to see if they complement each other and, when used together, give an even better performance enhancement.

After you have decided on how best to fix the original problem, document what you have learned so that when a similar situation arises in the future, you, or whoever is responsible for the system at that time, know where to look for the problem and what may provide the best solution.

Done!

REVIEW

Many factors contribute to the performance of a database system. The platform it runs on must be adequate to begin with. Assuming an adequate starting system, the load on a system tends to grow with time. Depending on the nature of the increased load, different components of the system may start restricting performance. The problem may lie in the application. If it is not accessing data efficiently, it can degrade network throughput for everyone, in addition to being slow to deliver your query results to you. Using and optimizing indexes may help you receive results sooner. Coding to minimize the amount of network traffic you generate helps other users as well as yourself. Coding to minimize the effect of the locks you place on database resources can also yield a big performance improvement for other users. Hopefully, those other users reciprocate by dealing with locks efficiently, so system performance improves for you, too.

Some performance problems arise because of a memory configuration that does not match the needs of the applications that are running against the database. This is the province of the DBA, who can determine where data is physically stored on a system that uses both RAM and disk storage.

To address performance problems, follow a procedure that first determines the probable cause of the problem, next decides on a course of action that should fix the problem, and then takes the action, noting how effective it was. If performance is now adequate, great! If not, make a new hypothesis about the cause and, based on the knowledge you gained from trying your first solution, go through the step-by-step procedure again.

QUIZ YOURSELF

1. What is the main thing that a database server does? (See "System Sizing and Capacity Planning.")
2. When can a DBA stop being concerned about capacity planning? (See "System Sizing and Capacity Planning.")

3. Would it make sense to create indexes for a table that has 47 records? (See "Application Tuning.")

4. Why does use of the SERIALIZABLE isolation level have a negative impact on overall system performance? (See "Application Tuning.")

5. Why can adding more RAM to a server improve its performance? (See "DBMS Tuning.")

Accessing Databases over the Internet

Session Checklist

✔ The advantages of putting a database on the Web

✔ Overcoming obstacles

✔ Determining needed capability

✔ Providing adequate security

✔ Choosing the right implementation

**30 Min.
To Go**

Up until now I have talked about database systems in their traditional environment, which is a client/server system on a local area network. In this environment, the database and the "back-end" portion of the DBMS reside on the server, while the application program and the "front-end" portion of the DBMS reside on multiple client machines. This is a congenial environment for you, the application developer, because you know exactly what hardware makes up the client computers and what operating system is running on them. These things are generally standardized within an organization.

Why Put a Database on the Web?

The Web is a new environment for database applications. Businesses are making their catalogs available over the Web and even conducting sales transactions. Larger sites, instead of building and maintaining hundreds or thousands of HTML pages, are creating a few screen templates and putting their variable content into a database. When a site visitor accesses a page, the template is displayed and appropriate content is pulled up from the database to fill it, which can save thousands of hours of page development and ongoing maintenance. More and more, Web sites are becoming template-based and data-driven.

Now that the World Wide Web has become the electronic nervous system of the planet, database access over the Web has become critical. There are some architectural similarities between database use in a client/server system and database use over the Internet. There are some differences, too. First let's look at the similarities.

- In both cases, the user sits at a client machine and the database resides on a server machine.
- Application programs use SQL to communicate with the database.
- You can build the user interface of the Web-based system to look just like the user interface of an equivalent client/server system.
- You can build the functionality of the Web-based system to do everything that an equivalent client/server system can do.

There are important differences between database on a client/server system and database on the Web. They include:

- In a client/server system, the developer controls both the client and the server environments, and the application resides on the client. In a Web-based system, the developer does not control the client. All you can be sure of is that the client hosts a Web browser that understands HTML.
- In a client/server system, most of the database manipulation logic runs on the client. In a Web-based system, most of the database manipulation logic runs on the server.
- Client/server systems are entirely located within the physical confines of a single organization. Security is not a major issue for most client/server installations. Web-based systems are accessed by users located all over the world, some of whom could be hostile. Security is a very major issue for most Web-based installations.

Due to the differences between client/server and Web-based systems, Microsoft and other vendors have developed special technologies to meet the needs of Web-based systems. Microsoft's entry in this field is Active Server Pages (ASP) working in conjunction with ActiveX Data Objects (ADO). There are a number of tools that provide similar capabilities for non-Windows platforms. PHP is an open source example of such a tool. (PHP, created by Rasmus Lerdorf, stands for *Personal Home Page* because he originally used it to add capability to his personal home page.) I briefly describe each of these technologies and put them in context.

Meeting the Challenges

There are two worlds: the world of database, where you speak SQL, and the world of the Web, where you speak HTML. To make a database accessible from the Web, you must bridge that language gap. Depending on which DBMS you are using and which operating system it is running under, you will make different choices. If you are running a Microsoft DBMS, such as SQL Server or Access, on a Microsoft operating system, such as one of the various flavors of Windows, the combination of ASP and ADO may be the best choice for a technology to bridge the language gap.

What does ASP do?

ASP is Microsoft's way of adding dynamic behavior to Web sites. Plain vanilla HTML produces static Web pages. Static Web pages merely display text and graphics. Far more engaging are dynamic Web pages that interact with the user. User interaction requires that the Web page contain executable programs or scripts. Such scripts can either execute on the client machine or on the server. ASP is a technology for server-side scripting. ASP code, written in Microsoft's VBScript scripting language, executes on the server and sends any results to the client in the form of HTML. In this way, it doesn't matter what browser the user has; if it can handle HTML, it can handle the output of an ASP script. This bypasses the problem caused by the fact that the Web developer has no control over the capabilities of the users' browsers. All the "heavy lifting" is done on the server.

Accessing databases with ADO

Although Microsoft first developed ODBC and encouraged the rest of the industry to accept it as a standard, they then went on to develop a newer technology called *Object Linking and Embedding-DataBase* (OLE-DB). OLE-DB does essentially the same thing that ODBC does, but is capable of dealing with a wider variety of data sources. It also has not had the widespread acceptance that ODBC has enjoyed, being largely restricted to connecting to Microsoft databases.

I discuss ODBC in Session 17.

ActiveX Data Objects (ADO), another Microsoft technology, provides the interface between an application program and OLE-DB providers. OLE-DB providers connect directly to the data sources that the application uses. If an OLE-DB provider is not available for the specific data source you want to use, an OLE-DB provider with an ODBC interface is available from Microsoft that enables you to connect to any ODBC-compatible data source. Figure 26-1 shows how the various components of such a system fit together.

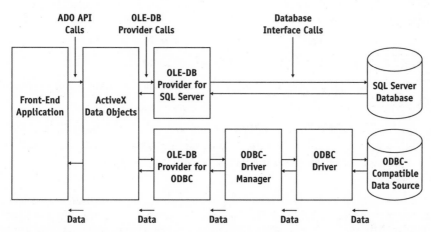

Figure 26-1 *Accessing data through ADO and OLE-DB*

If you are developing in a Microsoft environment, and you want to make database content available to users equipped with browsers on client machines that are connected to your server either via the Internet or an organizational intranet, you will probably be best served by using ASP/ADO technology. The downside of this solution is that migration to a non-Microsoft platform may be difficult.

JDBC

*20 Min.
To Go*

ODBC is not well suited for interfacing to applications written with the Java programming language, and OLE-DB is not available on non-Microsoft platforms. Because Java is often the language of choice for data-driven Web applications, and because many database servers are Unix or Linux-based, it was important that a more suitable interface for Java applications be created. SunSoft created the specification for Java DataBase Connectivity (JDBC). Functionally, JDBC is very similar to ODBC, but it is specifically designed to work with Java applications. Like ODBC, JDBC provides access to a wide range of SQL databases as well as spreadsheets and other flat file data sources.

Figure 26-2 shows how a Java application interfaces to a data source using JDBC.

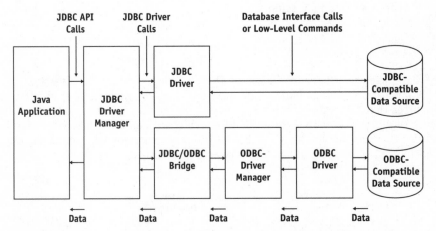

Figure 26-2   *Java application to data source communication path*

The JDBC Driver Manager can connect to a data source either through a JDBC driver or through an ODBC driver via a JDBC/ODBC bridge.

A JDBC/ODBC bridge is a software component that translates JDBC commands into equivalent ODBC commands that the database understands. It makes the reverse translation when the database returns the results.

For Web-based applications, Java code in the form of an applet is embedded in a Web site's HTML and downloaded with the HTML to a client's browser when the client visits the Web site. A Java Virtual Machine (JVM) in the browser executes the Java code. The applet can send SQL statements to the data source, and it can also invoke stored procedures on the Web server. Executing stored procedures on the server can significantly boost performance, as opposed to performing the same function from the client.

Session 18 covers triggers and stored procedures.

PHP

PHP is a scripting language that you can use for server-side scripting in a Unix or Linux environment in the same way that you would use ASP scripting in a Microsoft environment. You can even use PHP on a Windows server, making it a good choice for cross platform deployment.

The PHP code is embedded in an HTML page on the server. The code is interpreted and replaced with the results of the script. What gets downloaded to the client is pure HTML, with embedded values where the embedded PHP scripts had been.

Here's an overview of the main steps involved in PHP-mediated database access:

- A site visitor's browser requests a Web page by connecting to a URL.
- The Web server checks and finds that the requested file is a PHP script, and interprets it accordingly.
- PHP commands establish a connection to the database and request the content that is to be displayed on the Web page.
- The database sends the requested content to the PHP script.
- The PHP script stores the content in variables and embeds those values in the HTML for the requested Web page, then sends the HTML to the Web server.
- The Web server sends the content, now in the form of HTML to the visitor's browser.

How Much Traffic Will It See?

*10 Min.
To Go*

When you make a database accessible on the Web, you know much less about your user community than you do on a local area network. On a local area network, you know how many client machines are connected to the network, so you know that the number of simultaneous accesses to your database cannot exceed that number. The Web is different. Under normal circumstances, you may receive five or six accesses per day. However, if your site suddenly becomes popular, your traffic can jump to tens of thousands of simultaneous accesses. It is difficult to predict what the load on your database may be, let alone prepare for it.

Predicting traffic is important because some implementations are limited in the amount of traffic they can handle. Microsoft Access 2000, for example, is probably not a good choice for a Web site that has any possibility of heavy traffic. However, you can prototype your site using Access, then when you start to approach the limits of that product, move up to SQL Server 2000. There is a smooth migration path from one to the other. MySQL also has limitations that you should understand thoroughly. That is not to say it is a bad choice for a Web database. Many Web sites that experience moderately heavy traffic use MySQL as a back-end database. MySQL is noted for its speed as well as for being free. If you don't need the features it lacks, or can program around them, MySQL may be a good Web database for you. Oracle is probably the most robust choice, but SQL Server and IBM's DB2 are also good choices for heavy volume Web sites.

MySQL and PostgreSQL, being open source software products, typically do not have the tightly integrated set of auxiliary programs and support tools available that the commercial database products have. Because the databases themselves are free, to balance things out you have to pay somewhere. In the immortal words of Robert A. Heinlein, "There ain't no such thing as a free lunch (TANSTAAFL)."

Protecting Your Database

Of course, a Web database system has all the security and data integrity concerns that I mention in Session 23 and Session 24 in the context of a multi-user client/server system. In addition, with a Web database, you have much more to worry about. For a public Web site, you have no control over who your users are or what kind of computer they are using to connect to you. Even a password-protected, limited access site may be vulnerable to cracking, followed by mischievous damage, or theft of proprietary information.

In addition to all the normal protective measures discussed in Session 23, you need to at least install a firewall between your database server and the Web. A *firewall* is a combination of hardware and software that intercepts every packet of data coming in from the Web, rejecting anything that it considers suspicious. No firewall affords complete protection, but everything you can afford to do to enhance the security of your database is probably worthwhile. Ask yourself the following question, "What's the worst that can happen if my worst enemy or a misdirected fanatic should take control of my database?" The answer to that question should serve as your guide in deciding how much protection you should put into place.

What Products Will Meet Your Needs?

All the DBMS products on the market have strengths and weaknesses compared to their competition. The right choice for you depends on your specific needs, both now and in the foreseeable future. Right from the beginning of your development effort, it is important that you choose a DBMS and development environment that meets the needs of your Web site both now and in the future. Try to forecast your Web site's popularity and the type of operations that will be performed on your database. Choose a product that meets the needs of your forecast without burdening you with the huge costs that come with overcapacity. Keep in mind that if your requirements should grow beyond your current expectations, products that are scalable to accommodate increased needs are preferable to those that do not have a clear migration path.

- **Microsoft Access 2000** is relatively inexpensive and easy to use, but is not appropriate for an enterprise level database. It runs only under Microsoft's Windows operating systems, so is not an option for Unix users. It supports a small number of concurrent users (255) and holds up to 2 GB of data per table. If you are confident that your site will not be heavily trafficked by database users, at least at first, this may be a good choice. If you discover later that you are experiencing more usage than you anticipated, there is a smooth upgrade path from Access to Microsoft SQL Server 2000.

- **MySQL** runs on a broad array of operating systems, including all of the popular Unix variants as well as Microsoft Windows. MySQL lacks some key features that other products have, such as nested queries, but it is fast and free. If you are a savvy developer who doesn't need a lot of support and are building a data-driven Web site on a limited budget, MySQL may be the platform to build it on. There is a developer community that is gracious in giving help to newcomers.

- **PostgreSQL**, like MySQL, is an open source product. It has many of the features that MySQL lacks. As yet, its use is not as widespread as is that of MySQL. It runs under several variants of Unix, including Linux, but does not run under any of the Microsoft operating systems. It is free and features good performance. It may not be quite as fast as MySQL, but that may be due to the fact that it is more full-featured. PostgreSQL can be a good choice for a limited-budget but high-talent organization whose Web site may grow to the enterprise level (thousands of simultaneous connections).

- **Microsoft SQL Server 2000** is an enterprise-class DBMS that is used by many large and well-known companies. It runs only under Microsoft Windows operating systems. If you are running only Microsoft operating systems on your servers, you may want to consider using a Microsoft DBMS too, so that you have only one place to call if problems arise. If you are an all-Microsoft shop, when you call Microsoft's technical support, they will not be able to point the finger any anyone else.

- **Oracle 9i** is the current version of the leading enterprise-class DBMS. Huge sites with massive traffic have been using Oracle databases for years. Oracle 9i is available on the most popular Unix variants, including Linux, as well as Microsoft's Windows 2000 operating system.

- **DB2** (from IBM) is another worthy entry in the DBMS market. Inexpensive versions run on small platforms and more robust versions provide enterprise-class performance on more powerful computers. Like Oracle, DB2 runs on most of the popular Unix flavors and on the Microsoft operating systems.

Done!

REVIEW

The only way to provide large amounts of information on the Web is to store the information in a database and display selections from it at the request of site visitors. Because databases and the Web operate using two very different languages, one challenge in getting the two to work together is to get them talking to each other. Scripts written in scripting languages such as ASP, PHP, or others can provide this needed communication.

A second challenge is the fact that the Web is a wild, uncontrolled place. To protect your database from intentional or accidental damage, you must put extraordinary measures into place, such as firewalls that monitor traffic coming in from the Web and stop any data packets that may pose a threat.

The DBMS you choose as the base for a Web-based database application may be different from the one you would choose for an in-house client/server system. Scalability becomes a more important consideration, as does security. Choose the DBMS product that provides the best combination of features that you need, at a cost you can afford, both up front, and in terms of ongoing maintenance.

QUIZ YOURSELF

1. Why did Sunsoft develop JDBC? (See "Meeting the Challenges.")

2. Where is ASP code executed? (See "Meeting the Challenges.")

3. When a Web-surfer visits an ASP-based data-driven Web site, a Web page is sent from the server to the surfer's client computer. What does the Web page consist of? (See "Why Put a Database on the Web?")

4. Where is PHP code executed? (See "Meeting the Challenges.")

5. Why is security more of a concern on the Web than it is on a company intranet? (See "Protecting Your Database.")

PART

V

Sunday Morning Part Review

1. Name three ways that data redundancy can hurt you.

2. What characteristic must a table have to ensure entity integrity?

3. In creating an INVOICE table, what constraint would you use to assure that the amount entered in the TotalRemitted column does not exceed the amount entered in the TotalCharge column?

4. What are modification anomalies?

5. What is a composite key?

6. When can you be sure that a table is in domain-key normal form?

7. Who has primary responsibility for the maintenance and health of a database?

8. What rights can a database object owner grant to another user?

9. In the context of privilege granting, what is a role?

10. At what stage in the life of a database system do most problems occur?

11. What is the effect of a read lock in a multi-user system?

12. Which transaction isolation level provides the least protection against unwanted user interactions?

13. What does a database server spend most of its time doing?

14. Which index generally provides the fastest access to a single row in a database table?

15. Is performance better if a large database is entirely located on a single large hard disk or if it is spread across multiple smaller disks that have the same performance characteristics?

16. Why would you want to put a database on a large, information-rich Web site?

17. What is ASP?

18. Why is security more of a concern for a Web database than it is for a database residing on a corporate network?

PART

VI

Sunday Afternoon

Cursors

Session Checklist

✔ Moving through a data table with a cursor

✔ Telling SQL you want to use a cursor

✔ Retrieving a result set

✔ Operating on data one row at a time

✔ Finishing a cursor operation gracefully

**30 Min.
To Go**

S QL differs from other popular computer languages in a fundamental way — the way it deals with data. Most computer languages you probably have used or heard about, such as Visual Basic, Java, C, or C++, are procedural languages, which deal with data one item at a time. Typically, you write a procedure that uses a code loop to perform an operation on one table row; then the execution loops around to perform the same operation on the next table row. The procedure continues looping until it has processed all the rows that it is supposed to process. SQL typically does not work that way.

SQL is a *set-oriented language*, meaning that it operates on table data a set at a time rather than a row at a time. A WHERE clause determines which rows in a table are to be processed; then the SQL statement deals with all the designated rows at once. For example, a SELECT statement returns all the rows in a table that meet the condition specified in the WHERE clause. An UPDATE statement makes the indicated change to all the rows that meet the condition specified in the WHERE clause. A DELETE statement deletes all the rows that meet the indicated condition specified in the WHERE clause. A single execution of a single statement affects multiple table rows.

As we have seen in previous sessions, SQL's normal set-oriented mode of operation is very effective in producing useful results. There are occasions however, when it is desirable to process a table in the row-by-row manner characteristic of the procedural languages. SQL supports this mode of operation with a feature called a *cursor*.

What Cursors Do

A cursor is a pointer to a single row in a database table. Using a cursor in conjunction with a SELECT statement, SQL can retrieve a single row and then pass it off to the host language for processing. Host languages are designed to deal with data, one item at a time. Alternatively, you can use a cursor to locate a specific row to update or delete.

Using a cursor is a multi-stage operation. First you must declare the cursor so that your DBMS recognizes the fact that it exists. Next you must open the cursor to make it active. At this point, it still hasn't done anything. Next you execute a FETCH statement, which accesses the row pointed to by the cursor. At this point you can perform a SELECT, UPDATE, or DELETE statement on the row the cursor is pointing to. Finally, when you are finished with the cursor, you can close it.

A typical use of a cursor goes as follows:

- SQL DECLARE CURSOR statement. It declares the retrieval that will be made.
- SQL OPEN cursor statement. An SQL SELECT statement retrieves a result set and a cursor points to the "space" just before the first record in the set.
- Procedural code starts a loop
- SQL FETCH statement takes data from the row the cursor is currently pointing to in the result set, and stores it in variables.
- Procedural code checks the loop condition. If it is satisfied, it repositions the cursor and loops. If the condition is not satisfied, it exits the loop.
- SQL CLOSE statement closes the cursor

Declaring a Cursor

Because the primary purpose of cursors is to allow SQL to retrieve a single row from a table so that a host language can process it, I assume in the following examples that the SQL we are using is embedded in a program written in a host language. When you embed an SQL statement in a host language program, you have to inform the host language compiler that it is about to encounter an SQL statement. You do this with the EXEC directive. The host language compiler does not attempt to compile any line starting with the EXEC directive, but instead passes it directly to the DBMS for execution. The DECLARE CURSOR statement has the following syntax:

```
EXEC SQL DECLARE <cursor name> [ SENSITIVE | INSENSITIVE | ASENSITIVE ]
    [ SCROLL ] CURSOR [ WITH HOLD ] [ WITH RETURN ]
    FOR <query expression>
    [ <order by clause> ]
    [ FOR (READ ONLY | UPDATE OF <column name> [ , column name, ... ] ;
```

I explain what each part of this statement means. Keywords and phrases enclosed in square brackets are optional. If they are omitted, a default value is assumed.

Defining scope with the query expression

The query expression can be any legal SELECT statement. It retrieves the result set that the cursor walks through during the FETCH phase of the process. Although the query expression is included in the DECLARE statement, it is not actually executed until the cursor is opened. The DECLARE statement, as the name implies, is merely a declaration. It does not actually do anything.

Sorting retrieved rows with an ORDER BY clause

Perhaps you want the cursor to step through the rows of the result set in some specific order. The easiest way to make that happen is to have the result set sorted before the cursor even becomes involved. You can do this with the optional ORDER BY clause. This way, you can move the cursor ahead one record every time you execute the loop that contains the FETCH statement.

Suppose you wanted to retrieve hire dates from the EMPLOYEES table and then process the information retrieved in some manner with procedural code. You want the records to be processed in alphabetical order by employee last name followed by employee first name. You can declare a cursor as follows:

```
EXEC SQL DECLARE Emp1 CURSOR FOR
    SELECT EmployeeID, FirstName, LastName, HireDate
        FROM EMPLOYEES
    ORDER BY LastName, FirstName ;
```

This declaration sets things up for the retrieval of records from the EMPLOYEES table, sorted by employee last name, then sorted by first name within the scope of any duplicated last names.

Controlling table changes with an updatability clause

The last clause in the DECLARE syntax statement given above is the optional updatability clause. When you access a table row with a cursor, you can specify whether the row is updatable or not. The default behavior, which occurs if you do not include an updatability clause, is for the retrieved rows to be updatable, meaning they can be changed with an UPDATE statement or deleted with a DELETE statement. To restrict the updatability to specified columns, put an updatability clause in your DECLARE statement, similar to the following example:

```
EXEC SQL DECLARE Emp1 CURSOR FOR
    SELECT EmployeeID, FirstName, LastName, HireDate
        FROM EMPLOYEES
    ORDER BY LastName, FirstName
    FOR UPDATE of FirstName, LastName, Hiredate ;
```

This structure allows updates to all the table's fields except its primary key, EmployeeID. If you want to prevent changes or deletions entirely, use the READ ONLY keywords:

```
EXEC SQL DECLARE Emp1 CURSOR FOR
    SELECT EmployeeID, FirstName, LastName, HireDate
        FROM EMPLOYEES
    ORDER BY LastName, FirstName
    FOR READ ONLY ;
```

Multiple open cursors may cause problems

It is possible for multiple cursors on the same table to be declared and open at once, but this can be a dangerous thing. The code that is using the first cursor can perform an operation that interferes with the operation of the code using the second cursor or vice versa.

One way to protect yourself from harmful interactions is to declare your cursor to be INSENSITIVE. When you have an INSENSITIVE cursor, SQL creates a separate result table that is not accessible to any other cursors that may be open. You do your operations on that separate table. If your declare your cursor to be SENSITIVE, then SQL does not create a separate table, and changes made using other cursors are visible to you, possibly affecting your results. The default sensitivity is ASENSITIVE. When you use an ASENSITIVE cursor, SQL may or may not create a separate table. Different implementations may behave differently.

Because without checking the specifications of your implementation you cannot tell whether a separate result table is being created or not, it is a good idea to declare your cursors as INSENSITIVE unless you specifically want your results to be affected by what other programs are doing at the same time. In that case you should declare your cursor to be SENSITIVE.

**20 Min.
To Go**

Scrolling the cursor

When you declare a cursor, you can specify that it be scrollable. If you don't so specify, with the SCROLL keyword, the cursor is only able to step through the result set one record at a time, starting with the first and ending with the last. In many cases, this is exactly the behavior you want. However, you may want to have more control than that. You may want to fetch rows from the result set in some order other than a strict sequence. If you do want to process rows in a different order, put the SCROLL keyword into your DECLARE statement.

Keeping a cursor open

If you are performing a series of transactions that all use the same cursor, you can keep it open after your transaction closes with a COMMIT, by using the WITH HOLD clause. Such a holdable cursor, will however be closed if your transaction closes with a ROLLBACK.

If a cursor definition includes a WITH RETURN clause, it is a result set cursor. A result set cursor that is declared in an SQL-invoked procedure returns a result set if the cursor is still open when the procedure ends.

Opening a Cursor

When you OPEN a cursor, the SELECT statement that makes up the query expression executes, producing a result set. At the same time, the cursor comes into existence and points to the position just before the first record in the result set. The syntax is:

```
EXEC SQL OPEN <cursor name> ;
```

An example similar to the one in the previous section would continue as follows:

```
EXEC SQL DECLARE Emp1 INSENSITIVE CURSOR FOR
    SELECT EmployeeID, FirstName, LastName, HireDate
        FROM EMPLOYEES
    WHERE HireDate < :startdate
    ORDER BY LastName, FirstName
    FOR READ ONLY ;
startdate = '1992-01-01' ;        // A host language statement
EXEC SQL OPEN Emp1 ;
startdate = '1997-01-01' ;        // Another host language statement
```

The DECLARE CURSOR statement is insensitive to any other activity that takes place on the same table at the same time because the OPEN statement makes its own copy of the table. The WHERE clause restricts the rows retrieved to those with a HireDate before January 1, 1992. The result set is sorted by last name, and if there is any duplication of last names, by first name.

The second host language statement

```
startdate = '1997-01-01'
```

has no effect. It is ignored because the OPEN statement freezes the values of all variables. Any processing of the result set is done using the first value of startdate.

**10 Min.
To Go**

Fetching Data with a Cursor

After a cursor is open, you can direct it to point to a record in the result set. For a scrollable cursor, there are six different orientation options: NEXT, PRIOR, FIRST, LAST, ABSOLUTE, and RELATIVE. They have the following meanings:

- **NEXT** — Fetch the record immediately following the current cursor position.
- **PRIOR** — Fetch the record immediately before the current cursor position.
- **FIRST** — Fetch the first record in the result set.
- **LAST** — Fetch the last record in the result set.
- **ABSOLUTE N** — Fetch the record that is N positions away from the first record in the result set.
- **RELATIVE N** — Fetch the record that is N positions away from the current cursor position.

To illustrate the orientation options:

- FETCH ABSOLUTE 7 retrieves the seventh record in the result set.
- FETCH RELATIVE 7 retrieves the seventh record beyond the current cursor position.
- FETCH RELATIVE -7 retrieves the record seven positions before the current cursor position.
- FETCH ABSOLUTE -7 retrieves the record seven positions before the end of the result set.
- FETCH ABSOLUTE 1 produces the same effect as FETCH FIRST. Both statements position the cursor at the first record in the result set.
- FETCH ABSOLUTE -1 and FETCH LAST position the cursor at the last record in the result set.

Here's an example of a FETCH, using our EMPLOYEES table:

```
EXEC SQL FETCH NEXT FROM emp1
    INTO :empid,
         :first,
         :last,
         :hire ;
```

This statement puts all the data items fetched from the current row of the result set into host variables, where they are available for host language processing.

If you did not declare the cursor to be FOR READ ONLY, you can update the row the cursor is pointing to, or you can delete it. To do so, the syntax is a little different from what it is for a normal UPDATE or DELETE statement.

To update the row at the current cursor position use the following syntax:

```
UPDATE <table name>
    SET <column name>=<value expression>[,<column name>=<value
expression>,...]
    WHERE CURRENT OF <cursor name> ;
```

The only columns you can update are those that were named in the query expression, because they are the only columns in the result set. If the cursor is not pointing to a row in the result set when the UPDATE statement is executed, no update is performed and an error indication is returned.

Session 29 covers error handling.

To delete the row at the current cursor position, the syntax is:

```
DELETE FROM <table name> WHERE CURRENT OF <cursor name> ;
```

If the cursor is not pointing to a row in the result set when the DELETE statement is executed, no deletion is performed and an error indication is returned instead.

Closing a Cursor

When you are finished with a cursor, close it immediately. An open cursor makes you vulnerable to data corruption. Closing a cursor is easy. The syntax is:

```
CLOSE <cursor name> ;
```

In our example, it would be:

```
CLOSE emp1 ;
```

REVIEW

Cursors provide a way to overcome the incompatibility between set-oriented SQL and row-oriented procedural host languages. A cursor forces SQL to act in a row-oriented manner rather than its natural set-oriented mode of operation. Forcing SQL to act in an unnatural, row-oriented way is a multi-stage process. To use a single cursor, you must first declare it, next open it, then fetch data from a row with it, and finally close it.

A cursor operates on the result set of a query. You can use a cursor to retrieve data from a table one row at a time, and then process the data with host language code. You can also update or delete the rows pointed to by the cursor. A scrollable cursor gives you great flexibility in accessing result set rows in any order you want.

Done!

QUIZ YOURSELF

1. What kind of statement must the query expression part of a DECLARE CURSOR statement be? (See "Declaring a Cursor.")

2. What does the host language compiler do when it encounters an EXEC SQL directive? (See "Declaring a Cursor.")

3. How can you be sure that retrieved rows will not be deleted? (See "Declaring a Cursor.")

4. What is the INSENSITIVE keyword good for? (See "Declaring a Cursor.")

5. When does the query expression in the cursor declaration retrieve a result set? (See "Opening a Cursor.")

6. If you had a cursor named cust1 that had been declared on the CUSTOMERS table, and a result set that included CustomerID had been returned, what statement should you use to put the CustomerID of the next to last record in the result set into a host variable named :winner? (See "Fetching Data With a Cursor.")

SQL in Common Development Environments

Session Checklist

✔ Features of Microsoft Access 2000

✔ Features of Microsoft SQL Server 2000

✔ Features of MySQL 4.0

✔ Features of PostgreSQL 7.1

✔ Features of Oracle 9i

✔ Recap of Missing SQL:1999 Features

*30 Min.
To Go*

QL is defined by the international ANSI/ISO standard SQL:1999. No commercially available database management system complies completely with the standard, although all DBMS vendors attempt to offer as many of the standard features as they can. There are several reasons why a particular product may differ from the standard:

- A product may have implemented a feature that was not standardized until later. The product has the feature, but with non-standard syntax.

- A standard feature is viewed to be of limited value to a product's user base and thus not worth the time and effort to implement it.

- There has not yet been enough time to implement recently standardized features.

- A product has proprietary features designed to offer an advantage over competitive products that offer only standard features.

For the above reasons, multiple products, all claiming SQL:1999 compatibility, may differ substantially in what they offer and how they offer it. In previous sessions, I have noted instances where Microsoft Access 2000, Microsoft SQL Server 2000, Oracle 9i, MySQL 4.0, and

PostgreSQL 7.1 have either provided or failed to provide a standard feature. In this session I give specifics on differences between the SQL:1999 specification and the capabilities of each of those products.

Microsoft Access 2000

Microsoft Access 2000 is the least complete database management system covered in this book. It has no aspirations of being an enterprise class DBMS. That's a job for its big brother SQL Server 2000. Access 2000 is designed for use by a single user or small workgroup. Furthermore, it assumes that it will be used largely by organizations that do not have ready access to database professionals. A great deal of effort has been expended in making the user interface as intuitive and easy to use as possible. Not only is Access 2000 easier to understand and to use than the other DBMS products I cover, it is less expensive to operate, too. Because Access 2000 is designed to run on a single computer, or at most a small LAN, it does not require a dedicated server. The server part of Access 2000 and the client part can both run on the same computer. One operational limitation of Access 2000 is the fact that it runs only under Microsoft Windows operating systems, so is not available on Unix machines.

Access data definition

You use a DBMS's data definition language (DDL) to build the structure of a database. With the DDL you can create, alter the structure of, and delete database objects. The standard SQL statements to do these things are CREATE, ALTER, and DROP. You can embed these statements in a VBA host language program, or perform the same functions from the keyboard. Access 2000 provides graphical tools for creating, altering, and dropping tables. You can also CREATE, ALTER, and DROP tables by entering SQL statements, but the method of doing so is a little unusual. You must pretend you are building a query, as described in the sidebar on building queries in Session 2.

Start by selecting the option to create a query in Design View. After you open the Query in the Design View window, switch to SQL View in the View menu. This displays an editing window. You can delete whatever is in it and type in an SQL CREATE, ALTER, or DROP command. When you then click on the exclamation point to execute the SQL you have entered, the database engine performs the creation, alteration, or drop as directed.

Access offers nearly all of the SQL:1999 data types or close equivalents. Missing are several of the Time types and the Interval type.

Access data manipulation

Data manipulation, as implemented by SQL's data manipulation language (DML) consists of four major operations:

- Adding new data to a table with the INSERT statement
- Changing existing data in a table with the UPDATE statement
- Deleting rows from a table with the DELETE statement
- Retrieving data from a table with the SELECT statement

You can perform all these SQL operations in a query's SQL view, as described in the previous section.

There are standard SQL:1999 features that Access 2000 does not support. Among them are the OVERLAPS predicate, the MATCH predicate, the SIMILAR predicate, the CASE expression, the INTERSECT set operator, the EXCEPT set operator, the NATURAL JOIN statement, the Column Name Join, all the Outer Joins, the IF structure, the CASE structure, the LOOP structure, the WHILE structure, the REPEAT structure, the FOR structure, triggers, and assertions. In addition, Access 2000 is not scalable to large databases or heavy transaction traffic.

Access database security

Rather than supporting the SQL GRANT and REVOKE statements, Access has its own security system for the granting and revoking of permissions to individuals and to members of a group through windows in its graphical user interface. For a cruder type of security, Access also offers password access to the database. This is an all-or-nothing type of access. If you have the password, you can do anything. And if you don't, you can't do a thing.

Access supports transactions, but does so using host language code rather than SQL statements. Consequently, it does not offer the control over isolation levels that SQL offers.

Microsoft SQL Server 2000

20 Min.
To Go

Microsoft SQL Server 2000 is a full-featured enterprise level database management system. It has all the capability needed to deal with very large files and high transaction rates. SQL Server 2000 is being used successfully in numerous large high-demand environments. It runs only under Microsoft Windows operating systems, so is not available on Unix machines.

SQL Server data definition

SQL Server provides full implementations of the CREATE, ALTER, and DROP DDL statements, for database objects such as tables and views. You can expect any SQL:1999 DDL statement that you enter into SQL Server 2000 to work as specified by the international standard.

SQL Server offers nearly all of the SQL:1999 data types or close equivalents. Only the Interval type is missing.

SQL Server data manipulation

SQL Server fully supports the SQL:1999 INSERT, UPDATE, DELETE, and SELECT DML statements. They all work as you would expect them to, based on the description in the SQL:1999 documentation.

There are standard SQL:1999 features that SQL Server 2000 does not support. Among them are the OVERLAPS predicate, the MATCH predicate, the SIMILAR predicate, the INTERSECT set operator, the EXCEPT set operator, the NATURAL JOIN statement, the Column Name Join, the CASE structure, the LOOP structure, the REPEAT structure, the FOR structure, and assertions. Most of these missing features are not offered by any of the other products covered in this book.

SQL Server database security

The GRANT and REVOKE statements are fully supported by SQL Server. Transactions are also fully supported and consistent with the definitions set out in the SQL:1999 standard.

MySQL 4.0

MySQL is an open source product that, structurally, is a file manager rather than a relational database management system. MySQL has a reputation for being very fast. Its speed is in part due to the fact that it is not a full implementation of SQL. Functionally, it performs most of the frequently used operations that true RDBMS systems perform. The features that it does not provide may or may not be important to you, depending on your application.

MySQL data definition

With MySQL you can CREATE, ALTER, and DROP database objects. MySQL provides all the DDL functionality you are likely to need.

MySQL offers most of the SQL:1999 data types or close equivalents. Missing are the National Character types, Bit and Bit Varying, Boolean, and the Interval type.

MySQL data manipulation

MySQL does not support nested queries, also known as *sub-selects*. Nested queries can be very valuable tools and their lack is a serious deficiency of MySQL.

There are additional standard SQL:1999 features that MySQL does not support. Among them are the OVERLAPS predicate, the MATCH predicate, the SIMILAR predicate, the CASE expression, the UNION set operator, the INTERSECT set operator, the EXCEPT set operator, Right Outer join, Full Outer join, the IF structure, the CASE structure, the LOOP structure, the WHILE structure, the REPEAT structure, the FOR structure, stored procedures, triggers, and assertions.

MySQL database security

MySQL's default table handler is not ACID compliant. Transactions are not supported. This is a major concern if data integrity is important to you. It supports atomicity, but not consistency, isolation, or durability. The Gemini table handler for MySQL from Nusphere Corporation is ACID compliant, but sacrifices some speed relative to the default table handler.

PostgreSQL 7.1

10 Min.
To Go

PostgreSQL is probably the most functionally complete of the open source database products. It is supported by several commercial enterprises, including PostgreSQL, Inc., and Red Hat, Inc.

PostgreSQL data definition

PostgreSQL provides complete DDL functionality, including full-featured CREATE, ALTER, and DROP statements.

PostgreSQL does not offer any of the National Character data types, Bit or Bit Varying, or the BLOB type. PostgreSQL includes a number of geometric data types that none of the other products covered in this book offer.

PostgreSQL data manipulation

PostgreSQL has a very complete set of data manipulation features. However, there are several standard SQL:1999 features that PostgreSQL does not support. Among them are the OVERLAPS predicate, the MATCH predicate, the SIMILAR predicate, the CASE expression, the Natural join statement, the Column Name Join, all the Outer Joins, the IF structure, the CASE structure, the LOOP structure, the WHILE structure, the REPEAT structure, the FOR structure, and assertions. Many of these are not provided by any of the other products covered in this book either.

PostgreSQL database security

PostgreSQL has solid support for both the granting and revoking of privileges and for high-volume transaction processing. It is ACID compliant and is secure enough to be safely used as an enterprise database system.

Oracle 9i

Oracle 9i has the most complete feature set of any of the products discussed in this book. Many of the largest, most mission-critical applications in the world run on Oracle databases. Aside from being the most feature-rich, Oracle databases are the most scalable of any covered in this book. They run on the desktop and also on the largest mainframe computers available. Clustering allows a database to be spread over multiple disk drives, eliminating bottlenecks and thereby enhancing performance.

Oracle data definition

Oracle offers nearly all of the SQL:1999 data types or close equivalents. Missing are the Time types (although TimeStamp types are present), and the Bit and Bit Varying types.

Oracle data manipulation

Oracle 9i provides the most complete set of data manipulation features of any product covered in this book. There are a few standard SQL:1999 features that Oracle 9i does not support. Among them are the OVERLAPS predicate, the MATCH predicate, the SIMILAR predicate, the Column Name Join, the REPEAT structure, the FOR structure, and assertions. None of these features are supported by any of the other products covered in this book.

Oracle database security

Oracle 9i provides full support for the granting and revoking of privileges to individuals and groups. Its transaction processing is among the most reliable available on the market today. Oracle supports failover solutions up to and including hot standby servers that provide a level of reliability and availability not approached by open source products such as MySQL and PostgreSQL. In mission-critical applications where downtime cannot be tolerated, Oracle databases shine.

Missing SQL:1999 Feature Recap

To make it easier to see which DBMS product lacks a particular feature and which product includes it, Table 28-1 lists features missing from at least one of the products covered in this book, showing which products have the feature and which do not.

Table 28-1   *Standard SQL:1999 Feature Comparison*

Feature	Access 2000	SQL Server 2000	Oracle 9i	PostgreSQL 7.1	MySQL 4.0
All Time types	No	No	No	No	No
Interval type	No	No	No	Yes	No
National CHAR type	No	Yes	Yes	No	No
Bit type	No	Yes	No	No	No
Bit Varying type	No	No	No	No	No
BLOB type	No	Yes	Yes	No	Yes
OVERLAPS	No	No	No	No	No
MATCH	No	No	No	No	No
SIMILAR	No	No	No	No	No
CASE expression	No	Yes	Yes	No	No
UNION	Yes	Yes	Yes	Yes	No
INTERSECT	No	No	Yes	Yes	No
EXCEPT (MINUS)	No	No	Yes	Yes	No
NATURAL JOIN	No	No	Yes	No	No
Column Name Joins	No	No	No	No	No

Feature	Access 2000	SQL Server 2000	Oracle 9i	PostgreSQL 7.1	MySQL 4.0
LEFT OUTER JOIN	No	Yes	Yes	No	Yes
RIGHT OUTER JOIN	No	Yes	Yes	No	No
FULL OUTER JOIN	No	Yes	Yes	No	No
IF	No	Yes	Yes	No	No
CASE structure	No	No	Yes	No	No
LOOP	No	No	Yes	No	No
WHILE	No	Yes	Yes	No	No
REPEAT	No	No	No	No	No
FOR	No	No	No	No	No
Triggers	No	Yes	Yes	Yes	No
Assertions	No	No	No	No	No
GRANT	No	Yes	Yes	Yes	Yes
REVOKE	No	Yes	Yes	Yes	Yes

It seems like there are a lot of "No" entries in Table 28-1, and there are. However, this should not be a cause for major concern. In many cases, for an operation that could have been performed with one of the missing features, an equivalent operation can also be performed with one or more of the supported features. If you absolutely need to have one of the features listed above, then you will be constrained to choose one of the DBMS products that has a "Yes" in the row of interest.

Some features, such as the OVERLAPS, MATCH, and SIMILAR predicates, are not supported by any of the covered products. You will have to find different ways to achieve the results you would normally use these predicates for. In other cases, such as with the UNION operator or the LEFT OUTER JOIN operator, you have multiple choices and can base your decision of what product to use on other factors.

Done!

REVIEW

The five DBMS products covered in this book differ in a number of ways. Every one of them is a member of a solid line of products with a long history of valuable service. None of them is appropriate for every possible database application. Each has its own advantages and disadvantages. Depending on the type of organization you are developing for and the types of applications that organization would like to have developed, one or another of the products featured in this book may be the best option available. There are other competitive products on the market besides those covered here that might also be worth considering. Think about the features that you absolutely must have and those that you might need in the future. Think about up front cost and the cost of ongoing maintenance and support. Think about scalability. Think about the availability of people who are familiar with and can develop applications using the chosen system. Think about the availability of documentation and support tools. After you have done a lot of thinking, choose a DBMS, install it, and start to work.

QUIZ YOURSELF

1. Of the five DBMS products covered in this book, which one would be least appropriate to support the back end database of a high transaction volume Web site? (See "Microsoft Access 2000.")

2. Which of the covered products will run on systems that use the Unix operating system? (See "MySQL 4.0," "PostgreSQL 7.1," Oracle 9i.")

3. Which system is not ACID compliant? (See "MySQL 4.0.")

4. Which product offers the largest choice of looping structures? (See "Oracle 9i.")

Error Handling

Session Checklist

✔ Identifying errors with SQLSTATE

✔ Dealing with whole classes of errors with the WHENEVER clause

✔ Storing error information in the diagnostics area

✔ Handling exceptions

**30 Min.
To Go**

I t is practically impossible to write an application program of even moderate complexity without errors. Even after you have completely debugged a program and verified that it is error free, it still may fail due to a network or hardware failure or due to receiving an invalid value from another program or from a user.

Because error conditions arise in even the world's most carefully written and heavily tested programs, you can expect them to arise in the ones that you write, too. When errors do arise, you need a way of dealing with them appropriately. The ones that you can anticipate can be handled automatically. The unexpected ones may cause you to terminate execution. At least you can do so gracefully rather than causing a system crash. SQL incorporates a robust error handling capability (which it calls *exception handling*) that starts with the SQLSTATE status variable.

SQLSTATE

SQLSTATE is a status variable that gets updated after every SQL statement is executed. It is a five-character field divided into a two-character class and a three-character subclass. Only the ASCII upper case letters A–Z and numerals 0–9 may appear in SQLSTATE. The two-character class gives a general indication of the success or failure of the immediately preceding SQL statement. The three-character subclass gives more detailed information.

The class code

Of all the legal class codes, 00 through ZZ, all but three indicate an exception condition that probably requires corrective action. The three non-exception codes are 00, 01, and 02. They have the following meanings:

- 00 means the preceding SQL statement executed successfully and everything is fine.
- 01 means the preceding SQL statement executed, but there is a warning indication. Everything may or may not be fine. Perhaps you should check.
- 02 means the preceding SQL statement executed but did not return any data. This may be fine or it may not. If you have been looping through a table with a cursor, it may mean that you have come to the end of the data and should break out of the loop.

All other class codes indicate an exception of some sort. Any class code that starts with the letter A through H or the numeral 0 through 4 is flagging a standard exception. All implementations of SQL ascribe the same meaning to these class codes. Class codes starting with I through Z or 5 through 9 are not standard. Each implementation has its own meaning for codes in these ranges.

Because the value of the SQLSTATE variable is updated after every SQL statement is executed, and because something can go wrong with every SQL statement that is executed, it makes sense to check the SQLSTATE class code for values other than 00, 01, and 02 after every SQL statement is executed. If you do get an exception code when you check, you can direct execution to an appropriate exception handling routine, rather than continuing on as if everything is fine. Because it would be tedious to include exception checking code after every SQL statement in your application, SQL provides the WHENEVER directive as a mechanism to handle the checking for you.

The WHENEVER directive

Whenever the SQLSTATE status variable contains an exception code after the execution of an SQL statement, you probably want to branch out of the normal flow of execution to some sort of exception-handling routine. You can prepare for such an eventuality before the execution of your program begins by putting one or more WHENEVER directives in the declaration section of your program. Examples may be:

```
WHENEVER SQLWARNING CONTINUE ;
WHENEVER NOT FOUND GO TO loop_exit ;
WHENEVER SQLERROR GO TO exception_handler ;
WHENEVER SQLEXCEPTION GO TO exception_handler ;
WHENEVER SQLSTATE (22012) GO TO div_by_zero ;
WHENEVER CONSTRAINT (NAME_FK) GO TO name_reference ;
```

- When SQLSTATE's class is 01, SQLWARNING is set to TRUE. The first directive above says to ignore the warning and continue processing.
- When SQLSTATE's class is 02, NOT FOUND is set to TRUE. The second directive in the above list sends execution to the loop_exit label.
- When SQLSTATE's class is anything but 00, 01, or 02, both SQLERROR and SQLEXCEPTION are set to TRUE. SQLERROR is the older indicator, from the SQL-92 standard.

SQLEXCEPTION means exactly the same thing, but is new with the SQL:1999 standard. Some implementations may not support the SQLEXCEPTION syntax yet.

- An SQLSTATE of 22012 indicates that the previous SQL statement performed a division by zero. This is one of the standard codes that means the same thing in all implementations of SQL. If you suspect a division by zero may occur, you can write a specific routine to handle it and use the WHENEVER directive to send execution directly to that exception handler, should a division by zero occur. This feature is new with SQL:1999 and may not be implemented yet in many DBMS products.

- Whenever a specific constraint is violated, the WHENEVER CONSTRAINT (constraint_name) directive causes execution to transfer to the exception handling routine that you have written to handle that specific constraint violation. Once again, this directive is new with SQL:1999 and may not be implemented in most DBMS products for quite some time.

20 Min. To Go

The Diagnostics Area

The diagnostics area is an area of memory that the database engine sets aside for the storage of information that would be helpful in the event that an exception or warning occurs. There is room for multiple diagnostic entries, each one consisting of a header and zero or more detail areas. In Session 24, I discuss transactions and explained the SET TRANSACTION statement, which includes a DIAGNOSTICS SIZE clause. The number you specify for DIAGNOSTICS SIZE is the number of specific warnings or exceptions that can be recorded in a detail area. Because a the execution of a single SQL statement may cause several warnings before it generates an exception, multiple diagnostic entries may be relevant to debugging a particular problem.

The diagnostics header area

The header area contains eight fields, as shown in Table 29-1.

Table 29-1 *Diagnostics Header Area*

Fields	Data Type
NUMBER	INTEGER
ROW_COUNT	INTEGER
COMMAND_FUNCTION	VARCHAR (>=128)
COMMAND_FUNCTION_CODE	INTEGER
MORE	INTEGER
TRANSACTIONS_COMMITTED	INTEGER
TRANSACTIONS_ROLLED_BACK	INTEGER
TRANSACTION_ACTIVE	INTEGER

The NUMBER field is the number of detail areas that have been filled with diagnostic information about the current exception. The ROW_COUNT field holds the number of rows affected if the previous SQL statement was an INSERT, UPDATE, or DELETE.

The COMMAND_FUNCTION field describes the dynamic SQL statement that was just executed (if in fact the last SQL statement to be executed was a dynamic SQL statement). The COMMAND_ FUNCTION_CODE field gives the code number for the dynamic SQL statement that was just executed (if the last SQL statement executed was a dynamic SQL statement). Every dynamic function has an associated numeric code.

I cover dynamic SQL in Session 30. Don't worry about it for now.

The MORE field may be either a "Y" or an "N." *Y* indicates that there are more status records than the detail area can hold. *N* indicates that all the status records generated are present in the detail area. Depending on your implementation, you may be able to expand the number of records you can handle using the SET TRANSACTION statement, as described in Session 24.

The TRANSACTIONS_COMMITTED field holds the number of transactions that have been committed. The TRANSACTIONS_ROLLED_BACK field holds the number of transactions that have been rolled back. The TRANSACTION_ACTIVE field holds a "1" if a transaction is currently active and a "0" otherwise. A transaction is deemed to be active if a cursor is open or if the DBMS is waiting for a deferred parameter.

The diagnostics detail area

The detail area contains twenty-six fields, as shown in Table 29-2.

Table 29-2 *Diagnostics Detail Area*

Fields	Data Type
CONDITION_NUMBER	INTEGER
RETURNED_SQLSTATE	CHAR (6)
MESSAGE_TEXT	VARCHAR (>=128)
MESSAGE_LENGTH	INTEGER
MESSAGE_OCTET_LENGTH	INTEGER
CLASS_ORIGIN	VARCHAR (>=128)
SUBCLASS_ORIGIN	VARCHAR (>=128)
CONNECTION_NAME	VARCHAR (>=128)
SERVER_NAME	VARCHAR (>=128)

Fields	Data Type
CONSTRAINT_CATALOG	VARCHAR (>=128)
CONSTRAINT_SCHEMA	VARCHAR (>=128)
CONSTRAINT_NAME	VARCHAR (>=128)
CATALOG_NAME	VARCHAR (>=128)
SCHEMA_NAME	VARCHAR (>=128)
TABLE_NAME	VARCHAR (>=128)
COLUMN_NAME	VARCHAR (>=128)
CURSOR_NAME	VARCHAR (>=128)
CONDITION_IDENTIFIER	VARCHAR (>=128)
PARAMETER_NAME	VARCHAR (>=128)
ROUTINE_CATALOG	VARCHAR (>=128)
ROUTINE_SCHEMA	VARCHAR (>=128)
ROUTINE_NAME	VARCHAR (>=128)
SPECIFIC_NAME	VARCHAR (>=128)
TRIGGER_CATALOG	VARCHAR (>=128)
TRIGGER_SCHEMA	VARCHAR (>=128)
TRIGGER_NAME	VARCHAR (>=128)

The most important of the detail fields is the first one, RETURNED_SQLSTATE. It gives you the value of SQLSTATE, which, after you look up what that particular code means, tells you something helpful about what caused the exception. MESSAGE_TEXT may also be helpful, depending on the implementation. It can tell you what the SQLSTATE code means, or it may give even more specific information.

If a failing SQL statement produces multiple detail records, the first one listed is the most serious exception, rather than being the first to occur. Any exception that causes a rollback is listed first. Less serious exceptions are listed next, followed by no-data warnings (class 02) and other warnings (class 01).

Retrieving information from the diagnostics area

**10 Min.
To Go**

The diagnostics area is cleared every time an SQL statement is executed. That way you can be sure that any records you find in the diagnostics area pertain only to the most recently executed SQL statement. You can retrieve diagnostics header information with the GET DIAGNOSTICS statement. The syntax is:

```
GET DIAGNOSTICS :variable1 = <field1> [, :variable2 = <field2>]... ;
```

<field1> can be any of the header fields, such as MESSAGE_TEXT. The values you retrieve are placed into variables that you can later use to help determine what has happened. You probably also need to retrieve diagnostics detail information. The syntax to do that is similar:

```
GET DIAGNOSTICS EXCEPTION <condition number>
    :variable1 = <field1> [, variable2 = <field2>]... ;
```

In this case, <condition number> tells where this exception is located in the list in the detail area. Condition number 1 is the first and most serious exception; condition number 2 is the second and next most serious, and so on. <field1> represents any of the detail fields, such as RETURNED_SQLSTATE. :variable1 is the variable that receives the contents of <field1>.

Exception Handling

If after you execute an SQL statement the class portion of SQLSTATE holds anything but 00, 01, or 02, you have an exception condition. Something is wrong, and you need to take some action to deal with the problem. There are several ways to handle such a situation. The easy way is to abdicate responsibility and pass the problem off to someone else. Have your sub-procedure immediately return control to whatever procedure called it, along with the bad news that an exception has occurred. This doesn't really solve anything, but at least may lead to a graceful termination of the program.

A second way to handle an exception, particularly apt if you have some idea beforehand as to what kind of exception may have occurred, is to use one or more WHENEVER directives. Put a WHENEVER directive in your program's declaration section for every exception condition that you can anticipate, each one directing execution to a different exception handling routine.

A third possibility is to handle the exception on the spot with a compound SQL statement. A compound SQL statement is a sequence of simple SQL statements within a BEGIN/END block. Let's look at an example of how such a solution may work. Suppose the SQL statement we are attempting to execute is an UPDATE of a column named Quantity of the SMALLINT type in the INVENTORY table, where the ProductNumber is 15. We are concerned that the input value for Quantity that we receive may exceed the range of the SMALLINT data type. If it does, something is wrong, because no value of Quantity should ever be that high. We can use something similar to the following code:

```
BEGIN
    DECLARE QuantityOutOfRange CONDITION FOR SQLSTATE VALUE '88010' ;
    DECLARE EXIT HANDLER
        FOR QuantityOutOfRange
        RESIGNAL ;

    UPDATE INVENTORY
        SET Quantity = :newquantity
        WHERE ProductNumber = 15 ;
END
```

In this (fictitious) implementation, an SQLSTATE value of '88010' means "quantity out of range." First we make a declaration to that effect. Next we declare that if the "QuantityOutOfRange" condition occurs we want the handler to exit the BEGIN/END block and resume execution beyond the END keyword. If the exception condition with SQLSTATE = '88010' occurs, the RESIGNAL statement loads the diagnostics area with the appropriate exception information.

After the declarations have been made, the UPDATE statement is executed. If it executes successfully, the exception handler code is not invoked. However, if the value of :newquantity exceeds the maximum allowable for the SMALLINT data type, you can handle the exception raised with code that follows the END keyword.

Done!

REVIEW

Problems, called exception conditions, can crop up in applications you write. They can be due to bugs in your code or to environmental conditions at runtime. When exceptions do occur, you need a way of recognizing them, dealing with them, and hopefully overcoming them. To that end, SQL provides the SQLSTATE status variable and a diagnostics area where information about exceptions and warnings is stored. You can retrieve the information in the diagnostics area, and based on what it tells you, you can take action to overcome the problem. If you can't overcome the problem, you should at least be able to terminate execution of your application in a graceful manner.

QUIZ YOURSELF

1. In the SQLSTATE status variable, what does a class code of 02 mean? (See "SQLSTATE.")

2. If the status variable SQLWARNING is TRUE, what is the class code of SQLSTATE? (See "The WHENEVER directive.")

3. If a SQL statement generates more warnings and exceptions than the diagnostics area can hold, how do you know that you do not have all the error information? (See "The Diagnostics Area.")

4. How can you retrieve information about exceptions from the diagnostics area? (See "The Diagnostics Area.")

Dynamic SQL

Session Checklist

✔ The distinguishing features of interactive SQL

✔ The distinguishing features of embedded SQL

✔ The distinguishing features of module language SQL

✔ How dynamic SQL differs from static SQL

✔ Looking at prepared statements versus immediate statements

✔ Dealing with descriptors

✔ Processing a row at a time with dynamic cursors

**30 Min.
To Go**

There are four different forms of SQL. Throughout this book I have primarily talked about two of them, interactive SQL and embedded SQL. These are the two forms of SQL that most people use most of the time. The other two, module language SQL and dynamic SQL, are less common. In this session I give brief recaps of interactive SQL and embedded SQL, and then briefly explain module language SQL, before diving into dynamic SQL in more depth.

Interactive SQL

Interactive SQL is a real-time conversation between the user and the database engine. You enter an SQL statement from the keyboard and the database engine responds by executing it and possibly returning a result set to you. An example of interactive SQL may look something like the following:

```
SELECT *
FROM INVOICE
ORDER BY Salesperson, TotalCharge DESC;
```

There are advantages and disadvantages to this method of using SQL. The primary advantages are that the "programming" is simple and the response is immediate. There are two big disadvantages, also. One is that queries that you need to run a dozen times a day must all be typed in a dozen times a day. Data entry errors and terminal boredom are both inevitable. A second disadvantage is that a user whose primary job is something other than database programming must learn SQL syntax.

Embedded SQL

Interactive SQL may be fine for one-time queries to get a quick answer, but it is not a viable option for generating reports that are run on a regular basis, for insertions of multiple table rows, or for updates to multiple table rows. For those kinds of activities, you want to be able to write a program once, and then just run the program whenever you want to interact with the database. The most common method for doing this uses embedded SQL.

Even with the procedural features added by the SQL:1999 specification, SQL is not a full-function general purpose programming language. It is great for interacting with a database, but a typical application that includes database interaction also does a lot of other things that SQL does not do well. The solution is to embed SQL statements within an enveloping structure made up of commands written in a general-purpose host language such as Java, Visual Basic, or C++.

Because the host language's compiler will not be able to recognize the SQL statements embedded in the host language code, an EXEC SQL directive precedes each such statement. This causes the compiler to ignore the SQL and continue to compile the program. At runtime, when execution reaches the embedded SQL statements, they are passed directly to the database engine for execution.

Most people who access information in relational databases do so through application programs written in some host language, with embedded SQL.

Module Language SQL

Like embedded SQL, module language works with a program written in a procedural language. However, the SQL statements are not embedded in the procedural language code. Instead, all the SQL is stored in a separate program module. The procedural language program contains calls to the statements in the SQL module. The SQL is called and executed in the same way that a subprocedure would be called and executed.

Applications implemented with a procedural language and module language SQL have the same functional capability as applications written with a procedural host language and embedded SQL. Use whichever one your host language supports.

**20 Min.
To Go**

Dynamic SQL versus Static SQL

Like embedded SQL and module language SQL, dynamic SQL is also used in programs. It differs from them both, however, in that the content of dynamic SQL statements is not completely known until runtime. Part or all of an SQL statement is either supplied by the user, or by the host program, based on interim results of execution.

Application programs using embedded SQL or module language SQL are written, compiled, debugged, and then compiled again by highly skilled application developers long before they are executed in a production environment by users who are not necessarily experts in SQL, database, or any computer language. By the time the user sees a program, its functionality is completely specified and frozen. For that reason, applications that use either embedded SQL or module language SQL are said to be using *static* SQL. The user can do no more with it than was foreseen and implemented by the application developer.

The lack of flexibility of static SQL does not apply to interactive SQL, but interactive SQL is not appropriate in a production environment for the speed and reliability reasons stated above. Nevertheless, there are application areas where such flexibility is needed. For such applications, some of the information needed to perform a task is not available until runtime. Dynamic SQL provides a means to write, compile, and debug a program that leaves unspecified the items that are not available until runtime. Either the user or the program itself can add these missing items at runtime, forming complete SQL statements, which then execute and produce the desired results.

Dynamic SQL calls the missing items that are supplied at runtime *dynamic parameters* or *parameter markers*. A dynamic parameter is denoted by a question mark (?) in a dynamic SQL statement. Here's an example of a dynamic SQL statement that contains dynamic parameters:

```
INSERT INTO EMPLOYEES (EmployeeID, FirstName, LastName, HireDate)
    VALUES (:empid, ?, ?, ?) ;
```

This is an example of SQL that may be used in conjunction with a data entry form. The program supplies a unique EmployeeID with the :empid variable, and the user makes entries for a new employee's first name, last name, and hire date. After the entries are made, the INSERT statement is complete and can be sent to the database engine for execution.

Prepared Statements versus Immediate Statements

There are two types of dynamic SQL statements: prepared and immediate. Each is appropriate for a different situation. Use the PREPARE/EXECUTE statement pair when the SQL you are writing will be executed multiple times. Preparation is analogous to compilation. When you PREPARE a dynamic SQL statement, you analyze it for proper syntax and determine the types of any dynamic parameters. This operation also gives the statement a name and optimizes it. You need to prepare a dynamic SQL statement only once. The execution part needs to be repeated each time the statement is invoked. Prepared dynamic SQL is better for any statement that will be executed multiple times, any statement that includes dynamic parameters, or any statement that returns a result.

As an example, suppose you have captured a dynamic SQL statement in a string variable that is a valid SQL statement named statementstring. You can then do the preparation part of the operation with:

```
statementstring = 'INSERT INTO EMPLOYEES
    (EmployeeID, FirstName, LastName, HireDate)
    VALUES (:empid, ?, ?, ?)' ;
EXEC SQL PREPARE statementname
    FROM :statementstring;
```

Later in the program, perhaps within a loop structure that executes it multiple times, you can put the execution part:

```
EXEC SQL EXECUTE :statementname ;
```

Any dynamic SQL statement that has dynamic parameters or that returns a result set must be handled with the PREPARE/EXECUTE pair, even if you are going to invoke it only once.

Sometimes you want to execute a dynamic SQL statement (one that you are not completely sure about until runtime) only once, and you know that it will contain no dynamic parameters, and that it will not return a result. Statements that satisfy those criteria can be executed immediately. There is no benefit to separating it into a preparation part and an execution part. In this case, syntax would be something like the following:

```
EXEC SQL EXECUTE IMMEDIATE :statementstring ;
```

Dealing with Descriptors

**10 Min.
To Go**

Dynamic parameters can be either input parameters that your host language program is sending to the database engine or output parameters that are returning results to your host language program. Because your host language program is written in a procedural language, it is not able to handle a result set of more than one row. Thus your statement must either be used with a cursor, or it must be guaranteed to return no more than one row.

The database engine must be able to store the dynamic parameters, as well as important facts about them such as their data type and length, and whether they may contain null values. This information is stored in an SQL item descriptor area in memory. Several SQL statements deal with the item descriptor area.

- ALLOCATE DESCRIPTOR names and allocates space in memory for a descriptor.
- DESCRIBE puts information into the descriptor, based on user input.
- GET DESCRIPTOR retrieves the count of the number of parameters in the descriptor area, as well as facts about each parameter.
- SET DESCRIPTOR is a tool the programmer uses to set a field in a descriptor area to a predetermined value.
- DEALLOCATE DESCRIPTOR releases system resources that have been taken up by a descriptor.

The ALLOCATE DESCRIPTOR statement

To use a dynamic SQL statement, it must be completely described. That description must reside someplace in memory. The ALLOCATE DESCRIPTOR statement sets aside a block of space in the item descriptor area for each dynamic SQL statement in a program. The ALLO-CATE DESCRIPTOR statement takes the following form:

```
ALLOCATE DESCRIPTOR descriptor-name
    [WITH MAX occurrences] ;
```

After you declare a descriptor name with this statement, you can refer to it in subsequent DESCRIBE, SET DESCRIPTOR, GET DESCRIPTOR, and DEALLOCATE DESCRIPTOR statements. The optional WITH MAX occurrences clause specifies how many items to make space for. These items are the dynamic parameters that will be supplied at runtime. Table 30-1 lists all the things that must be specified about each dynamic parameter.

Table 30-1 *Dynamic Parameter Information Stored in SQL Item Descriptor Area*

Field Name	Field Data Type	Comment
TYPE	Exact numeric, scale 0	Code for the data type
LENGTH	Exact numeric, scale 0	Length in characters or bits for string types
OCTET_TYPE	Exact numeric, scale 0	Length in octets for strings
RETURNED_LENGTH	Exact numeric, scale 0	Length in characters or bits returned from DBMS for strings
RETURNED_OCTET_LENGTH	Exact numeric, scale 0	Length in octets returned from DBMS strings
PRECISION	Exact numeric, scale 0	Precision for numeric types
SCALE	Exact numeric, scale 0	Scale for exact numeric types
DATETIME_INTERVAL_CODE	Exact numeric, scale 0	Code for datetime/interval sub-type
DATETIME_INTERVAL_PRECISION	Exact numeric, scale 0	Precision of interval's leading field
NULLABLE	Exact numeric, scale 0	Is column nullable?
NAME	Character string, length <= 128	Name of associated database column
UNNAMED	Exact numeric, scale 0	Is name real, or supplied by DBMS?
COLLATION_CATALOG	Character string, length <= 128	Catalog name for column's collation

Continued

Table 30-1 *Continued*

Field Name	Field Data Type	Comment
COLLATION_SCHEMA	Character string, length <= 128	Schema name for column's collation
COLLATION_NAME	Character string, length <= 128	Collation name for column's collation
CHARACTER_SET_CATALOG	Character string, length <= 128	Catalog name for column's character set
CHARACTER_SET_SCHEMA	Character string, length <= 128	Schema name for column's character set
CHARACTER_SET_NAME	Character string, length <= 128	Collation name for column's character set
DATA	Specified by code in TYPE field	The actual data
INDICATOR	Exact numeric, scale 0	Value for indicator parameter

The first field in Table 30-1, TYPE, holds a numeric code that corresponds to the data type of the dynamic parameter that space is being allocated for. Table 30-2 shows what data types these numeric codes represent.

Table 30-2 *TYPE Codes*

Code	Data Type
Negative	Implementor-defined data types
1	CHARACTER
2	NUMERIC
3	DECIMAL
4	INTEGER
5	SMALLINT
6	FLOAT
7	REAL
8	DOUBLE PRECISION
9	DATE, TIME, or TIMESTAMP
10	INTERVAL

Code	Data Type
11	Reserved for future use
12	CHARACTER VARYING
13	ENUMERATED
14	BIT
15	BIT VARYING
17	Abstract data types
30	BLOB
31	BLOB LOCATOR
40	CLOB
41	CLOB LOCATOR

The DATETIME_INTERVAL_CODE field in Table 30-1 also contains a numeric code. This code distinguishes between the various date and time types, if the dynamic parameter for which space is being allocated happens to be a date, time, or interval (type code = 9). Table 30-3 gives the codes that apply to the DATE, TIME, and TIMESTAMP types.

Table 30-3   *DATETIME Codes for DATE, TIME, or TIMESTAMP Data*

Code	Data Type
1	DATE
2	TIME
3	TIMESTAMP
4	TIME WITH TIME ZONE
5	TIMESTAMP WITH TIME ZONE

Table 30-4 holds the codes that appear in the DATETIME_INTERVAL_CODE field if the data type of the dynamic parameter is INTERVAL (type code = 10).

Table 30-4   *DATETIME Codes for INTERVAL Data*

Code	Data Type
1	YEAR
2	MONTH

Continued

Table 30-4	*Continued*
Code	**Data Type**
3	DAY
4	HOUR
5	MINUTE
6	SECOND
7	YEAR TO MONTH
8	DAY TO HOUR
9	DAY TO MINUTE
10	DAY TO SECOND
11	HOUR TO MINUTE
12	HOUR TO SECOND
13	MINUTE TO SECOND

Building a dynamic SQL statement

Once you have allocated space in the descriptor area for a descriptor table, the next step is to place information into that area, based in input from the user, and then turn that information into an SQL statement. This is an involved process that uses the host language within which your SQL is to be embedded. Here are the steps:

1. Declare variables to hold the name of the table, its primary key, and the columns you are going to affect.
2. Solicit from the user the names of the table and the columns of interest.
3. Construct the dynamic SQL statement as a character string and assign the string to a host variable.
4. Create the EXEC SQL PREPARE directive that prepares the statement for execution.
5. Determine the data types of all the values that the user will enter. This involves use of the ALLOCATE DESCRIPTOR, DESCRIBE, and GET DESCRIPTOR statements. The SET DESCRIPTOR statement allows you, the programmer, to specify descriptor values rather than soliciting them from the user.
6. Solicit from the user the entry of the values that will be inserted into the dynamic SQL statement.
7. Taking the user-entered values, construct a complete SQL statement.
8. EXECUTE the dynamic SQL statement.

9. After execution, when you are sure you won't need this prepared SQL statement and descriptor again, you can free up the system resources they are consuming with DEALLOCATE PREPARE and DEALLOCATE DESCRIPTOR statements.

Setting up and using the descriptor areas is extraordinarily complex, which means that using dynamic SQL is extraordinarily complex. Most application programmers never use dynamic SQL at all. In practically all cases, as a programmer, you know what you want to do when you write the program. You also know what to expect to be returned as a result set. Dynamic SQL is mostly used by systems programmers who write utilities. If you are ever called upon to write a program that incorporates dynamic SQL, your best chance of success is to find an example in a manual or an existing program that uses dynamic SQL in a way similar to what you need to do and copy it, modifying it appropriately. It is probably not worth the time it would take to become a dynamic SQL guru, unless you plan to use it frequently. On the other hand, it is good to know that this capability exists because you may encounter dynamic SQL in code that someone else has written and that you are now tasked with maintaining.

Cursors and Dynamic SQL

The dynamic SQL discussed in the preceding sections works for non-SELECT statements such as UPDATE, and for SELECT statements that are guaranteed to return no more than one row of result. To create a dynamic SQL statement that could possibly return a result set of more than one row, you have to use a cursor because the host language that you return the result to is not capable of handling data a set at a time. The syntax for a dynamic cursor is slightly different from the syntax for a static cursor that I describe in Session 27. The syntax is:

```
DECLARE cursor-name [INSENSITIVE][SCROLL] CURSOR
    FOR statement-name ;
```

The FOR statement holds the name of a character string rather than a query expression. Since the needed query expression may not be known at compile time, a character string is used as a placeholder. At runtime, the newly constructed query expression is substituted for the character string, then it is executed.

The dynamic OPEN cursor statement is similar to the static one, except for the fact that if dynamic parameters appear in the cursor expression, they must be listed, as shown here:

```
OPEN cursor-name [USING dynamic-parameter-list] ;
```

The dynamic FETCH statement is of the form:

```
FETCH [[orientation] FROM] cursor-name
    USING dynamic-parameter-list ;
```

When you are finished with the dynamic cursor, you can close it with:

```
CLOSE cursor-name ;
```

Done!

REVIEW

There are four different ways of using SQL with a database, interactive, embedded, module language, and dynamic. Of these, embedded SQL is the most frequently used. Embedded is a form a static SQL, which is compiled in an operation that is separate from its execution. This has the effect of streamlining the execution of a database application, but means that the contents of the SQL statement must be completely known at compile time. In some applications, particularly utility programs, the content of an SQL statement may not be known until runtime. In such cases, static SQL cannot do what is needed.

Dynamic SQL can be partially specified (prepared) beforehand, and partially specified at runtime. This mode of operation is valuable when the same statement must be executed multiple times, possibly with a different set of dynamic parameters each time. Some types of dynamic SQL statements (those that do not include dynamic parameters, and that do not return a result) can be specified completely at runtime and executed immediately.

Setting up a program to use dynamic SQL is complicated, but happily it is also rare. Most application objectives can be achieved with static SQL.

QUIZ YOURSELF

1. In what way does the use of interactive SQL differ from the other three ways of using SQL? (See "Interactive SQL.")

2. Which executes faster: a dynamic SQL statement that has been prepared, or an equivalent statement that was invoked with an EXECUTE IMMEDIATE directive? (See "Dynamic SQL versus Static SQL.")

3. Why may you not use EXECUTE IMMEDIATE to execute a SELECT statement? (See "Dynamic SQL versus Static SQL.")

4. Why must you use a dynamic cursor with a dynamic SELECT statement that could possibly return a result set of more than one row? (See "Cursors and Dynamic SQL.")

PART

VI

Sunday Afternoon
Part Review

1. Which SQL statements operate on multiple table rows in a single operation?

2. Which of the commands associated with cursors actually retrieves a result set from a database?

3. When declaring a cursor, what clause should you add to prevent changes to the table row the cursor points to?

4. Why might a DBMS vendor purposely offer a feature that does not comply with the SQL:1999 standard?

5. What DDL functions does Microsoft SQL Server 2000 fully support?

6. Which of the covered DBMS products has the weakest database security?

7. What value of SQLSTATE means that the immediately preceding SQL statement executed without any detected error, exception, warning, or otherwise unusual outcome?

8. What conditions will cause SQLEXCEPTION to be set to FALSE?

9. What does it mean if the MORE field in the diagnostics header area contains a value of "Y"?

10. Why do host language debuggers have problems with applications that contain embedded SQL?

11. What are dynamic parameters?

12. What SQL statement would you use to set aside space in memory for the storage of dynamic parameters?

Answers to the Part Reviews

Friday Evening Review Answers

1. A flat file is composed of multiple fields, each one containing a specific category of data. Each field is assigned a predefined number of characters.

2. The application program must contain information about the physical structure of the flat file, not just its logical contents. If the file structure should ever change, the application will no longer work properly.

3. Metadata is data about data. It holds the knowledge of the structure of the data in a database. Since structural knowledge resides in the database rather than the application, structural changes will not necessarily cause the application to malfunction.

4. The relational model is based upon two-dimensional tables made up of columns and rows, similar to the columns and rows of an electronic spreadsheet.

5. SQL is the internationally recognized standard language for dealing with data in relational databases. It is a data sublanguage that does not contain all the functionality of a general purpose programming language such as C or Java.

   ```
   SELECT ContactName, ContactPhone FROM PROSPECTS ;
   SELECT ContactName, ContactPhone FROM PROSPECTS
           WHERE Country = 'Canada' ;
   ```

6. The precision of a number is the maximum number of digits that it may hold.

7. Use the REAL data type when the numbers represented may be either very large or very small.

8. TRUE, FALSE, and UNKNOWN.

9. Use of non-standard data types complicates the migration of an application from one database back end to another.

10. The CAST operator will translate one data type to another.

11. A fully qualified column reference is a column reference that explicitly states which table a column is from.

```
SELECT COUNT (*) FROM PROSPECTS ;
SELECT * FROM PROSPECTS
              WHERE SUBSTRING (Country FROM 1 FOR 1) = 'U' ;
```

12. A value expression must reduce to a single value.

Saturday Morning Review Answers

1. ```
   SELECT * FROM INVOICE
       WHERE TotalRemitted >= 200 ;
   ```

2. ```
   SELECT * FROM CUSTOMERS
   WHERE Country <> 'USA' AND ContactFax IS NULL ;
   ```

3. ```
   SELECT * FROM PROSPECTS
   WHERE Country NOT IN ('USA','Canada','UK','Germany','China') ;
   ```

4. ```
   SELECT * FROM PROSPECTS
   WHERE Address1 LIKE '%brook%' ;
   ```

5. You cannot use any of the comparison operators, such as the "equals" operator, with a NULL value because NULL means UNKNOWN.

6. Nested queries.

7. The EXISTS operator returns a TRUE value if the subquery it introduces returns a result. It returns a FALSE value if the subquery it introduces returns no result.

8. A UNIQUE operator that introduces a subquery will return a FALSE value if the result set returned by the subquery contains at least one duplicate record.

9. FALSE. The DISTINCT predicate will not return an UNKNOWN value.

10. TRUE. There is a one-minute overlap.

11. Use a MATCH UNIQUE, MATCH UNIQUE SIMLE, or a MATCH UNIQUE FULL predicate.

12. The SIMILAR operator operates on regular expressions that reduce to character strings, while the LIKE operator operates only on character strings.

13. The CASE conditional expression performs a test, and depending on the outcome, selects one of multiple values to return.

14. The statement updates the Country column of the PROSPECTS table by replacing every instance of the value 'USSR' with the NULL value.

15. The COALESCE expression returns the first non-NULL value in its list of arguments.

16. A row value constructor returns an entire row of values rather than a single value as does a value expression.

17. ```
    SELECT CustomerID, COUNT(CustomerID) FROM INVOICE
           GROUP BY CustomerID ;
    ```
    ```

18. SELECT CUSTOMERID, COUNT(CustomerID) FROM INVOICE
       GROUP BY CustomerID
       HAVING CustomerID < 2000 ;

19. SELECT * FROM INVOICE
      ORDER BY TotalCharge DESC ;

Saturday Afternoon Review Answers

1. All the tables related by the UNION, INTERSECT, and EXCEPT operators must have the same structure. Tables related by joins need not have the same structure.

2. SELECT DepartmentManager FROM NASTAFF
UNION
    SELECT DepartmentManager FROM EUROSTAFF ;

3. Rows that appeared in both the AUTHORS table and the EDITORS table would be returned.

4. Table aliases are declared in the FROM clause.

5. The syntax of a cross join and of an equi-join of the same two tables is the same except for the fact that the equi-join includes a WHERE clause that compares for equality a column of the first table with a column of the second table.

6. An equi-join and a condition join of the same two tables are the same except for the fact that the WHERE clause of the equi-join must compare two columns for equality. The condition join can use any of the conditional operators. Thus an equi-join is a special case of a condition join.

7. Theoretically there is no limit to the number of levels of nesting you may have in a nested query, but there is a practical limit that is set by the specific implementation you are using.

8. Only SELECT statements are allowed in subqueries of a nested query.

9. One of the two types of nested query may execute faster on your system than the other does.

10. A screen form is the best facility to provide users for data entry.

11. The application must put the users entries into variables and use those variables are arguments in an SQL INSERT statement.

12. The unnamed fields are filled with the NULL value.

13. Host language debugging tools do not know how to deal with the embedded SQL statements.

14. Programs that use embedded SQL are easier to understand because program listings show the flow of execution in a linear manner without branching out to a procedure in a separate SQL module.

15. RAD tools cannot perform complex database operations. For those you need SQL.

16. Use of the ATOMIC keyword prevents some of the statements in a block from executing successfully and one failing, leaving the database in a corrupted state.

17. A REPEAT loop will always execute at least once, regardless of the state of the termination condition. A WHILE loop may not execute at all, if the termination condition is already satisfied when the loop is entered.

18. The IF structure is the most widely supported branching and looping structure.

Saturday Evening Review Answers

1. When you use native drivers for database management systems, your application must use different application program interface (API) code for each one of them. If later you need to support a new DBMS, you will need to alter your program code to accommodate the new API.

2. Application, Driver Manager, Drivers, Data Sources

3. The Driver Manager determines which driver to load.

4. Everything that stays on the server does not have to be sent over the network to clients. Fewer network round trips translates to better performance.

5. Recompile the stored procedure to make sure it is compatible with the new table structure.

6. Triggers are often used to enforce business rules.

7. You would use the ALTER TABLE statement to add a column to an existing table.

8. A NULL value is unknown, and thus it may duplicate the value of the primary key of another row in the table. This must not be allowed.

9. You may want to make a view of a single table in order to eliminate from the result set of a retrieval on the view all the rows that are not relevant to the purpose of the retrieval. You may also want to use a view to make the values in some columns available to certain users but to hide other columns.

10. Scope creep hurts your wallet the most when you are working on a fixed price contract.

11. The E-R model's entities and attributes become tables and columns in the relational model.

12. It does not make sense to build an index for a table that has a small number of rows.

Sunday Morning Review Answers

1. Data redundancy wastes storage space, prolongs execution time, and makes the database vulnerable to inconsistencies when updates to not reach all copies of the redundant data.

2. The table must be entirely consistent with the entity it models.

3. CHECK NOT (TotalRemitted > TotalCharge)

4. Modification anomalies are problems that corrupt the data in a table when you modify it with either an insertion or a deletion.

5. A composite key is a key that is made up of more than one column.

6. A table is in domain-key normal form if every constraint on the table is a logical consequence of the definition of keys and domains.

7. The database administrator has primary responsibility for the maintenance and health of a database.

8. A database object owner may grant SELECT, INSERT, UPDATE, DELETE, REFERENCES, USAGE, and GRANT privileges to another user.

9. A role is a function in the organization. Everyone who has that role can be granted the same access privileges with a single operation.

10. Most problems occur when the system is new, or when a major system component has changed.

11. A read lock placed on a database object by a user prevents all other users from reading the contents of that database object until the lock is released.

12. The READ UNCOMMITTED isolation level provides the least protection against unwanted user interactions.

13. A database server spends most if its time inputting and outputting data (I/O).

14. An index on a table's primary key generally provides the fastest access to a single desired row.

15. Performance is better if a large database is stored across multiple disks.

16. With a database and templated design, you can build and maintain a large Web site faster and cheaper than would be possible if each page were custom coded.

17. ASP is a server-side scripting language that pulls data from a database and converts the results to HTML for transmission to the requesting client.

18. Security is more of a concern for a Web database because you have no control over the people who will access it or over their intentions.

Sunday Afternoon Review Answers

1. SELECT, UPDATE, and DELETE operate on multiple table rows.

2. The OPEN statement retrieves a result set from the database.

3. FOR READ ONLY

4. A vendor may purposely offer a non-standard feature to competitive advantage over other products that do not offer such a feature.

5. SQL Server 2000 fully supports the CREATE, ALTER, and DROP DDL statements.

6. MySQL has the weakest database security. It's default table handler is not ACID compliant.

7. 00000

8. SQLSTATE class codes of 00, 01, or 02 will cause SQLEXCEPTION to be set to FALSE.

9. If the MORE field of the diagnostics header area contains a value of "Y" there were more status records returned from the execution of the preceding SQL statement than the diagnostics area is configured to hold.

10. Host language debuggers expect to encounter native host language commands, not alien SQL statements.

11. Dynamic parameters are parts of a dynamic SQL statement that are not added to the statement until runtime.

12. ALLOCATE DESCRIPTOR

What's on the CD

This appendix provides you with information on the contents of the CD that accompanies this book. (For the latest and greatest information, please refer to the ReadMe file located at the root of the CD.) Here is what you will find:

- System Requirements
- Using the CD with Windows and Linux
- What's on the CD
- Troubleshooting

System Requirements

Make sure that your computer meets the minimum system requirements listed in this section. If your computer doesn't match up to most of these requirements, you may have a problem using the contents of the CD.

For Windows 9x, Windows 2000, Windows NT4 (with SP 4 or later), Windows Me, or Windows XP:

- PC with a Pentium-compatible processor running at 120 Mhz or faster
- At least 64 MB of total RAM installed on your computer; for best performance we recommend at least 128 MB
- A CD-ROM drive

Note: The computer will run fine on computers equipped with AMD Duron and Athlon chips.

For Linux:

- PC with a Pentium-compatible processor running at 90 Mhz or faster
- At least 64 MB of total RAM installed on your computer; for best performance we recommend at least 128 MB
- A CD-ROM drive

Note: The computer will run fine on computers equipped with AMD Duron and Athlon chips.

Using the CD with Windows

To install the items from the CD to your hard drive, follow these steps:

1. Insert the CD into your computer's CD-ROM drive.
2. A window appears with the following options. Install, Explore, and Exit.

   Install: Gives you the option to install the supplied software and/or the author-created samples on the CD-ROM.

   Explore: Allows you to view the contents of the CD-ROM in its directory structure.

   Exit: Closes the autorun window.

Note: If you do not have autorun enabled or if the autorun window does not appear, follow the steps below to access the CD.

1. Choose Start ➪ Run.
2. In the dialog box that appears, type **d:\setup.exe**, where *d* is the letter of your CD-ROM drive; this will bring up the autorun window described above.
3. Choose the Install, Explore, or Exit option from the menu. (See Step 2 that precedes this set of steps for a description of these options.)

Using the CD with Linux

To install the items from the CD to your hard drive, follow these steps:

1. Log in as **root**.
2. Insert the CD into your computer's CD-ROM drive.
3. Mount the CD-ROM.
4. Launch a graphical file manager.

What's on the CD

The following sections provide a summary of the software and other materials you'll find on the CD.

Author-created materials

All author-created material from the book including code listings and samples are on the CD in the folder named "Author".

Applications

The following applications are on the CD:

- **MySQL.** Open source version of MySQL for Linux and Unix. For more information, check out www.mysql.com.
- **MySQL.** Alternative site for open source version of MySQL for Linux and Unix. For more information check out www.mysql.org.
- **PostgreSQL.** Open source version of PostgreSQL for Linux and Unix. For more information, check out www.postgresql.org.

PostgreSQL Installation Instructions

To help clarify the PostgreSQL installation process, I'm including additional instructions, both the short and long version.

Short version

```
./configure
    gmake
    gmake install
    adduser postgres
    su - postgres
    /usr/local/pgsql/bin/initdb -D /usr/local/pgsql/data
    /usr/local/pgsql/bin/postmaster -D /usr/local/pgsql/data >logfile 2>&1 &
    /usr/local/pgsql/bin/createdb test
    /usr/local/pgsql/bin/psql test
```

Long version

The long version is broken into subsections.

Requirements

In general, a modern Unix-compatible platform should be able to run PostgreSQL. The platforms that had received explicit testing at the time of release are listed in the section called Supported Platforms below. In the doc subdirectory of the distribution there are several platform-specific FAQ documents you might wish to consult if you are having trouble.

The following prerequisites exist for building PostgreSQL:

- GNU make is required; other make programs will not work. GNU make is often installed under the name gmake; this document will always refer to it by that name. (On GNU/Linux systems GNU make is the default tool with the name make.) To test for GNU make, type **gmake -- version**. If at all possible you should use version 3.76.1 or later.

- You need an ISO/ANSI C compiler. Recent versions of GCC are recommendable, but PostgreSQL is known to build with a wide variety of compilers from different vendors.

- gzip

- The GNU Readline library for comfortable line editing and command history retrieval will automatically be used if found. You may wish to install it before proceeding, but it is not required. (On NetBSD, the libedit library is readline-compatible and is used if libreadline is not found.)

- Flex and Bison are not required when building from a released source package because the output files are pre-generated. You will need these programs only when building from a CVS tree or when the actual scanner and parser definition files were changed. If you need them, be sure to get Flex 2.5.4 or later and Bison 1.28 or later. Other yacc programs can sometimes be used, but doing so requires extra efforts and is not recommended. Other flex programs will definitely not work.

- To build on Windows NT or Windows 2000 you need the Cygwin and cygipc packages. See the file doc/FAQ_MSWIN for details.

If you need to get a GNU package, you can find it at your local GNU mirror site (see www.gnu.org/order/ftp.html for a list) or at ftp://ftp.gnu.org/gnu.

Also check that you have sufficient disk space. You will need about 30 MB for the source tree during compilation and about 5 MB for the installation directory. An empty database takes about 1 MB, later it takes about five times the amount of space that a flat text file with the same data would take. If you are going to run the regression tests you will temporarily need an extra 20 MB. Use the df command to check for disk space.

If you are upgrading

The internal data storage format changes with new releases of PostgreSQL. Therefore, if you are upgrading an existing installation that does not have a version number "7.1.x", you must back up and restore your data as shown here. These instructions assume that your existing installation is under the /usr/local/pgsql directory, and that the data area is in /usr/local/pgsql/data. Substitute your paths appropriately.

1. Make sure that your database is not updated during or after the backup. This does not affect the integrity of the backup, but the changed data would of course not be included. If necessary, edit the permissions in the file /usr/local/pgsql/data/ pg_hba.conf (or equivalent) to disallow access from everyone except you.

2. To dump your database installation, type **pg_dumpall > outputfile**.

   If you need to preserve the OIDs (such as when using them as foreign keys), then use the -o option when running pg_dumpall. pg_dumpall does not save large objects. Check the Administrator's Guide if you need to do this.

   Make sure that you use the pg_dumpall command from the version you are currently running. 7.1's pg_dumpall should not be used on older databases.

3. If you are installing the new version at the same location as the old one, shut down the old server before you install the new files:

   ```
   kill -INT `cat /usr/local/pgsql/data/postmaster.pid`
   ```

Versions prior to 7.0 do not have this postmaster.pid file. If you are using such a version you must find out the process id of the server yourself, for example, by typing **ps ax | grep postmaster**, and supply it to the kill command.

On systems that have PostgreSQL started at boot time, there is probably a start-up file that will accomplish the same thing. For example, on a Red Hat Linux system one might find that **/etc/rc.d/init.d/postgresql stop** works.

4. If you are installing in the same place as the old version, then it is also a good idea to move the old installation out of the way, in case you still need it later on. Use a command like this:

   ```
   mv /usr/local/pgsql /usr/local/pgsql.old
   ```

After you have installed PostgreSQL, create a new database directory and start the new server. Remember that you must execute these commands while logged in to the special database user account (which you already have if you are upgrading).

```
/usr/local/pgsql/bin/initdb -D /usr/local/pgsql/data
/usr/local/pgsql/bin/postmaster -D /usr/local/pgsql/data
```

Finally, using the new psql, restore your data with:

```
/usr/local/pgsql/bin/psql -d template1 -f outputfile
```

You can also install the new version in parallel with the old one to decrease the downtime. These topics are discussed at length in the Administrator's Guide, which you are encouraged to read in any case.

Installation procedure

1. **Configuration.**

   The first step of the installation procedure is to configure the source tree for your system and choose the options you would like. This is done by running the configure script. For a default installation simply type **./configure**. This script will run a number of tests to guess values for various system-dependent variables and detect some quirks of your operating system, and finally creates several files in the build tree to record what it found.

   The default configuration will build the server and utilities, as well as all client applications and interfaces that only require a C compiler. All files will be installed under /usr/local/pgsql by default. You can customize the build and installation process by supplying one or more of the following command line options to configure:

   - **--prefix=PREFIX:** Install all files under the directory PREFIX instead of /usr/local/pgsql. The actual files will be installed into various subdirectories; no files will ever be installed directly into the PREFIX directory. If you have special needs, you can also customize the individual subdirectories with the following options.

- **--exec-prefix=EXEC-PREFIX:** You can install architecture-dependent files under a different prefix, EXEC-PREFIX, than what PREFIX was set to. This can be useful to share architecture-independent files between hosts. If you omit this, then EXEC-PREFIX is set equal to PREFIX and both architecture-dependent and -independent files will be installed under the same tree, which is probably what you want.
- **--bindir=DIRECTORY:** Specifies the directory for executable programs. The default is EXEC-PREFIX/bin, which normally means /usr/local/pgsql/bin.
- **--datadir=DIRECTORY:** Sets the directory for read-only data files used by the installed programs. The default is PREFIX/share. Note that this has nothing to do with where your database files will be placed.
- **--sysconfdir=DIRECTORY:** The directory for various configuration files, PREFIX/etc by default.
- **--libdir=DIRECTORY:** The location to install libraries and dynamically loadable modules. The default is EXEC-PREFIX/lib.
- **--includedir=DIRECTORY:** The directory for installing C and C++ header files. The default is PREFIX/include.
- **--docdir=DIRECTORY:** Documentation files, except "man" pages, will be installed into this directory. The default is PREFIX/doc.
- **--mandir=DIRECTORY:** The man pages that come with PostgreSQL will be installed under this directory, in their respective manx subdirectories. The default is PREFIX/man.

  Note: To reduce the pollution of shared installation locations (such as /usr/local/include), the string"/postgresql" is automatically appended to datadir, sysconfdir, includedir, and docdir, unless the fully expanded directory name already contains the string "postgres" or "pgsql". For example, if you choose /usr/local as prefix, the C header files will be installed in /usr/local/include/postgresql, but if the prefix is /opt/postgres, then they will be in /opt/postgres/include.
- **--with-includes=DIRECTORIES:** DIRECTORIES is a colon-separated list of directories that will be added to the list the compiler searches for header files. If you have optional packages (such as GNU Readline) installed in a non-standard location you have to use this option and probably the corresponding--with-libraries option.

  Example:--with-includes=/opt/gnu/include:/usr/sup/include.
- **--with-libraries=DIRECTORIES:** DIRECTORIES is a colon-separated list of directories to search for libraries. You will probably have to use this option (and the corresponding--with-includes option) if you have packages installed in non-standard locations.

  Example:--with-libraries=/opt/gnu/lib:/usr/sup/lib.
- **--enable-locale:** Enables locale support. There is a performance penalty associated with locale support, but if you are not in an English-speaking environment you will most likely need this.
- **--enable-recode:** Enables single-byte character set recode support. See the Administrator's Guide about this feature.

- **--enable-multibyte:** Allows the use of multibyte character encodings. This is primarily for languages like Japanese, Korean, and Chinese. Read the Administrator's Guide for details.

- **--with-pgport=NUMBER:** Set NUMBER as the default port number for server and clients. The default is 5432. The port can always be changed later on, but if you specify it here then both server and clients will have the same default compiled in, which can be very convenient.

- **--with-CXX:** Build the C++ interface library.

- **--with-perl:** Build the Perl interface module. The Perl interface will be installed at the usual place for Perl modules (typically under /usr/lib/perl), so you must have root access to perform the installation step (see step 4). You need to have Perl 5 installed to use this option.

- **--with-python:** Build the Python interface module. You need to have root access to be able to install the Python module at its default place (/usr/lib/pythonx.y). To be able to use this option, you must have Python installed and your system needs to support shared libraries. If you instead want to build a new complete interpreter binary, you will have to do it manually.

- **--with-tcl:** Builds components that require Tcl/Tk, which are libpgtcl, pgt-clsh, pgtksh, pgaccess, and PL/Tcl. But see below about --without-tk.

- **--without-tk:** If you specify --with-tcl and this option, then programs that require Tk (that is, pgtksh and pgaccess) will be excluded.

- **--with-tclconfig=DIRECTORY,--with-tkconfig=DIRECTORY:** Tcl/Tk installs the files tclConfig.sh and tkConfig.sh which contain certain configuration information that is needed to build modules interfacing to Tcl or Tk. These files are normally found automatically at their well-known location, but if you want to use a different version of Tcl or Tk you can specify the directory where to find them.

- **--enable-odbc:** Build the ODBC driver package.

- **--with-odbcinst=DIRECTORY:** Specifies the directory where the ODBC driver will expect its odbcinst.ini configuration file. The default is /usr/local/pgsql/etc or whatever you specified as --sysconfdir. A default file will be installed there. If you intend to share the odbcinst.ini file between several ODBC drivers then you may want to use this option.

- **--with-krb4=DIRECTORY, --with-krb5=DIRECTORY:** Build with support for Kerberos authentication. You can use either Kerberos version 4 or 5, but not both. The DIRECTORY argument specifies the root directory of the Kerberos installation; /usr/athena is assumed as default. If the relevant headers files and libraries are not under a common parent directory, then you must use the --with-includes and --with-libraries options in addition to this option. If, on the other hand, the required files are in a location that is searched by default (e.g., /usr/lib), then you can leave off the argument. Configure will check for the required header files and libraries to make sure that your Kerberos installation is sufficient before proceeding.

- **--with-krb-srvnam=NAME:** The name of the Kerberos service principal. "postgres" is the default. There's probably no reason to change this.

- **--with-openssl=DIRECTORY:** Build with support for SSL (encrypted) connections. This requires the OpenSSL package to be installed. The DIRECTORY argument specifies the root directory of the OpenSSL installation; the default is /usr/local/ssl. Configure will check for the required header files and libraries to make sure that your OpenSSL installation is sufficient before proceeding.

- **--with-java:** Build the JDBC driver and associated Java packages. This option requires Ant to be installed (as well as a JDK, of course). Refer to the JDBC driver documentation in the Programmer's Guide for more information.

- **--enable-syslog:** Enables the PostgreSQL server to use the syslog logging facility. (Using this option does not mean that you must log with syslog or even that it will be done by default; it simply makes it possible to turn this option on at run time.)

- **--enable-debug:** Compiles all programs and libraries with debugging symbols. This means that you can run the programs through a debugger to analyze problems. This enlarges the size of the installed executables considerably, and on non-gcc compilers it usually also disables compiler optimization, causing slowdowns. However, having the symbols available is extremely helpful for dealing with any problems that may arise. Currently, this option is considered of marginal value for production installations, but you should have it on if you are doing development work or running a beta version.

- **--enable-cassert:** Enables assertion checks in the server, which test for many "can't happen" conditions. This is invaluable for code development purposes, but the tests slow things down a little. Also, having the tests turned on won't necessarily enhance the stability of your server! The assertion checks are not categorized for severity, and so what might be a relatively harmless bug will still lead to postmaster restarts if it triggers an assertion failure. Currently, this option is not recommended for production use, but you should have it on for development work or when running a beta version. If you prefer a C or C++ compiler different from the one configure picks then you can set the environment variables CC and CXX, respectively, to the program of your choice. Similarly, you can override the default compiler flags with the CFLAGS and CXXFLAGS variables.

  Example: env CC=/opt/bin/gcc CFLAGS='-02 -pipe' ./configure

2. **Build.**

   To start the build, type **gmake**. (Remember to use GNU make.) The build can take anywhere from five minutes to half an hour. The last line displayed should be `All of PostgreSQL is successfully made. Ready to install.`

3. **Regression tests.**

   If you want to test the newly built server before you install it, you can run the regression tests at this point. The regression tests are a test suite to verify that PostgreSQL runs on your machine in the way the developers expected it to. Type **gmake check**. It is possible that some tests fail, due to differences in error message wording or floating point results. The file src/test/regress/README and the Administrator's Guide contain detailed information about interpreting the test results. You can repeat this test at any later time by issuing the same command.

4. **Installing the files.**

Note: If you are upgrading an existing system and are going to install the new files over the old ones then you should have backed up your data and shut down the old server by now, as explained in the section called "If you are upgrading" above.

To install PostgreSQL type **gmake install**. This will install files into the directories that were specified in Step 1. Make sure that you have appropriate permissions to write into that area. Normally you need to do this step as root. Alternatively, you could create the target directories in advance and arrange for appropriate permissions to be granted.

If you built the Perl or Python interfaces and you were not the root user when you executed the above command then that part of the installation probably failed. In that case you should become the root user and then do

gmake -C src/interfaces/perl5 install

gmake -C src/interfaces/python install

Due to a quirk in the Perl build environment the first command will actually rebuild the complete interface and then install it. This is not harmful, just unusual. If you do not have superuser access you are on your own: you can still take the required files and place them in other directories where Perl or Python can find them, but how to do that is left as an exercise.

The standard install installs only the header files needed for client application development. If you plan to do any server-side program development (such as custom functions or datatypes written in C), then you may want to install the entire PostgreSQL include tree into your target include directory. To do that, type **gmake install-all-headers**. This adds a megabyte or two to the install footprint, and is useful only if you don't plan to keep the whole source tree around for reference. (If you do, you can just use the source's include directory when building server-side software.)

Client-only installation: If you want to install only the client applications and interface libraries, then you can use these commands:

gmake -C src/bin install

gmake -C src/interfaces install

gmake -C doc install

To undo the installation use the command gmake uninstall. However, this will not remove the Perl and Python interfaces and it will not remove any directories.

After the installation you can make room by removing the built files from the source tree with the gmake clean command. This will preserve the choices made by the configure program, so that you can rebuild everything with gmake later on. To reset the source tree to the state in which it was distributed, use gmake distclean. If you are going to build for several platforms from the same source tree you must do this and re-configure for each build.

Post-installation setup

This section is divided into subsections.

Shared libraries

On some systems that have shared libraries (which most systems do) you need to tell your system how to find the newly installed shared libraries. The systems on which this is not necessary include FreeBSD, HP/UX, Irix, Linux, NetBSD, OpenBSD, OSF/1 (Digital Unix, Tru64 UNIX), and Solaris.

The method to set the shared library search path varies between platforms, but the most widely usable method is to set the environment variable LD_LIBRARY_PATH like so: In Bourne shells (sh, ksh, bash, zsh):

LD_LIBRARY_PATH=/usr/local/pgsql/lib

export LD_LIBRARY_PATH

or in csh or tcsh:

setenv LD_LIBRARY_PATH /usr/local/pgsql/lib

Replace /usr/local/pgsql/lib with whatever you set --libdir to in Step 1. You should put these commands into a shell start-up file such as /etc/profile or ~/.bash_profile. Some good information about the caveats associated with the method can be found at www.visi.com/~barr/ldpath.html.

On some systems it might be preferable to set the environment variable LD_RUN_PATH before building. If in doubt, refer to the manual pages of your system (perhaps ld.so or rld). If you later on get a message like psql: error in loading shared libraries libpq.so.2.1: cannot open shared object file: No such file or directory, then this step was necessary. Simply take care of it then.

Environment variables

If you installed into /usr/local/pgsql or some other location that is not searched for programs by default, you need to add /usr/local/pgsql/bin (or what you set --bindir to in step 1) into your PATH. To do this, add the following to your shell start-up file, such as ~/.bash_profile (or /etc/profile, if you want it to affect every user): PATH=$PATH:/usr/local/pgsql/bin

If you are using csh or tcsh, then use this command: set path = (/usr/local/pgsql/bin path)

To enable your system to find the man documentation, you need to add a line like the following to a shell start-up file: MANPATH=$MANPATH:/usr/local/pgsql/man

The environment variables PGHOST and PGPORT specify to client applications the host and port of the database server, overriding the compiled-in defaults. If you are going to run client applications remotely then it is convenient if every user that plans to use the database sets PGHOST, but it is not required and the settings can be communicated via command line options to most client programs.

Getting started

The following is a quick summary of how to get PostgreSQL up and running once installed. The Administrator's Guide contains more information.

1. Create a user account for the PostgreSQL server. This is the user the server will run as. For production use you should create a separate, unprivileged account ("postgres" is commonly used). If you do not have root access or just want to play around, your own user account is enough, but running the server as root is a security risk and will not work.

   adduser postgres

2. Create a database installation with the initdb command. To run initdb you must be logged in to your PostgreSQL server account. It will not work as root.

   root# mkdir /usr/local/pgsql/data

   root# chown postgres /usr/local/pgsql/data

   root# su - postgres

   postgres$ /usr/local/pgsql/bin/initdb -D /usr/local/pgsql/data

   The -D option specifies the location where the data will be stored. You can use any path you want, it does not have to be under the installation directory. Just make sure that the server account can write to the directory (or create it, if it doesn't already exist) before starting initdb, as illustrated here.

3. The previous step should have told you how to start up the database server. Do so now. The command should look something like:

   /usr/local/pgsql/bin/postmaster -D /usr/local/pgsql/data

   This will start the server in the foreground. To put the server in the background use something like

   **nohup /usr/local/pgsql/bin/postmaster -D /usr/local/pgsql/data **

       </dev/null >server.log 2>&1 </dev/null &

   To stop a server running in the background you can type:

   kill `cat /usr/local/pgsql/data/postmaster.pid`

   In order to allow TCP/IP connections (rather than only Unix domain socket ones) you need to pass the -i option to postmaster.

4. Create a database:

   Type **createdb testdb**. Then type **psql testdb** to connect to that database. At the prompt you can enter SQL commands and start experimenting.

What now?

- The Tutorial should be your first reading if you are completely new to SQL databases. It should have been installed at /usr/local/pgsql/doc/html/tutorial.html unless you changed the installation directories.

- If you are familiar with database concepts then you want to proceed with the Administrator's Guide, which contains information about how to set up the database server, database users, and authentication. It can be found at /usr/local/pgsql/doc/html/admin.html.

- Usually, you will want to modify your computer so that it will automatically start the database server whenever it boots. Some suggestions for this are in the Administrator's Guide.

- Run the regression tests against the installed server (using the sequential test method). If you didn't run the tests before installation, you should definitely do it now. This is also explained in the Administrator's Guide.

Supported platforms

PostgreSQL has been verified by the developer community to work on the platforms listed below. A supported platform generally means that PostgreSQL builds and installs according to these instructions and that the regression tests pass.

Note: If you are having problems with the installation on a supported platform, please write to <pgsql-bugs@postgresql.org> or <pgsql-ports@postgresql.org>, not to the people listed here.

OS	Processor	Version	Reported	Remarks
AIX	4.3.3RS6000	7.1	2001-03-21, Gilles Darold (<gilles@darold.net>)	see also doc/FAQ_AIX
BeOS	x86	7.1	2001-02-26, Cyril Velter (<cyril.velter@ libertysurf.fr>)	requires new 5.0.4BONE networking stack
BSD/OS 4.01	x86	7.1	2001-03-20, Bruce Momjian (<pgman@ candle.pha.pa.us>)	
Compaq Tru64	Alpha	7.1	2001-03-26, Adriaan Joubert (<a.joubert@ albourne.com>)	4.0-5.0, cc and gcc
UNIX FreeBSD 4.3	x86	7.1	2001-03-19, Vince Vielhaber (<vev@hub.org>)	
HP/UX	PA-RISC	7.1	2001-03-19, 10.20 Tom Lane (<tgl@sss.pgh. pa.us>), 2001-03-22, 11.00, 11i Giles Lean (<giles@nemeton.com.au>)	32- and 64-bit on 11.00; see also doc/ FAQ_HPUX
IRIX 6.5.11	MIPS	7.1	2001-03-22, Robert Bruccoleri (<bruc@acm.org>)	32-bit compilation model
Linux 2.2.x	Alpha	7.1	2001-01-23, Ryan Kirkpatrick (<pgsql@rkirkpat.net>)	

OS	Processor	Version	Reported	Remarks
Linux 2.2.x	armv4l	7.1	2001-02-22, Mark Knox (<segfault@hardline.org>)	
Linux 2.0.x	MIPS	7.1	2001-03-30, Dominic Eidson (<sauron@ the-infinite.org>)	Cobalt Qube
Linux 2.2.18	PPC74xx	7.1	2001-03-19, Tom Lane (<tgl@sss.pgh.pa.us>)	Apple G3
Linux	S/390	7.1	2000-11-17, Neale Ferguson (<Neale. Ferguson@softwareAG-usa.com>)	
Linux 2.2.15	Sparc	7.1	2001-01-30, Ryan Kirkpatrick (<pgsql@ rkirkpat.net>)	
Linux	x86	7.1	2001-03-19, Thomas Lockhart (<thomas@ fourpalms.org>)	2.0.x, 2.2.x, 2.4.2
MacOS X	PPC	7.1	2000-12-11, Peter Bierman (<bierman@ apple.com>), 2000-12-11, Daniel Luke (<dluke@ geeklair.net>)	Darwin (only) Beta-2 or higher
NetBSD 1.5	Alpha	7.1	2001-03-22, Giles Lean (<giles@nemeton.com.au>)	
NetBSD 1.5E	arm32	7.1	2001-03-21, Patrick Welche (<prlw1@cam.ac.uk>)	
NetBSD	m68k	7.0	2000-04-10, Henry B. Hotz (<hotz@jpl. nasa.gov>)	Mac 8xx
NetBSD	PPC	7.1	2001-04-05, Henry B. Hotz (<hotz@jpl. nasa.gov>)	Mac G4
NetBSD	Sparc	7.1	2000-04-05, Matthew Green (<mrg@eterna. com.au>)	32- and 64-bit builds

Continued

OS	Processor	Version	Reported	Remarks
NetBSD 1.5	VAX	7.1	2001-03-30, Tom I. Helbekkmo (<tih@ kpnQwest.no>)	
NetBSD 1.5	x86	7.1	2001-03-23, Giles Lean (<giles@nemeton.com.au>)	
OpenBSD 2.8	Sparc	7.1	2001-03-23, Brandon Palmer (<bpalmer@ crimelabs.net>)	
OpenBSD 2.8	x86	7.1	2001-03-21, Brandon Palmer (<bpalmer@ crimelabs.net>)	
SCO UnixWare 7.1.1	x86	7.1	2001-03-19, Larry Rosenman (<ler@lerctr.org>)	UDK FS compiler; see also doc/FAQ_SCO
Solaris 2.7-8	Sparc	7.1	2001-03-22, Marc Fournier (<scrappy@ hub.org>), 2001-03-25, Justin Clift (<justin@ postgresql.org>)	see also doc/FAQ_Solaris
Solaris 2.8	x86	7.1	2001-03-27, Mathijs Brands (<mathijs@ilse.nl>)	see also doc/FAQ_Solaris
SunOS 4.1.4	Sparc	7.1	2001-03-23, Tatsuo Ishii (<t-ishii@sra.co.jp>)	
Windows NT/2000 with Cygwin	x86	7.1	2001-03-16, Jason Tishler (<Jason.Tishler@ dothill.com>	with Cygwin toolset, see doc/FAQ_MSWIN

Unsupported platforms

The following platforms have not been verified to work. Platforms listed for version 6.3.x and later should also work with 7.1, but we did not receive explicit confirmation of such at the time this list was compiled. We include these here to let you know that these platforms could be supported if given some attention.

OS	Processor	Version	Reported	Remarks
DGUX 5.4R4.11	m88k	6.3	1998-03-01, Brian E Gallew (<geek+@cmu.edu>)	6.4 probably OK
MkLinux DR1	PPC750	7.0	2001-04-03, Tatsuo Ishii (<t-ishii@sra.co.jp>)	7.1 needs OS update?
NextStep	x86	6.x	1998-03-01, David Wetzel (<dave@turbocat.de>)	bit rot suspected
QNX 4.25	x86	7.0	2000-04-01, Dr. Andreas Kardos (<kardos@repas-aeg.de>)	Spinlock code needs work. See also doc/FAQ_QNX4.
SCO OpenServer 5	x86	6.5	1999-05-25, Andrew Merrill (<andrew@compclass.com>)	7.1 should work, but no reports; see alsodoc/FAQ_SCO
System V R4	m88k	6.2.1	1998-03-01, Doug Winterburn (<dlw@seavme.xroads.com>)	needs new TAS spinlock code
System V R4	MIPS	6.4	1998-10-28, Frank Ridderbusch (<ridderbusch.pad@sni.de>)	no 64-bit integer
Ultrix	MIPS	7.1	2001-03-26	TAS spinlock code not detected
Ultrix	VAX	6.x	1998-03-01	No recent reports. Obsolete?
Windows 9x, ME, NT, 2000 (native)	x86	7.1	2001-03-26, Magnus Hagander (<mha@sollentuna.net>)	client-side libraries (libpq and psql) or ODBC/JDBC, no server-side; see Administrator's Guide for instructions

Troubleshooting

If you have difficulty installing or using any of the materials on the companion CD, try the following solutions:

- **Turn off any anti-virus software that you may have running.** Installers sometimes mimic virus activity and can make your computer incorrectly believe that it is being infected by a virus. (Be sure to turn the anti-virus software back on later.)

- **Close all running programs.** The more programs you're running, the less memory is available to other programs. Installers also typically update files and programs; if you keep other programs running, installation may not work properly.

- **Reference the ReadMe.txt:** Please refer to the ReadMe file located at the root of the CD-ROM for the latest product information at the time of publication.

If you still have trouble with the CD, please call the Hungry Minds Customer Care phone number: (800) 762-2974. Outside the United States, call 1 (317) 572-3993. You can also contact Hungry Minds Customer Service by e-mail at techsupdum@hungryminds.com. Hungry Minds will provide technical support only for installation and other general quality control items; for technical support on the applications themselves, consult the program's vendor or author.

Index

Continued

Hungry Minds, Inc.
End-User License Agreement

READ THIS. You should carefully read these terms and conditions before opening the software packet(s) included with this book ("Book"). This is a license agreement ("Agreement") between you and Hungry Minds, Inc. ("HMI"). By opening the accompanying software packet(s), you acknowledge that you have read and accept the following terms and conditions. If you do not agree and do not want to be bound by such terms and conditions, promptly return the Book and the unopened software packet(s) to the place you obtained them for a full refund.

1. **License Grant.** HMI grants to you (either an individual or entity) a nonexclusive license to use one copy of the enclosed software program(s) (collectively, the "Software") solely for your own personal or business purposes on a single computer (whether a standard computer or a workstation component of a multi-user network). The Software is in use on a computer when it is loaded into temporary memory (RAM) or installed into permanent memory (hard disk, CD-ROM, or other storage device). HMI reserves all rights not expressly granted herein.

2. **Ownership.** HMI is the owner of all right, title, and interest, including copyright, in and to the compilation of the Software recorded on the disk(s) or CD-ROM ("Software Media"). Copyright to the individual programs recorded on the Software Media is owned by the author or other authorized copyright owner of each program. Ownership of the Software and all proprietary rights relating thereto remain with HMI and its licensers.

3. **Restrictions on Use and Transfer.**

    (a) You may only (i) make one copy of the Software for backup or archival purposes, or (ii) transfer the Software to a single hard disk, provided that you keep the original for backup or archival purposes. You may not (i) rent or lease the Software, (ii) copy or reproduce the Software through a LAN or other network system or through any computer subscriber system or bulletin-board system, or (iii) modify, adapt, or create derivative works based on the Software.

    (b) You may not reverse engineer, decompile, or disassemble the Software. You may transfer the Software and user documentation on a permanent basis, provided that the transferee agrees to accept the terms and conditions of this Agreement and you retain no copies. If the Software is an update or has been updated, any transfer must include the most recent update and all prior versions.

4. **Restrictions on Use of Individual Programs.** You must follow the individual requirements and restrictions detailed for each individual program in Appendix B of this Book. These limitations are also contained in the individual license agreements recorded on the Software Media. These limitations may include a requirement that after using the program for a specified period of time, the user must pay a registration fee or discontinue use. By opening the Software packet(s), you will be agreeing to abide by the licenses and restrictions for these individual programs that are detailed in Appendix B and on the Software Media. None of the material on this Software Media or listed in this Book may ever be redistributed, in original or modified form, for commercial purposes.

8. **General.** This Agreement constitutes the entire understanding of the parties and revokes and supersedes all prior agreements, oral or written, between them and may not be modified or amended except in a writing signed by both parties hereto that specifically refers to this Agreement. This Agreement shall take precedence over any other documents that may be in conflict herewith. If any one or more provisions contained in this Agreement are held by any court or tribunal to be invalid, illegal, or otherwise unenforceable, each and every other provision shall remain in full force and effect.